*FOREVEI* _____ *CATS*

(Published in 2022)

"I have truly enjoyed reading Jamie Vaught's articles and books that he has written over the years. When it comes to the University of Kentucky basketball, his insights have been remarkable as well as informative and entertaining. But even more important, however, is the friendship I have enjoyed with Jamie over the many years he covered my career and the interviews I have done with him. "

— *Jack Givens, former Kentucky Wildcat star and current TV broadcaster*

"Despite his lofty accomplishments as the author of six books, Jamie Vaught remains one of the nicest guys on the UK media beat. In *Forever Crazy About The Cats*, we get a candid glimpse of not only why he's so passionate about Kentucky Basketball but also why he's such an inspiration to so many. It's a book worth reading and a story you don't want to miss."

— *Dr. John Huang, award-winning author of Kentucky Passion*

"I have finished the book and really enjoyed it. I found it really entertaining with the sidebar stories about a number of individuals associated with UK. Jamie is a superstar in how he has overcome adversity in doing such a great job on this book. Congratulations!"

— *Jim Host, member of the National College Basketball Hall of Fame and Sports Marketing pioneer*

"Who could possibly find and share so many Kentucky Wildcat basketball stories as famed sportswriter Jamie Vaught? This one is his best of many great ones. In this latest work, we finally get to know the miracle man who 'listens' with his heart."
*—Bill Cunningham, retired Kentucky Supreme Court Justice and author*

"If you are a University of Kentucky sports fan, then longtime sportswriter Jamie Vaught has another book about UK basketball that I think you will enjoy. He shares stories about Adolph Rupp, Joe Hall, Cawood Ledford, Dan Issel, Fran Curci, Mark Stoops, Maci Morris, Oscar Tshiebwe and others. I loved the book!"
*— Larry Vaught, Kentucky sportswriter*

"Jamie's latest book goes beyond the ordinary and includes personal experiences to go along with his love for the Wildcats. It really puts into perspective Jamie's ability to overcome his hearing loss and achieve his goals without seeking self-pity. It's a must read and will keep you engaged from the first to the last page. Well-done and perhaps one of his best projects to date."
*— Keith Taylor, Kentucky Today*

"If you're a UK sports fan—and nearly everyone in Kentucky is—then you'll want to get your hands on sportswriter Jamie Vaught's newest book. Yes, it's about sports, but it's also about the author's personal journey in overcoming a severe disability to pursue his dream. Somerset Community College is proud to have been a part of making his dream come true. Great read with some unexpected twists. Roberto Clemente? Wow!"
*—Stuart Simpson, retired professor, Somerset Community College*

"As usual, Jamie Vaught has provided special insight into Kentucky basketball through the eyes of individuals who have had special access to this storied program over the years; and this volume also includes rare snippets about the football program as well! However, the thing that sets *Forever Crazy About the Cats* apart is the behind the scenes view that the author provides about his struggles—since birth—to overcome a hearing disability that left him near deaf. The obstacles that he has faced, and overcome, rival those with which any Kentucky team has had to contend over the years. An inspirational story.

*— W. Bruce Ayers, retired president, Southeast Kentucky Community and Technical College*

"In *Forever Crazy about the Cats*, Jamie Vaught provides a great read for Wildcat fans of every generation. There are new insights and stories not only about the biggest names, but also those that fans may be getting to know for the first time. In either case, Jamie's decades of experience covering the Cats will show as he tells the stories in an interesting and entertaining style. A side trip into his friendship with Pittsburgh Pirates Hall of Famer Roberto Clemente adds to his journey, as does a special connection to former Kentucky football coach Blanton Collier. In this book, his sixth, he also offers some powerful personal accounts of the challenges he faced while dealing with severe hearing loss as he built successful careers in sportswriting and teaching. *Forever Crazy about the Cats* is educational, inspiring and fun."

*— Keith Elkins, former journalist at Lexington's WLEX-TV who once served as studio host for UK Sports Network*

Praise for
*CHASING THE CATS*
(Published in 2020)

"This is an absolutely wonderful book and a must read for any Kentucky fan. Jamie Vaught displays in *Chasing the Cats* a brilliant insight to UK basketball and a beautiful writing style sure to please basketball fans everywhere. I don t remember a book I have enjoyed more. Just a rich and riveting read."
— *Paul Finebaum, SEC Network/ESPN*

"Jamie has put together again another terrific composite of UK history. You have to have a special love for Kentucky hoops to assemble these stories. Enjoy!"
— *Mike Pratt, ex-Kentucky Wildcat standout*

"Jamie Vaught has spent his career covering the Kentucky Wildcats as thoroughly as anyone and he knows the stories behind some of the biggest names in the history of the program. By introducing us to their stories, Jamie takes us along on his Kentucky basketball journey with him, and it is a great ride with a tremendous human being."
— *Matt Jones, founder of Kentucky Sports Radio*

"No one knows Kentucky basketball better than Jamie Vaught. He has communicated his passion for UK basketball to me by email and clippings for years. The Wildcats and John Calipari are lucky to have him tell the story of UK basketball."
— *Jim O'Brien, the U.S. Basketball Writers Hall of Fame (2003 Class)*

## Also by Jamie H. Vaught

*Crazy About the Cats: From Rupp to Pitino*

*Still Crazy About the Cats*

*Cats Up Close: Champions of Kentucky Basketball*

*Krazy About Kentucky: Big Blue Hoops*

*Chasing the Cats: A Kentucky Basketball Journey*

*Forever Crazy About the Cats: An Improbable Journey of a Kentucky Sportswriter Overcoming Adversity*

# Unforgettable Journey with the Cats

## Inside Kentucky Hoops Madness

Jamie H. Vaught

*Unforgettable Journey with the Cats: Inside Kentucky Hoops Madness*

Copyright © 2025 by Jamie H. Vaught

All rights reserved.

ISBN: 979-8-9993875-0-9 (paperback)
ISBN: 979-8-9993875-1-6 (hardcover)
ISBN: 979-8-9993875-2-3 (ebook)

Published by KySportsStyle360, LLC
Printed in the United States of America

In memory of my parents

# Contents

Acknowledgments      1

1. The Press Conference      4

2. Part One: Wildcats in Wild & Wacky ABA      29
   (Louie Dampier, Cliff Hagan & more)

3. Part Two: Wildcats in Wild & Wacky ABA      52
   (Dan Issel, John Y. Brown III & more)

4. Shot Heard Around Kentucky      86
   (Paul Andrews)

5. From Hyden to Hall of Fame      108
   (Tim Couch)

6. From London to NBA      136
   (Reed Sheppard)

7. Aussie Superstar      155
   (Georgia Amoore)

8. First Lady      183
   (Lee Anne Pope)

9. Growing Up in the Appalachian Mountains      209
   (Trent Noah)

10. Lefty's Prize Pupil      233
    (Kenny Brooks)

11. Italian Magician                         263
    (Rick Pitino)

12. Pope Brings Hope & Passion               283
    (Mark Pope)

About the Author                             313

# Acknowledgments

As the book title indicates, the overriding theme of my seventh book is about various individuals associated with the Kentucky Wildcats, mostly men's basketball during the post-Rupp years. The new volume also includes stories about University of Kentucky women's basketball as well as the former Wildcats who played in the old American Basketball Association. A chapter on Tim Couch, arguably the greatest player in UK football history, was thrown in for good measure.

Writing for this new volume has been a labor of love for the past two years, and it wouldn't have been possible to have it done without the help of many wonderful and cooperative folks. It's very difficult to believe this is my seventh book on UK basketball during a period of nearly 35 years as the first one came out in November of 1991. Looking back, my work ethic must have gone through the roof in a big way! In addition to my family responsibilities and full-time college professorship over the years, I somehow found the time to do some writing and covering the UK games. I don't mind the hard work involved on the project because I love writing. Like my mother and grandmother, writing is definitely in my blood. I simply can't stop writing books or articles. And I love to meet and write about interesting athletes and coaches.

I would like to thank many individuals who provided comments or kindly agreed to be interviewed for a chapter. The helpful folks who were kind enough to lend a hand or two for photos or setting up interviews include several from UK Athletics — Cami Moore Williams, Megan Summers, Deb Moore, Greg Welsh and Tony Neely, as well as individuals from other universities — Carter Brown (Virginia Tech Athletics), Chris Brooks (James Madison Athletics), John Bilello (JMU Athletics), and Tyson Jex (Brigham Young Athletics). Special thanks to Landry Collett for reaching out to his friend and former high school teammate Tim Couch. Also, I would like to thank outstanding photographers — Middlesboro's Danny Vaughn and Pineville's Wayne Mason — for pictures of former high school stars Trent Noah and Reed Sheppard, both from the 13th Region.

Without all of them, my book No. 7 wouldn't be around. Also special thanks to Darrell Bird of *The Cats' Pause* for permission to use a photo of Reggie Hanson and me for the back cover. In addition, special thanks to Mike DeCourcy of the *Sporting News* for locating a person who dealt with archives and permissions. I'm grateful to Bob Hille, also of the *Sporting News*, for permission to use one of the magazine's front covers. Also, thanks to Peter Gardner, editor of BYU's *Y Magazine*, for permission to use some passages from the school's alumni publication.

In addition to new interviews with many folks, selected passages, including several ABA stories, from my previous books were used. The background material and statistics from UK basketball and football media guides, and Basketball-Reference.com were helpful. In addition, Jon Scott's *Big Blue History* website was valuable for statistics and box scores. I had exclusive book interviews with UK coach Mark Pope in 2025 and 1998, as well as a couple of other interviews via email during the 2000s and covered nearly all of Pope's postgame news conferences at Rupp

Arena and several on the road during the 2024-25 season. Portions of transcripts of players' and coaches' press conferences provided via the universities and ASAP Sports were utilized as well. I also used brief quotes or material from my syndicated columns, which once appeared in several media outlets or newspapers in Kentucky. I also had quotes from other sources, and credit is given within the book where appropriate.

Special thanks go to my book editors — college professors Caroline Mayes Cooper, Astor Simpson and Jamie Jones — who checked the manuscript for grammar, spelling, punctuation and typographical errors, and provided critical feedback. I also sincerely hope that I haven't left out anyone else in this section. If so, I'm so sorry. Thanks to my wife, Deanna, and others for putting up with me during this book project. Lastly, but most importantly, I want to express thankfulness to the Lord for guidance and support every step of the way in my entire life. Without Him, I'd be lost in this crazy world. And thank you, Big Blue Nation!

*JHV*
*August 2025*

# 1

---

# The Press Conference

*April 14, 2024.*

It was the memorable date that marked the beginning of the Mark Pope era at the University of Kentucky as the school officially introduced the former Wildcat standout as the men's head basketball coach at a press conference before a large Rupp Arena crowd of over 20,000. It was a beautiful and sunny day that could have been declared a state holiday for the Big Blue Nation.

"Truly amazing.....There are programs that don't get this kind of crowd for five games," said UK athletics director Mitch Barnhart as he prepared to introduce Pope. "UK is here for a press conference. That is awesome."

The 6-foot-10 Pope, a popular captain of UK's 1996 national championship team, came to UK from Brigham Young, where he compiled a five-year coaching record of 110-52, including two appearances in the NCAA Tournament. Before BYU, Pope was the head coach at Utah Valley for four years. A second round NBA Draft selection by the Indiana Pacers in 1996, he played nine years in pro basketball, including six seasons in NBA. After his playing days, Pope spent three years in medical school, leaning toward pediatric ER medicine, at Columbia University in New York City before changing his mind. In 2009, he began his coaching career at Georgia, joining Mark Fox's staff as assistant director of basketball operations.

*Newly-hired coach Mark Pope and Athletics Director Mitch Barnhart smile during Pope's introductory press conference at Rupp Arena. (Photo by Jamie H. Vaught)*

Shortly after Barnhart presented the new coach a UK jersey (with No. 23), Pope said as he began his remarks, "We see these introductory press conferences all the time. Nobody in the world has ever seen anything like this. But I'm about to break tradition. At every one of these press conferences, the coach comes up and stands there with the AD and takes a picture with a jersey that they made that ends up in a closet somewhere. We're not doing that.

"Hey, this jersey (with No. 41) comes from a hallowed place in my home because it is a jersey I got to wear with my teammates in the national championship game in the Meadowlands of New York. And that's not just a jersey that will go in the closet. It is a jersey that has blood, sweat, and tears and love, and it is all of us together.

"When Mitch called me and talked to me about being the head coach here at Kentucky, I understand the assignment. We are here to win banners."

For this book, we invited numerous folks, including members of the news media as well as a couple of faithful fans along with two former Wildcats, to discuss their thoughts about Pope's memorable press conference. Below is what they had to say.

## Drew Franklin

"Mark Pope's introductory press conference at Rupp Arena was a shocking event, especially after the mixed reaction to the hire three days earlier," said Kentucky Sports Radio's Franklin. "The initial response to Mitch Barnhart's pick overall was frustration and lukewarm, but Big Blue Nation quickly united around Pope before his formal introduction on that memorable Sunday in Rupp Arena.

"I will always remember the scene outside the arena with fans lining entire city blocks on High and Vine Streets, hoping to get in. Inside, fans raced to grab a seat as the bleachers quickly filled to the top. The turnout was better than anyone, even Mitch Barnhart, could've imagined. I thought Pope could draw 3,000-4,000 and call it a success. Never in my or anyone else's wildest dreams could he fill Rupp Arena, yet he did. The enthusiastic crowd showed excitement and optimism around Pope and sent a message to the rest of college basketball, saying Pope had a unified BBN behind him."

Asked to describe the press conference in just one word, Franklin said, "Revival."

## Grover Sales

"Pope is the best hire UK could make," said Sales, a former UK basketball student manager who attended the press conference. "I have known him since he played at UK. The crowd was underestimated by UK officials. He is a refreshing change from (John) Calipari."

One word: "Exhilarating"

## Wyatt Huff

"Mark Pope's introductory press conference was absolutely unbelievable," said Huff, who writes for Kentucky Wildcats on SI.com. "To say that he understands what it means to be at Kentucky would be an understatement. To see the Big Blue Nation pack Rupp for a press conference is unlike anything I have ever seen. The buzz and energy in that place was incredible. BBN was roaring for Pope the moment they got in there.

"It was one of the more special events I have ever gotten the privilege to attend as media. That was the first look at Mark Pope at Kentucky and his vision of everything he plans to do here. Pope is the perfect person for the job, and his attitude and philosophy is really infectious. He loves this place, and his love and appreciation trickles down to the players. I'll never forget that Sunday when Big Blue Nation was introduced to Mark Pope."

One word: "Unforgettable"

## Alan Cutler

"Press conference was a great show where you hoped Pope would be the captain of the program the way he was captain of a national championship team," said Lexington's Cutler, a retired TV broadcaster who is still working as the host of his daily radio show.

One word: "Exciting"

*A media credential for Mark Pope's introductory press conference.*

## Samantha Money

"Mark Pope's introductory press conference was filled with a kind of excitement and hope that I don't think Big Blue Nation realized it needed so badly until a new face of Kentucky basketball entered Rupp Arena," said Money, sports anchor/reporter for Bowling Green's News 40 Sports/WNKY. "Plenty of basketball games inside the historic building have been packed before with thousands of fans eager to watch a game during the season, but this eagerness to hear Mark Pope speak his first words as the head coach of the Wildcats was different. It exceeded all amounts of excitement and hope that Rupp Arena had seen in a handful of years.

"During the press conference, Mark Pope spoke at the podium not for himself, but for the passionate fans that surrounded him. His words visibly restored the excitement and fun that fans had been missing while being a part of BBN. 'Hope in Pope' is a phrase that was heard all throughout the arena during that day, but it truly is the easiest way of describing how fans felt seeing the former Wildcat humbly accepting and acknowledging his new responsibility in Lexington. Pope portrayed at the press conference exactly who he has always been: a guy who genuinely loves Kentucky basketball and is determined to bring that love and honor of wearing a UK jersey back to Rupp."

One word: "Inspiring"

## Maci Morris

Morris, a former star for UK women's team, didn't attend Pope's press conference, but she saw numerous videos online. "I was not shocked at all at BBN's turnout," she said. "I think the fans have been wanting something new for the past couple of years and to bring in someone who understands what it means to represent the University of Kentucky. The fans were extremely excited."

One word: "Impressive"

## Jim Host

"I have never seen an outpouring of support as I saw when Mark Pope was introduced as UK's next men's basketball coach at Rupp Arena," said Lexington's Host, a member of the National College Basketball Hall of Fame and a sports marketing pioneer. "It was better in enthusiasm than having a crowd in Rupp Arena welcoming a team back who had just won a national championship (in 1996). Don't ever remember an event like this that had thousands of fans outside who could not get in.

"To be honest, I was not excited until I spent some time with him. I remember him well when he was a key member of the 1996 national championship team. My head to head conversation came a week after he was named. He was very praise worthy of Coach Cal and the job he had done but then talked about his coaching philosophy. He has boundless energy, enthusiasm and knows the expectations of UK fans. I firmly believe based on what I have seen so far is that he will outpace what the pundits think he will do in his first year. "

One word: "Unreal"

## Jeff Piecoro

"The event was surreal. I mean, this was an introductory press conference," said Piecoro, a Lexington television broadcaster. "Thousands of fans packed the streets around Rupp Arena and waited — some for hours — to see the new coach. Mark Pope came in on a bus full of former Wildcat heroes and, at that moment, the direction of Kentucky basketball changed forever. It was beautiful to behold, almost like a religious experience."

## Keith Farmer

"I have covered a lot of amazing events in my time, but that one was so unexpectedly cool," said Farmer of Lexington's WLEX-TV and *BBN Tonight*. "I had thoughts in my head about the type of crowd I might see. It far exceeded that with not just the sheer numbers but also the energy inside Rupp Arena. After having the chance to sit down with Coach Pope for one of his first interviews, I was told that he had a grand entrance planned. When the bus pulled in and all of those former players started coming off there to the roar of the crowd, it was electric. And when Pope came off the bus with national championship trophy, I didn't know how it could get louder. Still can't believe they aren't replacing the Rupp Arena roof."

One word: "Electric"

## Aaron Gershon

"It was something that you would only see or expect from Kentucky," said Gershon, now a former writer for *The Cats' Pause*. "Having to do my job in front of 20,000 people is something I never would've expected, but if there was one scenario it would be exactly that — welcoming a national champion home as the program's next head coach."

One word: "Unreal"

## Paul Saffer

"I thought there would be 2,000 to 3,000 people there," said Saffer, a UK basketball fan since 1955. "I was excited how fast the arena began to fill up. I knew it would be a big crowd when the seats behind the temporary stage were filling up. Those fans would have the worst seats, but they were running to claim a seat. I have been to many events over the years, but that was the most amazing thing I ever saw. When Pope was named the UK coach, I was surprised. I expected, like a lot of UK fans, we would hire a veteran coach.

"I remember when he (Pope) played at UK but had not followed his career. Of course, when I heard his passion for UK basketball I thought he would understand what it meant to us. Understanding how much we love UK basketball is a critical part of the job. It's much more than just Xs and Os. The UK coach has to understand and relate to UK fans worldwide."

## Lee Howard

"On the day of the Mark Pope introductory press conference, I arrived at Rupp Arena around 2:45 p.m. I arrived early because I was scheduled to appear on CBS national radio at 3 p.m. to discuss Kentucky's hiring of Pope," said Howard of Lexington's WKYT-TV. "I wanted to ensure I was out of traffic and in a spot where I could be parked and talk.

"On a typical Kentucky basketball game day, I park across the street from Rupp, but on this day, I pulled around back and into the parking garage below the arena. Because of where I parked, I didn't get a good sense of the crowd outside waiting to enter the building. I remember the CBS radio host asking me what I thought the reception would be for Pope, and I told him I was unsure. I assumed it would be mostly positive, but there had also been some public outcry over the hire, so there could be mixed reactions. I was wrong.

"When I entered the arena, it appeared the athletics department was preparing to host around 8 or 10 thousand fans. Half of the seats were roped off and situated behind the stage that was set up. But as it grew closer to the start time, a buzz in the arena made it feel like something special was about to occur. There were young and old fans, many with signs and custom t-shirts welcoming the next Kentucky basketball coach. That's when word started circulating that thousands of people were waiting in line outside and they may not all get in before it was time to begin the press conference.

"In my 20 years in sports media, I've attended many introductory press conferences, but this one felt much more like a pep rally. It felt surreal as the fans continued to pour in, and the Rupp Arena staff opened more and more seats until there was standing room only in the building. It felt like every person in Lexington had arrived except for the fire marshal. We were all waiting on a charter bus to drive onto the floor carrying Pope and a busload of former UK basketball players. It reminded me of a time a decade prior when I stood in Rupp waiting on the 2012 national championship team to pull a bus into Rupp for a celebration. It was indeed a celebration, not only for a new head basketball coach but also for the storied past of the UK program. Players from various generations exited the bus, with Pope exiting last while hoisting the 1996 national championship trophy.

"That moment felt like a turning point for a program that had grown frustrated and weary over the past several seasons. Pope's comments and answers to questions were exactly what the fan base needed to hear from him. He left little doubt with the BBN that Mitch Barnhart had made the right hire. He said he understood the assignment: to win banners. When most new head coaches try to temper expectations, Mark Pope did the opposite. That day, he gained the trust of the wildest and craziest fan base in college basketball."

One word: "Rehabilitating"

*Anxious Rupp Arena crowd waiting for Coach Mark Pope's press conference to begin. (Photo by Jamie H. Vaught)*

*Former UK stars Jeff Sheppard and Rex Chapman listen during Mark Pope's introductory press conference. (Photo by Jamie H. Vaught)*

*New coach Mark Pope speaks at packed Rupp Arena. (Photo by Jamie H. Vaught)*

## Rick Bozich

"The crowd at Mark Pope's press conference was incredible," said Bozich, now a retired sportswriter from Louisville. "Amazing. Spectacular. It showed me how excited Kentucky fans were to embrace a former player from the Rick Pitino era to run the program again. They loved Pope's approach as a player, and they were primed to embrace his blue collar approach to winning as a coach. They wanted to make sure the college basketball world (understood) there was no disappointment that Scott Drew and Danny Hurley were not the guys to follow John Calipari."

One word: "Scintillating"

## Lyndsey Gough

"I was unfortunately not in attendance for Mark Pope's press conference as I was anchoring our coverage in studio that evening. However, I did watch it all on the stream and social media," said Lexington WKYT-TV's Gough. "When I saw what was unfolding, I couldn't believe it. As a lifelong Kentuckian, a fan, and an alum,

I've seen the Big Blue Nation show up in force, but I couldn't have imagined a full arena for a press conference, but maybe I should have, since Mark Pope is one of their own.

"I remember looking at social media in between my shows and seeing that it was actually being delayed because there were so many people outside that they were still trying to get in and into seats. I couldn't believe the photos I was seeing of just how full it was and how people turned out. It was truly fun and exciting to watch, all the little surprises sprinkled in — like bringing in the trophy, etc. — and I loved seeing how they were able to connect the past and present. The entire thing really got folks excited and that carried all the way into the season, which isn't easy to do.

"Of course, Pope nailed the press conference. He said and did all the right things. The fans embraced it. They embraced his family, and the family embraced them right back. It really was a special thing to see."

One word: "Exciting"

## Tyler Thompson

"I live in Nashville, and when the press conference was announced, I knew I had to drive up to Lexington to be there in person," said Thompson, editor-in-chief for Kentucky Sports Radio. "The media was allowed to park in the Rupp Arena garage, so I didn't see the crowd until I walked onto the floor. Even 45 minutes before the event started, it was clear the building would be at capacity despite UK only anticipating a crowd of 5,000 to 7,000. The energy was infectious as fans, some in Pope costumes and custom shirts, streamed in and danced to the 90s playlist. You truly had to see it to believe it.

"After another disappointing March and a divisive breakup with John Calipari, the fan base was finally coming together, with the moment Mark Pope stepped off the bus with the 1996 championship trophy serving as the catharsis."

One word: "Revival"

## Jeff Sheppard

"The day of the press conference was emotionally overwhelming," said Sheppard, who was one of many former Wildcat standouts who rode the bus to inside Rupp Arena. "Rex Chapman was my all-time favorite Wildcat and my childhood hero. Mark Pope is one of my best friends in the world, my UK roommate, my snow sledding partner, and my 1996 NCAA national championship teammate. (Son) Reed Sheppard is my all-time favorite Wildcat now. Sorry, Rex.

"Dr. Greg White and I had just finished up lunch at Corto Lima (in Lexington) as we drove past the huge group of fans that were waiting outside of Rupp Arena. Little did I know at that time that Mark Pope was in the crowd already thanking the BBN for attending the event. (The officials from) media relations (office) asked the former players to arrive several hours early to mingle and get instructions on the day. Just getting to see everyone before the event and enjoy so many laughs, hugs, and old stories was priceless.

"When all of the former players filled the bus to drive into Rupp to replicate the 1996 bus entrance celebrating the NCAA championship, I realized how unique being a former UK basketball player is. Additionally, Mark asked all of the 1996 team to huddle up in the very back of the bus. Therefore, we got to spend 15 minutes or so together on the bus ... together as a team....very special. When the bus pulled into Rupp Arena, we heard a roar from that crowd that was different than anything I had ever heard in that place. I played five years of basketball games at Rupp. I had just finished a year of cheering for my son at Rupp. I had even taken my daughter (Madison) when she was 10 years old and her friends to the Jonas Brothers concert at Rupp, but I have never experienced an ovation of passion like what I experienced at the press conference.

"The high point for me was actually a very uncomfortable moment then but now, my favorite memory. As Mark Pope addressed the most passionate college fan base in the country, Mark in his very special way was describing his vision as a coach to 'Shepherd' his players. However, he felt the need to strategically pause and allow that word — Shepherd or Sheppard, still not sure what his notes said that day — 'marinate' in the air at Rupp Arena. Well done, Mark.

"At this point, my son Reed and my wife Stacey were sitting in Los Angeles, getting ready to start his pre-draft NBA training process. Although Reed had already made his decision to leave UK and go to the NBA privately, Reed had not yet announced his decision publicly. Therefore, Mark along with everyone else at Rupp Arena except me took the opportunity to share their opinion about Reed's possible return to UK for a 'one more year' chant. So, there I was with my college roommate and new UK head basketball coach addressing a fan base that has been incredible loyal, kind, and passionate to me and my family for the last 32 years of my life. And guess who I got to stand next to during the entire press conference that day? Rex Chapman, my friend, childhood hero, and newest advocate and loyal supporter of my son, Reed. I'm not sure I have any words to describe the emotions I felt at that moment. But I will never forget it."

One word: "Hope"

## Keith Taylor

"The press conference was surreal to see and experience," recalled Taylor of *Kentucky Today*. "A full house at Rupp Arena for a press conference and not a UK basketball game and the enthu-siasm of coach Mark Pope further electrified the crowd after a coaching search that took a few twists and turns. The experience was one I will never forget, especially seeing Pope arrive on a bus carrying the NCAA championship trophy from 1996, and his teammates and former UK players at his introduction added a memorable touch to the press conference. If anyone doubted Pope was the right hire, those concerns were gone by the end of the presser."

One word: "Amazing"

*Mark Pope (Photo by Jamie H. Vaught)*

## Kenny Walker

"I was not at the press conference. Everyone assumes that I was there," said Walker, a two-time UK All-American who starred in the NBA. "I actually watched it on TV. I thought it was awesome, a guy who played at Kentucky and now he's being introduced as the head coach of his alma mater. I couldn't believe the size of the crowd, but then I thought this is what Kentucky is all about. Mark Pope understands what it means to put on that uniform and what it means for the University of Kentucky and all of our fans who support the program. Mark Pope is a class act and he will represent the University of Kentucky and our tradition like all of the other great coaches that we've had before him. It was a home run hire."

One word: "In the words of Dick Vitale, awesome, baby! with a capital A."

## Larry Vaught

"I have covered University of Kentucky basketball for 51 years and cannot remember another time when Big Blue Nation went from being terrified and unsure about the future to euphoric about the future in a 72-hour period," said Vaught, a long-time Kentucky sportswriter, in 2025. "However, that's exactly what happened from the time Mark Pope was announced as UK's next coach to that remarkable Sunday press conference at Rupp Arena with an overflow crowd of Big Blue fans cheering every word that Pope uttered.

"People lined up outside Rupp Arena like it was a top five show-down going on. I thought UK athletics director Mitch Barnhart took a huge gamble having an introductory press conference in Rupp Arena, but it turned out to be the feel-good moment UK fans needed to reunite. No way will I ever forget the noise as Pope walked off that bus holding the 1996 national championship trophy just like I had seen him do 28 years ago. It was one of the most magical moments in the illustrious history of Kentucky basketball."

One word: "Unbelievable"

## Cole Parke

"I remember leaving the event in higher spirits than I possibly could have imagined," said Parke, a former *Kentucky Kernel* writer now with *The Cats' Pause*. "As journalists, it's our responsibility often to remain as impartial as possible, but I can not deny that I have lived my entire life in central Kentucky and was raised as a Wildcat fan on top of having covered them for four years now as a career. Before I'd even left the premises, I wrote out a decent-length column titled 'It's a new era for Kentucky basketball, and it's a breath of fresh air.' In it, I described how Pope scratched just about every itch Kentucky fans had from SEC Tournament importance to the entire culture of the program. Chatting with other media members, it was clear my takeaways weren't just my own, but those of most who attended the event.

"As almost silly as it is to say, I don't know that I've ever attended an event quite like that one before and I don't know if I ever will again. The packed house, forcing the arena crew to open up more and more sections, the passion, the energy, the history of the trophies and returning legends, Pope's words, etc. It was truly special."

One word: "Fresh"

## Reed Sheppard

"I was not at the press conference," said Sheppard, a former Wildcat star who privately at the time was preparing for NBA. "I did see videos and pictures from the press conference, and it was pretty cool. I don't think a lot of colleges and fanbases could do that, and that just shows how great and crazy the Kentucky fans are and how excited they are to have Coach Pope be the new coach."

*Newly-hired Kentucky coach Mark Pope poses with UK cheerleaders and dancers after finishing his introductory press conference at Rupp Arena. (Photo by Jamie H. Vaught)*

## Tony Neely

"The event itself was remarkable — the energy of the fans, the number of former players who came, Mitch's introduction, and Coach Pope's captivating presence on stage combined for an incredible experience," said Neely, Assistant AD for Athletics Communications and Public Relations. "The atmosphere was electric, and it was a giant embrace of the past, present and future of Kentucky basketball."

Asked if the university had plans to have the press conference at the Joe Craft Center like the school did with coaches John Calipari and Kenny Brooks, instead of Rupp Arena, Neely commented, "Rumors began Sunday night (April 7) that Coach Calipari was leaving, so on Monday, we began preparations. However, it was kind of like hosting a dinner party in which you didn't know the guest of honor, how many guests were coming, or when they would arrive. Our athletics director Mitch Barnhart wanted to have the fans involved, and he felt that the interest would be beyond what we could host at the Craft Center, so we decided on Rupp Arena. Nathan Schwake and the promotions and marketing team, Scott Geisinger and the event management team, and Deb Moore and the media/communications team began putting together a plan that evolved as the week went on, literally up to the event itself.

"We thought if several thousand fans showed, it would be an incredible turnout. But, as they do so often. the Big Blue Nation went far and beyond that. The first person was in line at 8:30 a.m. for an event scheduled to begin at 4:30. Seeing the long lines, we opened the doors sooner than we planned and the fans kept coming. Our usher group, the Committee of 101, made sure every seat was used, and the fans did a great job of packing themselves in side-by-side. It was amazing to see the place fill up, and we eventually had to close the doors."

One word: "Transcendent"

## Cameron Mills

"When we drove in on the bus, we were asking people in the back, 'How many people are out there?' because a couple days before, the fans weren't completely on board (with Mark Pope). All of the ex-players were, especially the ones that played with him," recalled Mills, who played with Pope on UK's 1996 national championship team. "So when they opened up for a press conference, some of us (were), and I know Mark was, worried about how many people would show up. We're in the back in the bus, nothing but players and some managers, and we're asking, 'How many people are out there?' The last number we got was about 5,000, and so we were blown away that 5,000 people showed up for the press conference. Then we drove out and there were obviously more than 5,000 people there. There were what 22,000, not 20,000, whatever? And then we started hearing, this came later, that they had to turn 5,000 away at the gate.

"So it was an amazing feeling. Nathan Schwake with UK Sports Marketing is the one that did a great job of trying to recreate the moment of us driving into Rupp after the 1996 championship. But it was shocking and shocking in a very good way. It made all of us, even those of us that didn't know Mark well — the players who played before him and after him — feel great about the reaction from BBN.

"The funny thing is that once we got into the press conference, Mitch introduced him and then Mark started speaking. But we forgot it was a press conference, so when Mark gave his speech and just had the fans going crazy with saying everything that I think they had wanted to hear for a long time about the SEC Tournament matters. His perfect statement of 'We know the as- signment,' meaning the coaching staff. He knows the assignment. It's to hang more banners. If we get more kids to the NBA, great, and we will. Mark obviously isn't against that. He wants to do that, but the goal at Kentucky is to hang banners. So, it got everybody kind of frothing at the mouth with excitement. Then the funny, frustrating thing to me was that we had a press conference, which was really the whole point of this thing. I mean that was really all it was supposed to be, but 22,000 people showed up, and it became a pep rally.

"When Mitch or Mark or whoever it was, may have been Deb Moore or Tony Neely, I don't remember, the people that handled the media stopped at the pep rally and said, 'All right, let's take some questions from members of the media,' I was looking around like, 'Why?' Everybody in the media, I know fairly well, and love almost all of them. So, I'm sitting there thinking, 'We don't need them. Show them the door, get them out of here. We're having a pep rally in here.' It was kind of like we showed up for a press conference and it turned into a pep rally and then it needed to go back to a press conference. But for those of us enjoying the moment, it was like, 'What do we want to hear from these knuckleheads for?' I know they've got their questions, but just let Mark keep talking."

One word: "Overwhelming"

*Cameron Mills (UK Athletics Photo)*

On UK's announcement of Pope as the new coach on Friday morning, April 12,  Mills added,  "When it was announced, it was a surprise to a lot of people because we went from (Dan) Hurley to (Scott) Drew, both great coaches, both of whom said no. Then to a lot of people, it appeared like a big drop to Mark Pope. And what I kept hearing from fans is, 'Look, he's never won an NCAA tournament game.' Well, that's true, but if you look at Danny Hurley, for example, his winning percentage before he got to UConn was 67 percent. That was his winning percentage as a Division I coach. Mark Pope's winning percentage before he got to Kentucky, before he got to a high D-I, blue blood school, was 69 percent, so he had a better winning percentage.

"I was thrilled (with Pope). I think all of us who played with him were thrilled not just because he was an ex-player or an ex-teammate of ours. I think because a lot of us, the '96 team, the '95 team in particular, knew Mark personally and knew the kind of person he was and knew the kind of coach he was because you didn't have to be around Utah Valley or BYU and watch Mark coach to know. Even when he was playing, all of my teammates wanted to be coaches; that wasn't Mark. Mark didn't want to be a coach. I mean, he went to medical school. To me, that's the most amazing part of the whole story, other than him winding up back at Kentucky, is that he quit medical school at the beginning of his fourth year at Columbia of all places because he wanted to go into coaching. I think what I remember his quote being is that he felt like he could impact more people and more young people as a coach.

"So, for those of us who know him and knew him back when he was 22 years old, that made complete sense. Him being a doctor made complete sense, too. But we were thrilled beyond belief because number one, he was an ex-player, he's one of us, same thing.

"(We) knew how incredibly intelligent he was, how positive he was, how unbelievably motivated he was, how hardworking he was. I mean, he's got a work ethic that outdoes everybody. And this isn't bias or favoritism. His work ethic, I would put up against anybody, any coach in Division I, any coach period. He just outworks everybody and that's the kind of player he was.

"The only thing I will say that I'll give myself a little credit here. I do have backup that will verify this is the day I found out Cal was leaving, I found out from a Delta gate agent at the airport because I had an early 6:00 a.m. flight and I was checking in, heading to Alabama. And the Delta gate agent said, 'Can you believe this about Cal?' And I said, 'What?' because he (had said he) was staying. And then they told me he was leaving for Arkansas, and I didn't believe him. I thought, 'No, I'm sure that's just rumor.'

"Then as time went on that morning, meaning I went from checking in to going through TSA to getting on the plane. Now I'm sitting with people and we're in Lexington so they're all wanting to talk to me about, 'Who do you think we ought to get? What do you think? Can you believe this?' So, now it's real and I'm answering all these questions from people sitting beside me, people in the back of the plane who are getting on and seeing me and wanting to know. A member of my board of directors of my ministry, Craig Parker, texted me at 6:30 in the morning, 'Who is the next person going to be?' No one should be texting me at 6:30 in the morning. But he's texting me because this is obviously big news for crazy Kentucky fans. And I texted back to Craig and I said, 'I have no idea what Mitch is thinking. Don't know who is on Mitch's short list, don't know who is on his long list. But, honestly, I think he ought to go after Mark Pope.'

"And this was a week before. This was right after Cal had left. So I think everyone figured or assumed he was going to go after Hurley and Drew. Of course, (Billy) Donovan's name kept coming up. (Rick) Pitino's name even came up as a possibility, which I think was maybe a stretch of a possibility at that point. I don't think it would be at this point but again, we've got Mark. But I remember texting Craig because Craig has sent me several emails and texts saying, 'No one will believe me that you called it a week before.' And I didn't call it as though it's going to happen. I just said, 'If I had my pick, it would be Mark Pope.' That was completely out of the blue. It wasn't 'Well, we might be getting

Mark Pope so yeah, that's who I would want.' It was, 'I want Mark Pope.' Not trying to speak for all of my ex-teammates, but I think all of us would think the same thing.

"But this is the one that makes the most sense. He'd had success in Division I. He'd climbed the ladder from Utah Valley to BYU (which joined the Big 12). In his first year of Big 12, he had beaten (No. 11) Baylor, (No. 7) Kansas and Texas. I love the idea of instead of going out and getting a Hurley or a Drew, established national championship coaches, let's go get the next national championship coach. And the mere fact that it happened to be a former teammate, a friend and someone that I just thought would absolutely smash it here was just icing on the cake."

# 2

## Part One: Wildcats in Wild & Wacky ABA

(Louie Dampier, Cliff Hagan & more)

Over five decades ago on a Saturday night — February 28, 1970, to be exact — the author saw his very first pro basketball game in person. I felt like I was in heaven. My eighth-grade classmate and I even stayed around long enough after the game to obtain cherished autographs from the players like Louie Dampier, Jim "Goose" Ligon, Wayne Chapman (whose two-year-old toddler, Rex, would be a future UK and NBA star), among others, while my somewhat frustrated parents waited in the car for nearly one hour in the parking lot. That was in Louisville, the home of the Kentucky Colonels, not some city in the National Basketball Association. The Colonels played in the American Basketball Assocation, and I loved them. That was even before two UK stars — Dan Issel and Mike Pratt — joined the franchise in 1970.

I was a huge fan of ABA, which featured a couple of radical innovations — a three-point field goal (which at the time did not exist in the NBA or college basketball) and the red-white-blue "beach" ball. I certainly didn't like the well-established NBA very well with that ugly black-looking ball on a black-and-white TV set. Added John Y. Brown III in a 2025 interview, "The NBA was like watching basketball in black and white and the ABA was like watching basketball in technicolor." It was his father, John Y. Brown Jr. , who once owned the Colonels.

That night in 1970, we saw the Colonels defeat the Don Freeman-led Miami Floridians 115-111 before a small Convention Center crowd of about 3,000 during the pre-Issel years. Six-foot-9 forward Gene Moore had 28 points and 22 rebounds, and Dampier gunned in 24 points. Future hall of famer Earl Strom was one of the two referees who officiated the very physical contest. The ABA was a growing league which eventually stole stars and coaches from the rival NBA, and signed college standouts like Issel, North Carolina's Charlie Scott and Jacksonsville's Artis Gilmore to fat contracts.

After that memorable game, we began to make two or three trips to Louisville every season from our rural hometown of Science Hill in Pulaski County to watch the Colonels during my high school years. Occasionally, I even sneaked to the hardwood floor a couple of times with my cheap Kodak camera (with basic print film) and sat with other photojournalists to take pictures of my beloved Colonels. Each time, though, after sitting for around 10 minutes or so on the floor, a media relations official from the team or a security guard would catch me, forcing me to return to my seat since I didn't have a proper photo or media credential. The photos, of course, were very poor quality and dark, but I managed to get decent shots of 7-foot-2 star Artis Gilmore of Kentucky and San Diego coach K.C. Jones of the Boston Celtics fame.

Earlier, in 1967, when the league first began playing, it featured former Kentucky Wildcats like Dampier (Colonels), Cliff Hagan (a former NBA star who became the player-coach for the Dallas Chaparrals) and Cotton Nash (Colonels). Even ex-UK coach John

Calipari's former boss at Kansas, Larry Brown, was a 5-foot-9 playmaker for the New Orleans Buccaneers, leading the ABA in assist during the 1967-68 campaign. Former Wildcat and NBA veteran Adrian Smith of the 1958 national championship team played for the Virginia Squires in 1971-72. ABA had other teams like Pittsburgh Pipers (who became the league's first champion in 1968, featuring ABA MVP and future hall of famer Connie Hawkins), New Jersey Americans, Anaheim Amigos, Minnesota Muskies, Oakland Oaks, to name several. And I religiously read a weekly ABA column written by Jim O'Brien in *The Sporting News*. His entertaining column sometimes took up the entire page. The weekly magazine also published ABA box scores and statistics along with occasional cover stories on the top stars from the "radical" league, which also featured the sexy, bikini-clad ball girls from the Miami franchise.

That was during the pre-ESPN and pre-Internet days, and it wasn't easy to find ABA stories. The league wasn't seen on national television very often, either. O'Brien's column in *The Sporting News* was my only ABA source in addition to reading the *Louisville Courier-Journal*, which provided excellent coverage of the Colonels. O'Brien, who now lives in the Pittsburgh area, is often referred to as the "Mr. ABA" because he wrote countless articles in many national publications about the league.

"It was a good association for me," said O'Brien, now a retired journalist who was also the founding editor of *Street & Smith's Basketball Yearbook* for many years. "Writers were welcomed with open arms by most ABAers. They were like boxing people in that regard. They needed the ink. There were so many characters in the league, so many 'head cases.' I liked Art Heyman, Chico Vaughn, Johnny Neumann, John Brisker and Wendell Ladner. I made so many friends in that league. I actually helped the Pittsburgh Pipers put their original team together and became a life-long friend of (ABA and NBA star) Connie Hawkins. I was responsible for nominating him and preparing the nomination package to promote his candidacy (for the Hall of Fame in the early 1990s) when I was serving on the nomination board of the Basketball Hall of Fame. Connie once told my daughter Sarah that I was 'the best little white dude he ever knew.' I take that as a compliment."

O'Brien, who has written over 20 books on sports in Pittsburgh, was asked who was ABA's most colorful character that he has ever met. "Wendell Ladner (of the Colonels) ranked right up there," he said. "His coach, Babe McCarthy, once said, 'Wendell doesn't know the meaning of the word "fear," and a lot of other words, too.' I thought (Indiana Pacers' coach) Slick Leonard was a great guy and an easy interview. He dressed like no other coach."

Remember Ladner? He was the good-looking guy who crashed into a glass water cooler near the bench during a playoff game between the Colonels and the Larry Brown-coached Carolina Cougars at Freedom Hall in Louisville. Luckily, I was there (with my parents) as a fan sitting about seven rows from the playing floor to witness the memorable crash, and Ladner ended up with many cuts and stitches. With my cheap camera, I even took pictures of the floor where broken glass and paper cups scattered among water. And *Sports Illustrated* ran a story about that 1973 game and Ladner's incident in the following week. A fan favorite, Ladner later was killed in an airplane crash in 1975.

Through his job as a writer of nationally-published ABA articles and columns, O'Brien got to meet all kinds of people in the ABA, including the ex-Kentucky Wildcats. He has had a good share of interesting interviews. As far as traveling or covering the games are concerned, O'Brien said his favorite ABA cities were Indianapolis and Louisville. "I loved to go to Indianapolis," said O'Brien. "The treatment there by everyone in the organization was first-class. Louisville was close behind for the same reasons. The Pacers and Colonels were easy to work with. The whole league was. I loved staying at the Executive Inn (in Louisville). It had high beds, I remember. It was my favorite hotel on the road."

His thoughts or memories of ex-UK standouts when they were with the Kentucky Colonels? "Louie Dampier and Dan Issel were two of my favorites from my ABA days," he said. "I don't remember dealing with Mike Pratt, although I do remember him and can see his face. I was covering a Pacers-Colonels playoff game at Freedom Hall one night. I was interviewing Issel after the game, and someone shoved a cream pie in my face, blinding me momentarily. I'll never forget that Issel offered me a towel and was apologetic about the incident."

Two years later, while attending a college all-star game in Las Vegas, O'Brien said he learned "it was the wife of the Colonels' coach, Hubie Brown, who had done the evil deed. So Issel is on my all-star team of good guys. (Colonels' management team) Mike Storen, Alex Groza, the Browns (John Y. Brown Jr. and his first wife, Ellie), and Dave Vance were as good as they get. They provided you with access. I was even inducted into the Kentucky Colonels for life, I think. I hope so. I like being a Kentucky Colonel."

The 6-foot-7 Groza was a former All-American at UK during the Fabulous Five years in the late 1940s. He spent several years with the Colonels and the San Diego Conquistadors as a coach and an executive. He was the one who replaced NBA legend Wilt Chamberlain as the new coach at San Diego in 1974.

What about Artis Gilmore, who earned the ABA's Rookie of the Year and MVP honors in 1972 and helped the Colonels to a stunning 68-16 mark? O'Brien said, "I always remember that Gilmore's wife's name was Enola Gay. That was the name of the plane that dropped the A-Bomb on Hiroshima. That was the name of the pilot's mother, I just learned in a book I read. (Mrs. Gilmore's parents had watched a movie about the bombing of Hiroshima while mother was pregnant.)

"I met Artis right after he signed with the Colonels at a party hosted by Ellie and John Y. Brown at their palatial estate. Gilmore had legs like tree trunks and was hard to move. He was from Chipley, Fla., in the Florida panhandle. He went to Gardner-Webb Junior College (in North Carolina) and then Jacksonville. He played with a guy there named Rex (Morgan who briefly played in the NBA). I got along fine with Gilmore. He was a real soft-spoken guy."

As many old-timers will recall, Gilmore was the one who helped Jacksonville beat Issel-led UK with a 106-100 victory in an NCAA Tournament showdown in 1970. Gilmore later played for the Chicago Bulls, among others, after ABA merged with the NBA in 1976. In 2011, Gilmore was selected to Naismith Basketball Hall of Fame.

After legendary coach Adolph Rupp's forced retirement from UK in 1972, the Baron had an opportunity to be a pro basketball coach. He turned down a coaching offer by

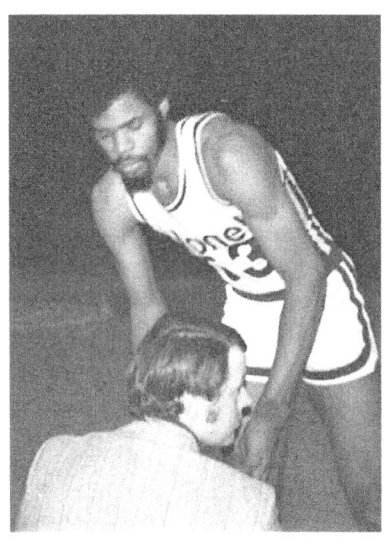

*Artis Gilmore (Vaught Family Photo Collection)*

Charles O. Finley, the owner of the Memphis club in the ABA, but he agreed to a three-year contract as a high-ranking executive with the Tams. "Charlie Finley called and told Daddy that he could be president, coach or general manager," said Herky Rupp, son of Adolph, in an interview many years ago. "All three or any combination he could choose. Daddy took the idea of being president/general manager, and he turned the coaching over to somebody else (Bob Bass). He had the chance to coach. All he had to say was, 'I'll do it.' And he didn't."

(During the late 1950s, Rupp also declined a head coaching offer by the old Cincinnati Royals of the NBA, as well as an ownership interest in the team.)

A member of U.S. Basketball Writers Hall of Fame, O'Brien remembers Rupp in the ABA when he spent one year with the

Tams (as president) and later with the Colonels. "I spoke to Rupp at Memorial Coliseum in Lexington," O'Brien said of Rupp who was in his early 70s at the time. "I was happy to be in his company. I have a picture to prove it. The (New York) Nets were playing the Colonels at the campus arena because they (the Colonels) had so many UK players on the team."

Herky Rupp said his father "enjoyed that (his years with the Colonels) because that was back home. He had Dan Issel, Mike Pratt, Louie Dampier and Ron Thomas (who likely was set to become the first black — instead of Tom Payne — to play basketball at UK, according to the younger Rupp). It was easier than going to Memphis in a Howard Johnson motel five days out of the week, and that got to be pretty tough."

About a year and half before Rupp passed away in December 1977 at the age of 76, the Colonels, who were one of the league's strongest franchises, unfortunately folded when NBA took four other ABA teams in a merger. Thanks to O'Brien's fine journalistic efforts, ABA managed to survive for nine years and become a thorn to NBA. Said O'Brien, "The ABA was a fun ride, a continuous adventure serial. (Hall of Fame coach) Alex Hannum said 'the red, white and blue ball belonged on the nose of a seal.' The NBA is now playing the ABA game."

## Chapman's ABA Memories

Wayne Chapman, a 6-foot-5 swingman who played on UK's 1963-64 freshman team with Louie Dampier and Pat Riley before transferring to Western Kentucky University, played four years in the ABA, including two years with the Kentucky Colonels, and he has some memorable stories about the new league. Chapman, who was named the Ohio Valley Conference Player of the Year in 1968, was a second-round draft pick by the Colonels.

While the Colonels were playing a game against the New York Nets at the 5,200-seat Island Garden Arena in West Hempstead, N.Y., the playing condition was much less than ideal, and the players and the fans practically froze. "It was really cold. We walked inside the place, and it was like 33 degrees," Chapman recalled. "They had these electric heaters that were behind the bench, and when you'd come out, you could put your hands down there and warm up. They (arena officials) were in a hurry, I guess, and they put the floor down on top of the ice rink without any insulation. So, water started coming up. It's not a great story, but it shows you a little bit about the condition. A guy named Levern Tart, who played for New York, went in for a layup, slid off the end of the floor and slid all the way to the end of the hockey rink and broke his jaw. The game was stopped. I remember we had a game called off there once, and it could have been that night. So, we played in some adverse conditions."

Chapman also remembers a wild incident at Indianapolis during the 1968-69 campaign. "We were playing the (Indiana) Pacers up at the old fairgrounds (9,111-seat Indiana State Fairgrounds) and a fight broke out between Jim Caldwell (of Kentucky) and George Peeples (of Indiana). They ran out underneath the stands all the way to the other exit and back to the floor again. Jim was chasing George. By the time they got back in, both teams were fighting. We went about four or five rows into the stands. The fans were into it. The owners were into it. The police were trying to break us up. I bet that fight lasted for 25 minutes. Fortunately, nobody was hurt. I remember Mamie and Joe Gregory owned the club at that time, and Joe, bless his heart, was getting the heck beaten out of him in the middle of the floor by somebody. Somebody hitting me over the head with a folding chair is the last thing I remember. It was an interesting fight."

In early 1971, Chapman had his biggest thrill of his ABA career while playing for the Denver Rockets (now Nuggets). That was when his mother saw him play. "Oh, Lord, my biggest moment in the ABA was, I guess, when my mother flew out to Denver and I think I got 38 (points). We didn't have television (coverage) back then, so she didn't get to see me play very often. The All-Star Game was the next week, and I had a tough time explaining to her why I wasn't on the all-star team. I was glad that she got to see me play at least once in the pros. My dad never did get to see me. He died my senior year in college. So, he didn't know anything about my professional career. We won (the game), and that was probably the best game I ever had."

Chapman later had a successful head coaching career on the high school and college levels in Kentucky. He guided Kentucky Wesleyan to a couple of national titles in NCAA Division II.

## Pat Boone

Legendary singer Pat Boone, who played high school basketball when he was the team captain during his senior year, still loves hoops, his favorite sport. The 91-year-old entertainer is very fond of his ABA days. "Basketball has always held a special place in my heart," Boone wrote in a Facebook post in 2025. "One of my proudest sports memories was helping launch the American Basketball Association. I was the only entertainer involved at the beginning and wound up owning the Oakland Oaks, led by none other than Rick Barry, one of the greats of the game. In just our second season, we won the ABA championship against the Indiana Pacers.

"Too many memories for one post. Thanks for letting me dribble down memory lane."

## Hagan's Coaching Days

In 1966, after he retired as a five-time all-star performer with NBA's St. Louis Hawks, former UK All-American Cliff Hagan became a radio and TV analyst for the Hawks franchise (which later moved to Atlanta in 1968) but he only stayed for one year. "I wasn't a natural at that," explained Hagan of his TV job. The 36-year-old Hagan then got a phone call from the Dallas Chaparrals of the new ABA, which began play for the 1967-68 season. It was a new league that had 11 teams.

"I flew down there, talked to them, and they wanted me to be a player-coach," said the future UK athletics director. "Well, I had sat out a year. I'd retired for a year. I had all the glory, you know, five-time all-star. Anyway, I decided to take the job. As I got into practicing with them, leading practice, I started playing with them. Well, I found out I knew how to pass the ball on a fast break. I knew how to play unselfish. Pass this way, go set a screen, then wait for the ball. Most players want to pass, they want to go toward the ball, and that's not basketball. It's passing, going away, setting a screen for somebody else. Well, I could do that and get some movement going on the court. Lo and behold, I still didn't want to play, but I did.

"The first game we played a California team (Anaheim Amigos, who later became the Los Angeles Stars before moving to Utah). They had a 7-foot center. I scored 40 points (actually a game-high 35 points) in the first game. How can I not play after that? Of course, they want me to play. I can still fade and get the hook shot, and I still had some quickness."

A gentleman off the hardwood floor, Hagan was an aggressive competitor on the floor when it came to basketball, becoming one of the league's leaders in personal fouls. Hagan also played in the first ABA All-Star Game in Indianapolis, scoring 10 points and becoming the first professional to participate in All-Star Games in both the ABA and NBA. Representing the Colonels in that game were Louie Dampier, former Western Kentucky University standout Darel Carrier (whose son, Josh, later played for coach Tubby Smith's Wildcats), and Randy Mahaffey.

*Then-UK athletics director Cliff Hagan, a former NBA and ABA standout, poses with the Wildcat mascot at Memorial Coliseum during the late 1970s. (UK Athletics Photo & Vaught Family Photo Collection)*

The Dallas franchise, which eventually became the San Antonio Spurs, did well under Hagan's leadership in the first year, posting a 46-32 mark for second place in the Western Division while the player-coach averaged 18.2 points in 56 games. The Chaparrals finished behind the first-place New Orleans Buccaneers, who were coached by former Mississippi State boss and future Kentucky Colonels coach Babe McCarthy. In 1968, Hagan was named the Texas Professional Coach of the Year. He stayed with Dallas until the midpoint of the 1969-70 campaign when he resigned from his coaching job and was replaced by general manager Max Williams.

Several ABA clubs had financial troubles. Not the Chaparrals, who had a strong ownership group. Hagan said he never had to worry about his paycheck bouncing. He couldn't remember his exact salary, but believed it was for a three-year pact at $30,000 each. "The Dallas Chaparrals had 20 owners and each of them had put up $200,000," he said. "So, that was enough for the program."

In the early 1970s, Hagan — who had some business interests, including his several restaurants which bear his name — eventually returned to his alma mater and became the assistant athletics director under AD Harry Lancaster, a former Rupp assistant, for a couple of years. One of Hagan's early responsibilities as assistant AD was to develop and implement the Blue & White Fund (now called the K Fund) for the new Commonwealth Stadium and then Rupp Arena. "I was the first assistant athletics director the university ever had," said Hagan, a Naismith Basketball Hall of Famer who eventually became UK athletics director in 1975.

## Larry Conley

After leaving Kentucky, Larry Conley decided to play pro basketball even though he wasn't drafted by anyone. He wanted to try his luck in the pro ranks. He made the season-opening roster with the new Kentucky Colonels in 1967. In addition to Conley, the Colonels had a couple of other former UK teammates in Louie Dampier and Cotton Nash.

But Conley didn't stay in pro basketball very long. A member of the National Guard, he had to join the Army during a riotous period when the United States fought in the Vietnam Conflict in the late 1960s. It was an experience he will never forget. "I got one game into the season, and I got my notice," Conley said. "I was shipped to Fort Polk, Louisiana, and did my basic training there, and I did my infantry training at Fort Dix, New Jersey. By the time I had finished all that training, that year was over with. The basketball year was over.

"It was also at a time when (Richard) Nixon was elected (President) in 1968. This was in the 1968 and '69 era, and when I look back on history, those two years have a lot of meaning to me. Those two years stand out more to me than any two years I think I'll ever remember in my lifetime only because of all the turmoil that went on. And he (Nixon) had made the promise about withdrawing the troops from Vietnam. After I had been in (the service) for about a year, they started pulling out of there.

"So, things kind of worked in reverse for me. I didn't go over. I ended up staying here in this country and finished out my training in the Army. It was such a turbulent period. We questioned everything that happened. We questioned authority. I can remember everything that went on at (UK) campus here, and our campus was fairly mild compared to some of the other ones around the country. It was certainly an interesting period."

That one game with the Colonels, by the way, was the only one Conley played in his very brief pro career. Interestingly, that was the Colonels' first contest ever in the history of the franchise. Conley played 18 minutes, scoring only two points, in a 117-95 loss to the host Indiana Pacers before a sellout crowd of over 9,000 at the State Fairgrounds Coliseum. Cotton Nash poured in 14 points and 10 rebounds for the Colonels, who were led by a 24-point, 13-rebound performance by ex-Murray State standout Stew Johnson. "I remember we had a big house that night," Conley commented. "It was crowded. And (former NBA star) George Mikan was the first commissioner of the ABA. He came to the game and said, 'This is really a historic moment.' He came into our locker room and talked to us. It was really interesting."

On using ABA's innovative red-white-blue basketball, Conley said he never got used to it. "(The ball) was the strangest thing to shoot with and you watch it twirl," he said. "It was like a kaleidoscope. You sit here and watch it, and it'd just spin and spin."

## Cotton Nash

In the long sports history, there have been numerous star athletes like Bo Jackson and Deion Sanders who participated in two pro sports on the major league level. And Cotton Nash of the UK All-American fame during the early 1960s is on that coveted list as he played major league baseball and pro basketball.

"*The Sporting News* had an article a few years back, and I was surprised to see the number of athletes who played both sports," Nash once said. "There were only about a dozen or so players who played both baseball and basketball. There were more who played both football and baseball. I don't think you can compare me to Bo Jackson (who played football and baseball). That is two different situations."

In pro baseball, Nash began in the California Angels' farm system before he was shipped to the Chicago White Sox in a 1967 trade involving veteran first baseman Bill "Moose" Skowron of Chicago. (Earlier in his career, Skowron had played in eight World Series championships, including seven with the New York Yankees.) Nash briefly played for the White Sox that season in a reserve role. Two years later, he appeared in the major leagues again with a different organization, the Minnesota Twins, in 1969 and '70. "I wasn't in the big leagues that long to really have any great moments," Nash said. A backup outfielder and first baseman, Nash played only 13 games with 16 at-bats in his career, hitting for an average of .188.

One of Nash's big-league managers was none other than con-troversial figure Billy Martin, who directed the Twins to the 1969 American League West Division championship as a rookie man-ager. "Billy Martin was a player's manager," Nash recalled. "If a player had to pick a guy they wanted as their manager, the ma-jority of them would say they wanted Billy Martin. He was not a front office manager. He couldn't get along with any front office. He always had conflict with the front office, but he was the best in relating to the players. And it was an experience just to play for him."

In 1964, the Los Angeles Lakers, coming off a 42-38 season, made Nash their second-round NBA draft pick. UCLA star Walt Hazzard was the team's first-round pick. And the Lakers, by the way, had future Hall of Famers Jerry West and Elgin Baylor on their roster. "I'm not really sure that the Lakers really wanted me at the time," said Nash. "Most teams were hesitant to draft me when they found out I was going to play two sports out of college. A lot of baseball teams were hesitant to talk to me or offer me a contract because I was going to play basketball, and the same went with the NBA teams. I should have been the first-round choice, but I wasn't because of that fact. The Lakers drafted me as an insurance policy because Elgin Baylor had been complaining of knee problems the year before. During the exhibition season, I did a lot of games. I started a lot in Elgin's place. He limped along during the exhibition season, which was about 20 games long. When the regular season started, something miraculous happened. His knees were just fine. He became healthy again. My role diminished because I was there as his insurance policy. They got rid of me (during the season), and I had signed with the (California) Angels."

After playing 25 games, averaging 2.1 points, for the Lakers, he went to the struggling San Francisco (now Golden State) War-riors, who would eventually finish with a woeful 17-63 mark for the 1964-65 season. Nash completed his first NBA season with a 3.0-point average in 45 games.

And he returned to baseball, trying his luck with the Angels organization. "I saw where the two-sport situation was taking away (my concentration and time) from both of them," Nash said. "It was getting to be impossible to do justice for either sport. I had to make a choice, so I chose baseball."

But two years later, a new pro basketball team came calling in 1967. The ABA's Kentucky Colonels pursued Nash. The club owner, Joseph Gregory, wanted him. He needed someone with a drawing power at the gate. Nash certainly fitted the bill as he was a major star at Kentucky. At first, Nash said no; he wasn't interested. But Gregory wouldn't give up. "They kept calling me all summer," Nash commented. "I thought it over and I gave them a figure that I would sign for, and I thought that would get rid of them. I didn't hear from them for a couple of weeks. Then about September, they agreed to my terms. So I said, 'What the hell, I might as well play.' I played my last game of the season in baseball, and then I played with the Colonels in Louisville. I didn't play the entire (1967-68 roundball) season as the White Sox camp was calling me to come for the spring training."

Asked about his salary with the Colonels, Nash smiled, "I'm not going to tell you what I made." But Nash reportedly was the highest-paid player on the squad in the neighborhood of $20,000. His high-scoring teammate, Louie Dampier, said he himself earned $15,000.

His only season with the Colonels was certainly interesting. "The league wasn't very well organized the first year," Nash said. "I remember playing one game in a hockey arena, and they laid the floor over the ice. The moisture settled on the floor and you could hardly move out there. Everybody was slipping and sliding around. You couldn't do anything about it. You'd wipe it off now and then, but it would come right back. We went like it was slow motion, just tiptoeing around.

"The first strange thing was getting used to that ball. Playing with that red, white and blue thing looked funny coming towards you sometimes. A lot of players had trouble with passing and trying to catch the ball. It was different. They had crazy promotions, but I don't remember what they were."

With the Colonels, who finished fourth in a five-team Eastern Division with a 36-42 mark, Nash saw action in 39 regular season games and averaged 8.5 points.

## Little Louie

In 1975, when John Y. Brown, Jr., and his first wife, Ellie, were the owners of the defending ABA champion Kentucky Colonels, they sold the team's most popular star, Dan Issel, to the new Baltimore Claws franchise for a reported $500,000. Stunned by unbelievable sale of Issel, the whole state of Kentucky was in a state of shock. The emotional fans and the media alike blasted the owners for this unthinkable action. Issel was The Colonels. He was The Franchise.

"That was one of the stupidest transactions ever made in pro basketball," recalled former Colonels star Louie Dampier, who was Issel's teammate for five years. "It was turmoil the next year. I had one more year left (at Kentucky before the NBA absorbed the remaining ABA teams in a pro basketball merger), and we kept bringing in everybody trying to replace Dan. We even brought in high-priced ball players, and we went through Tom Owens, Caldwell Jones and ended up with Maurice Lucas. Either the players didn't fit in with the team or had conflicts with (coach) Hubie Brown. We just had a poor season. It just wasn't a good move. The whole year was just a struggle."

The Colonels simply were never the same.

The Browns explained that the Issel transaction with Baltimore was purely a business decision, one of the most difficult they had made during their careers. Without the sale, they said the Colonels couldn't have remained in Louisville for the next few years. The owners had also considered selling one of the team's other stars, Artis Gilmore, instead of Issel. But they decided Gilmore, being a 7-foot-2 center, was more important to the team in the long run.

Without Issel, who eventually wound up with the Denver Nuggets as the Baltimore entry folded without playing a single game, the Colonels finished the 1975-76 campaign with a 46-38 mark, their worst in five years. Meanwhile, at Denver, Issel helped coach Larry Brown and his new Nuggets teammates post a 60-24 mark and reach the ABA championship series, which they lost to New York four games to two.

In 1967, the 6-foot Dampier became the very first Colonel in the Louisville franchise history when the two-time UK All-American signed a one-year contract for $15,000, including a bonus of $2,500. He would be the team's main attraction. His association with the Wildcats would help sell tickets. "The Colonels offered me that contract, and I took the security of that rather than taking a chance on going with Cincinnati," explained Dampier, who was a fourth-round draft pick by NBA's Cincinnati Royals but would have to go through the Royals' three-day rookie tryout camp. "I was real excited to sign that contract. To get paid to play basketball, I thought that was great. I thought maybe I'll last three years or six years and continue to play." Not so. When Dampier retired in 1979, he had played a total of 12 seasons in pro basketball, nine years with Kentucky in the ABA and three with the San Antonio Spurs in the NBA.

When the Colonels faced the Los Angeles Stars in November 1968, they featured a woman who made a very brief appearance as a player. In becoming the first female to play pro basketball, Penny Ann Early, a blonde jockey, made a one-second appearance by throwing in an inbounds pass during the second quarter of Kentucky's 111-107 loss to LA. The event drew a near-sellout crowd of 5,345 at Louisville's Convention Center. But the Kentucky players didn't like the publicity gimmick the team officials had put on. In fact, they were somewhat embarrassed about the event, especially Dampier, who hit a game-high 30 points.

"Thumbs down," said Dampier of the gimmick, pointing his thumb downward. "It was just explained to us that it was to draw some people in and get some publicity. She was a jockey who rode at Churchill Downs and they brought her in. She warmed up with us, sat on the bench and came in for Darel Carrier." Such an event was not uncommon in the early days of the ABA. The struggling league used all kinds of attractions to generate publicity, including ballgirls in bikinis who were employed by the Miami franchise.

In his pro career, Dampier had several coaches including a couple of Wildcat legends. His mentors at Kentucky and San Antonio included John Givens, Gene Rhodes, Alex Groza, Frank Ramsey, Joe Mullaney, Babe McCarthy, Hubie Brown and Doug Moe. Both Groza and Ramsey had been All-Americans at UK. Dampier said he didn't really have a favorite coach. "I feel like I'm a coachable player because I go along with whatever they want," he explained.

Early in the 1970-71 season, which was Issel's rookie year, the Colonels dismissed Rhodes as the coach, and Ramsey was hired by club president Mike Storen to guide the team on the floor. (In the interim, Groza, the team's business manager, coached the Colonels to two victories). Ramsey was returning to basketball after a six-year absence. Upon his retirement from the NBA in 1964, he had entered private business in his hometown of Madisonville, Ky.

Ramsey had a successful pro coaching debut when Kentucky defeated the Carolina Cougars 122-112 in Charlotte, N.C., as Issel and forward Cincy Powell each pumped in 28 points. The duo also grabbed 15 rebounds apiece. For the remainder of the regular season, the Colonels managed to post a 32-35 mark under Ramsey before catching fire in the playoffs. Kentucky advanced to the ABA championship series, but it lost to the Utah Stars in seven games. Issel captured the ABA scoring title with a 29.9-point average, edging former NBA superstar Rick Barry of the New York Nets by a fraction of a point. He also shared the league's Rookie of the Year honors with Virginia's Charlie Scott, a former pupil in coach Dean Smith's North Carolina program.

*Louie Dampier (right) is shown with UK coach Mark Pope and former Wildcat Jerry Hale in 2025. (UK Athletics Photo)*

It was Ramsey's only season at Kentucky. Joe Mullaney, the former Los Angeles Lakers coach, took over the helm the following season. Watching Ramsey on the hardwood floor, many fans had the impression that he did not enjoy or care about his coaching job. Dampier said that wasn't the case. "I think he enjoyed it," he said. "He's just such a laid back kind of guy that he wouldn't show it. One thing is that he didn't have pressure on him. That wasn't his goal in life to be a pro coach. He was approached (by the Colonels) and he had other things to fall back on that were probably more important to him — his businesses in Madisonville — rather than worrying about coaching."

Later, in 1974, Hubie Brown came to Louisville where he was named the Colonels coach, his first head coaching job in pro basketball. A disciplinarian, he had been an assistant with the successful Milwaukee Bucks of the NBA. When the 1974-75 season ended, Brown was a happy man as he guided the Colonels to their first league championship, defeating arch-rival Indiana in the finals. According to Dampier, that was the most fun season of his college or pro basketball career.

"The 1975 championship was the only championship I'd had at any level," he said, pointing to the championship ring on his finger. "After coming close a few times before, we finally did it. That was the happiest (moment), as far as pros or really through my whole career, because I finally got the championship. I personally had better seasons in scoring and assists, but we were in such complete control the whole year. Hubie Brown made it that way. He had a very analytical mind when it came to basketball, and he programmed what we did and what we would do. Sometimes it wasn't the most pleasant of circumstances because we got a little tired of continuous scouting reports, day to day, on the teams that we already knew quite well. He programmed us and he stuck to what he had scheduled for us and that proved to make us a very dominant team even though the (New York) Nets gave us a chase for a while.

"Toward the end of the year, we were one of the strongest teams in basketball and I think that showed in the way we went through the playoffs. Each of them (playoff series) was four to one. It was just an enjoyable season, even though we worked a little harder than we were used to. It paid off, and everything was fun when you were winning."

Speaking of Brown, he later became head coach for the Atlanta Hawks, the New York Knicks and the Memphis Grizzlies. Brown, who retired as a longtime TV analyst in 2025 at the age of 91, has said the 1975 Colonels were the best team he's ever coached in his career.

When the Colonels passed up an opportunity to join the NBA in 1976, Dampier obviously was very upset. Club owners John Y. Brown, Jr., and his wife, Ellie, said the price tag to join the established league was way too high at $3.2 million. They also thought the Louisville market was actually too small to support a pro basketball franchise even though the Colonels had been among the ABA's leaders in attendance figures for several years. "I was real disappointed because we could have been an NBA member," said Dampier. "I don't think they (owners) used the right or honest excuses for why we didn't do it. We knew the money was there, but they said that we didn't have a large enough market or good enough place to play in, which wasn't accurate. Freedom Hall is one of the nicest places there is to play basketball. Even before it was remodeled, it was a great place for players because the background was dark. It was a good shooting arena and sat almost 17,000.

"The interest would have been there (in the NBA) because teams only came in two times a year and that would have brought in all the stars. People could have seen a different star every game and wouldn't have to do like they did the last year in the ABA when we had seven teams. You might see the Virginia Squires twice in a week or once every two weeks. So, going with the NBA, (the league) would have had well over 20 teams. You know if a Magic

Johnson was coming in once, people would be there and you'd have a big crowd. If the Phoenix Suns only come in once, you'd have a big crowd. I think the attendance would have been there. The money was there. People would have supported it, and we would have had a good competitive team, too."

So, as the result of the so-called NBA-ABA merger, Dampier went to San Antonio where he played three more years primarily as a key reserve guard. However, things weren't the same. Texas was not home to Dampier. Kentucky was where he belonged, but there was nothing he could do. "I was not as happy as I would have been staying in Louisville," he said. "It was a good situation if l had to go to another team because I knew all the players on San Antonio. It was an ABA team. I knew the coach (Doug Moe). It was probably the best thing that could have happened to me that I did go down there. It's a beautiful city and I enjoyed it. But after three years of San Antonio, I was ready to go somewhere else."

Dampier retired in 1979 as one of the all-time NBA/ABA leading scorers with 15,279 points, many of them coming from his patented three-point bombs, with an average of 15.9 per game. In addition, Dampier and Issel finished their ABA careers as the league's top two all-time leading scorers. Dampier scored 13,726 points in nine years for an average of nearly 19 points, while Issel had 12,823 points, averaging almost 26 points in six seasons. In 2015, Dampier was voted in to the Naismith Basketball Hall of Fame, and Issel was his Hall of Fame presenter.

# 3

## Part Two: Wildcats in Wild & Wacky ABA

(Dan Issel, John Y. Brown III & more)

While at UK during the spring of 1970, when NBA and three-year-old ABA got into a bidding war for the top collegiate stars, Dan Issel sought coach Adolph Rupp for advice. The coach told Issel to make sure the franchise had strong financial backing. Some pro basketball teams, especially in the less-established ABA, were financially-strapped. Issel decided to remain in the state of Kentucky and signed a multi-year $1.4 million contract with the Colonels, who were one of the ABA's stronger franchises.

Issel's five-year pact, at the time, was reportedly the largest amount ever given to a pro basketball rookie. Kareem Abdul-Jabbar also had signed a reported $1.4 million contract with the Milwaukee Bucks in the previous year. Issel's Wildcat teammate Mike Pratt joined the Colonels for a reported $400,000. University of Tennessee's 6-foot-10 All-SEC center Bobby Croft also signed with Kentucky.

"The Colonels were a very sound team," said Issel, who graduated with a bachelor's degree in business. "They were owned by five men — Wendell Cherry and David Jones who had started Humana; John Y. Brown Jr., of course, who had the Kentucky Fried Chicken; Stuart Jay, who is a real successful lawyer in Louisville; and David Grissom, who was president of Citizens Fidelity Bank. So there was sound financial backing. If Coach Rupp hadn't known who the men behind the Colonels were, I don't think he would have given me the advice to sign with an ABA team, but he knew the Colonels were strong."

Issel, who is still UK men's all-time leading scorer with 2,138 points, said the Colonels and the ABA exaggerated his fat contract for public relations. "They played it up," he recalled. "It wouldn't be as big as they said it was. Of course, that was right when the ABA was getting competitive with the NBA and going after (top) players. They said the five-year deal was for $1.4 million, but there were a lot of investments that had to work out and things like that. My actual salary was $75,000 a year. I loved the fact that I got to stay in Kentucky and play professional basketball. So that was kind of a dream come true going right up the road and playing in Louisville."

Despite the horror stories about some teams failing to meet their payroll, Issel said he never worried about being paid during his ABA tenure. "I was always fortunate that I was with some teams (Kentucky and Denver) that had pretty good financial backing. We never had to worry about our payrolls, our check not cashing and clearing, and things like that. But there were a lot of shaky ABA teams financially. I know a lot of players in the ABA who did have to worry about their paychecks clearing. In fact, a friend of mine who was with the Virginia Squires told a funny story. He said everybody who played for the Squires went out and bought a real fast car because when they got their paychecks, only the first two or three guys to the bank would have their paychecks be good. Everybody bought a fast car so they could get to the bank quick.  But I never had to worry about that."

*Dan Issel (Photo by Jamie H. Vaught)*

With Issel and Pratt joining three-time All-ABA guard Louie Dampier as ex-Wildcats on board, the 1970-71 campaign was an exciting time for the Kentucky Colonels and the ABA.  Anticipating larger crowds because of Issel's popularity, the aggressive new ownership group decided to hold many of its home games at

16,933-seat Freedom Hall. In the previous three years since the ABA began in 1967, the Colonels usually played all of their home games at smallish 5,733-seat Convention Center in downtown Louisville. In addition, the Colonels, under the new leadership of innovative president and general manager Mike Storen, featured a modern look with new uniforms, new colors (from green to blue) and new logo. The franchise also signed new three-year contracts with Louisville's WLKY-TV (Channel 32) and powerful WHAS Radio. Lexington's WKYT-TV (Channel 27) also joined the Colonel Television Network, increasing statewide television coverage for the ABA club. The team received more local and regional newspaper coverage than it ever had before.

And the Colonels, occasionally, got national attention. The weekly *Sporting News* magazine had Issel on its cover (January 23, 1971), calling him the "Golden Boy," for a cover story about the upcoming ABA All-Star Game. In the mid-season classic, Issel had a remarkable game. He scored 21 points and snatched 11 rebounds in leading East to a 126-122 victory before a record 14,407 fans in Greensboro, North Carolina. The all-star game, which was nationally televised by CBS network, also featured ex-NBA superstars such as Joe Caldwell of the Carolina Cougars, Rick Barry of the New York Nets and Zelmo Beaty of the Utah Stars.

"Any (national) publicity that the ABA got then was kind of unusual because we played in a lot of small markets," Issel said. "We weren't in New York or Chicago or L.A. You know, we were on Long Island (where the New York Nets headquartered), and we were in Greensboro, Louisville and Indianapolis. So we didn't get a lot of publicity. It was real unusual when an ABA player would get on the cover of a national publication or get a story done in the national press."

The publicity-starved ABA didn't have a single nationally-televised contest until its third season (1969-70) when CBS carried its third annual All-Star Game in Indianapolis on a Saturday afternoon. The following season saw CBS televising several ABA games, showcasing the league's new superstars from the NBA and collegiate ranks, including Issel. Unlike today's television broadcasting industry, these were the days when the cable TV and streaming didn't even exist.

As a rookie, Issel encountered many interesting moments throughout the 1970-71 campaign. Sometimes the Colonels played in front of very small crowds when they faced some of the league's weaker franchises. Commented Issel, "I remember one night we were playing (the Texas Chapparals who used the name 'Texas' instead of 'Dallas' for only one year) in Dallas, and this is before they moved to San Antonio and became the San Antonio Spurs. During the national anthem, Louie (Dampier) took one side of the arena and I took the other side. We counted the crowd while they were playing the national anthem. And I don't remember the exact total, but it was 200 and something. That's how many people were at the gym."

The team also became embroiled in a controversy when the Colonels' departing trainer Bill Antonini, who earlier had served as a trainer for both the football and basketball teams at UK, made some comments, which first made the front page of the old *Louisville Times*. He charged the Colonels were having racial problems and that coach Frank Ramsey was doing a poor job of coaching. For several days, the city of Louisville was bombarded with media reports about the racial issue. Several black players, however, defended Ramsey, denying the trainer's charges. The Colonels had seven black players with five white players on the squad, according to the team's media guide. "We had a trainer who made a charge that I was a racist," Ramsey said in a 1994 interview. "That wasn't very pleasant. When that happened, I think it solidified the team. It allowed us to go on and go to the (ABA) finals."

The Colonels, which finished with a 44-40 worksheet in the regular season, advanced to the league's exciting championship series with the Utah Stars before dropping in seven games. As far as average home attendance was concerned, the Colonels fared well at the gate, drawing league's second-best 7,500 fans, behind Indiana's 8,200. "We always drew pretty well in Freedom Hall," said Issel.

Still the Colonels weren't satisfied. They didn't want to rest on their laurels. The Louisville franchise wanted an ABA championship, so they went out on a spending spree and signed 7-foot-2 Artis Gilmore, an intimidating shot blocker from Jacksonville who led the country in rebounding his junior and senior years. That meant Issel, who played at center as a 6-foot-9, 235-pound rookie, would be forced to move to forward in the following season.

In the 1971-72 season, Kentucky, with Issel and Gilmore in the lineup, improved dramatically, posting a remarkable regular season mark of 68-16, a league record. The fifth annual ABA All-Star Game was held in Louisville, and a record crowd of nearly 16,000 saw Issel capture the Most Valuable Player award. But the Colonels, guided by former Los Angeles Lakers mentor Joe Mullaney, didn't win the league crown. They didn't go very far in the postseason playoffs. The New York Nets, who finished the regular season with a 44-40 record, stunned the heavily-favored Colonels in seven games in the opening round. It would be three more years before Kentucky would win its first ABA championship. It was May 1975 when the Colonels, with coach Hubie Brown at the helm, finally captured the league title in defeating arch-rival Indiana Pacers in five games. Winning the league championship is the highlight of his career, Issel said. The ABA title will always be a special one for Issel; it's the only championship he has won in his long basketball career.

Even though his team won the championship, Kentucky owner John Y. Brown Jr. said he was still losing significant amount of money in operating the Colonels. To recover his losses, Brown decided that he would sell one of the Colonels stars — Artis Gilmore or Dan Issel. As mentioned previously, it was Issel who went to the Baltimore Claws franchise (formerly the Memphis Sounds) in a very controversial move. In the transaction, Brown got 6-foot-10 center Tom Owens and approximately $500,000 for Issel.

*Several ABA players, including superstars Julius Erving and Billy Cunningham, have graced the cover of The Sporting News magazine. Dan Issel of the Kentucky Colonels was the cover boy for the magazine's Jan. 23, 1971 edition. (TSN Archives)*

Issel said the 1975 trade was his most depressing moment of his pro basketball career. "I was very upset. Very upset," he commented. "We had just built a brand new home in Louisville after four years at the University of Kentucky, and five years with the Colonels. I thought I was going to live in Kentucky for the rest of my life. It was not only depressing in having to leave (Louisville), but it was depressing being in Baltimore because I would go to practice, and Cheri would try to go out and find a decent place to live. She couldn't find any place that she liked. We were (staying) in a hotel room with (daughter) Sheridan, a dog, and a parakeet, if I remember correctly. It was easily the most depressing moment."

Issel, however, wasn't the only one miserable. Issel's boss was having problems of his own. The highly-publicized trade got Brown in a big firestorm as he went through a giant public relations disaster. The Kentucky fans were outraged, feeling betrayed. To them, Issel was their hero. "(Brown) was getting very negative press in Louisville after he had sold me," Issel said. "The people were really upset in Louisville and the worse part is the people in Baltimore never paid John Y. the money for me they said they were going to pay." So, about a week later, without Issel's knowledge, Brown flew to Baltimore and checked in at the same hotel where Issel and his family were staying. And the phone rang in Issel's room. It was Brown. "He was the last guy that I expected to be hearing from," Issel said. "He said we need to talk, and I said okay."

"Can you come down to my room?" Brown asked.

"You're here?" said a confused Issel.

"Yeah, I'm here in the hotel in Baltimore."

After Issel arrived in Brown's hotel room, they had their conversation. Brown told Issel, "Here's the deal, if you said something that will get the people in Louisville off my back, I'll get you out of Baltimore and get you with a good team." Replied Issel, "You got a deal. Get me out of here!"

Popularly called "The Horse" because of his durability, Issel was on his way to the Denver Nuggets, one of ABA's best franchises. With him was a paycheck from the Baltimore Claws, who eventually folded without having played a single regular season game. "I got one paycheck that I didn't have a chance to cash before I left Baltimore," Issel said. "So I went to Denver and I went to the bank. I started a new account with this check I got from the Baltimore Claws. No good. It bounced. And (Denver owner) Carl Scheer had to make good on that check. But that is not a great way to get off a good relationship with a new bank — to open an account with a check that bounced."

While Denver coasted to ABA-best 60-24 mark during Issel's first year with the Nuggets, the ex-Colonel recalled a bizarre incident involving the financially-troubled Virginia Squires, who were in Denver to meet the Nuggets. "They were in a hotel in Denver. They had been there a time or two before, but hadn't paid their bill. (The hotel) put the teams' bags out on the street and wasn't going to let them stay there until they paid their bills. Our owner (and president/general manager), Carl Scheer, had to go down to the hotel and write a check for everything that the Squires owed them or they weren't going to let them come in and spend the night."

As for the 1975-76 season, Issel, who averaged 23 points and 11 rebounds, earned All-ABA honors for the fifth time, as the Nuggets went to the championship series before losing to high-flying superstar Julius "Dr. J" Erving and the New York Nets. About a month later, ABA sent four teams — Denver, Indiana, New York and San Antonio — to the NBA in a merger. Issel's former team, Kentucky Colonels, meanwhile, declined to join the NBA, saying the entry price of approximately $3 million was too high. It marked the unfortunate death of the Colonels and ABA. With the merger, ABA's popular innovations — the red, white and blue basketball, and the three-point field goal — disappeared.

The NBA rejected these so-called gimmicks, but it later embraced the three-point basket in 1979.

Many of ABA's star players continued to thrive in the older league. The newest NBA standouts included Issel, Gilmore, Erving, David Thompson, George McGinnis, Rick Barry, George Gervin, Billy Knight, to name a few. In his first year of NBA action, Issel finished as one of the league's top 10 scoring leaders, averaging 22 points. He also appeared in the NBA All-Star Game. By the way, a former ABA player captured the MVP honors in the All-Star classic. His name? Future Hall of Famer Julius Erving.

Issel would remain in Denver as a member of the NBA establishment for the rest of his playing career until 1985 when he retired at the age of 36. Toward the end of his last pro season as a player, Issel went through a so-called "farewell tour," receiving many gifts from several NBA clubs, including an exotic trip to Hawaii. The Nuggets also retired his famed "44" jersey number. In his 15-year pro career, Issel scored 27,482 points, ranking at No. 14 on the all-time ABA/NBA scoring list as of 2025.

Issel "was one of those people that they said was not big enough to play center at 6-foot-9," said Frank Ramsey, who coached the Colonels in Issel's rookie year. "Dan had a tremendous attitude about practice and working. They said he was too slow and couldn't jump, but by golly, look what he's done. He is now in the Basketball Hall of Fame. He had a tremendous career at Denver after the ABA (merged with the NBA). Dan is one fine individual."

While Issel was in the ABA, he knew a little girl who would someday become a well-known sportscaster. She was the oldest child of Mike Storen, who worked for the Kentucky Colonels as their top executive. That little girl is ESPN's Hannah Storm. Storm's dad also served as ABA commissioner for one year after a three-year stint with the Colonels. Issel said Storm didn't play or practice on the court with the players very much when she was small. "She would be at the games and (I would see her) when we went to the Storens for parties and things," recalled Issel. "I wasn't real close with her, but I definitely remember her when she was growing up." Later, she would interview Issel several times on TV.

When Rupp died in 1977, Issel wasn't able to attend the coach's funeral in Lexington. Issel, at the time, was still playing for the Nuggets. He learned of Rupp's death via a telephone call from Claude Vaughan, one of Rupp's close friends. "That was a sad day," Issel commented. "I loved Coach Rupp. He always did exactly what he told me he was going to do. A lot that I had and have, I think I owe to Coach Rupp, not only from the basketball angle and what he taught me about the game of basketball, but about being a human being — the work ethic and honesty. I learned an awful, awful lot from Coach Rupp."

## John Y. Brown III's Stories

When the younger John Brown was a young kid, growing up in Louisville during the late 1960s and early 1970s, his father, future Gov. John Y. Brown Jr., became a member of the ownership group that purchased the Kentucky Colonels in 1969. Brown III was a kid who had a basketball goal in his backyard and often played on warm summer nights under the bright flood lights. He was crazy about the Colonels and got to know many of their players.

"The Colonels were an integral part of my young life and I have so many wonderful memories," said Brown III, a UK College of Law graduate who followed his father in state politics as he twice was elected to the office of Secretary of State. "The story of my tears helping to save the Colonels (in 1973) is absolutely true, and I remember that day like it was yesterday. I think it was then that my father realized he'd made a mistake, and thousands of young Kentuckians across the state were broken-hearted and crying, too, over the loss. To his great credit, he fought successfully to cancel the deal with the Cincinnati group, and we kept the

Colonels several more years and finally secured that elusive but so well-deserved championship trophy (in 1975). Our two UK stars, Dan Issel and Louie Dampier, were the secret sauce. They 'Kentucky-ized' the team and were two of UK's all-time greats playing 42 home games a year for a beloved professional Kentucky team."

*John Y. Brown III, wearing a Kentucky Colonels uniform, shoots in the backyard with his parents, John and Ellie Brown, looking on at their Louisville home. (Brown Family Photo Collection)*

When Brown Jr. got the Colonels back, his wife, Ellie Brown, took over and established an historic all-female board of directors for the franchise, and the Colonels saw a dramatic increase in season ticket sales for the 1973-74 season. The average game attendance also increased by over 1,000.

The Colonels once had a player by the name of Jim Bradley, who later became a third-round NBA Draft pick by the Los Angeles Lakers in 1974. But before 6-foot-8 Bradley joined the team in the middle of the 1973-74 season, he had to try out in the backyard of Brown's house.

In a 2025 podcast with businessman and former Colonels player George Tinsley Sr., Brown III shared a story. "I remember one night David Vance (publicity director who later became the general manager) brought a player named Jim Bradley to the house at about 9:00 at night," Brown said. "It was dark and they were trying to decide (whether to pick him up or not), and my dad said, 'Well, let's go and see what you got.' I remember Jim Bradley was sitting with him (and saying), 'Well, what do you mean?' He (dad) said, 'Well, we've got a basketball goal outside my son shoots on.' I'd spray painted a free throw line, three-point line. Jim had on his platform shoes, and we put a flood light on so you could see him play, and he just starts shooting. He got this great one-hand shot, and I think Dan Issel once said of him, 'If you could put my heart in his body, we'd have the best player in the ABA.' After about 10 or 15 minutes, Dad said, 'Alright, let's sign him up.' Could you imagine anything like that happening today in the NBA?"

As Brown III told the author, the story "about adding Jim Bradley to the team is hilarious and captures the spirit of the league, the owners and players, as Jim was being asked to shoot around in our backyard at night wearing dress shoes and getting signed on.

"When the (fictional) movie *Semi-Pro* came out (in 2008), I went to opening night with my mom and (journalist) Billy Reed. We got dinner afterwards to talk about it all, and Billy said, 'I don't know why they felt the need to make up stories for the movie. There were so many real stories that were even more bizarre and funnier that actually happened.' "

On ABA, the younger Brown commented, "The real ABA history is rich and fascinating and has lots to teach and inspire. And, yes, there were plenty of clumsy and humorous moments along the way as well. I experienced it all through a child's eyes but could tell the NBA leaders viewed the ABA as a threat and knew the ABA had some of the sports X factors that they lacked. The Colonels coach, Hubie Brown, said the 1975 Kentucky Colonels were the best pro team he'd ever witnessed. My father put up $1 million for the 1975 NBA champs, the Golden State Warriors, to play the Kentucky Colonels, the ABA champs that year, for a 'World Championship Game' but the Warriors refused.

*John Y. Brown III (Brown Family Photo Collection)*

"I remember cringing as I listened to Red Auerbach (of the Boston Celtics fame) arrogantly try to minimize the caliber of ABA teams and players. It was infuriating. The ABA was more like the people's basketball league. It was like the NBA was the private school league comprised of boring set shots and bounce passes. The ABA was the public school league with more of a street ball flair that scared the NBA. ABA players truly were closer to their fans — they had to be. They would help sell season tickets in the offseason to keep their job.

"The ABA, in my mind, was just so darned interesting ... and quintessentially American. It was a ragtag group that felt they could be as good or better than the stuffy NBA and refused to be told no — no matter how steep the odds. It had an experimental and entrepreneurial culture that made them charming and beloved and impossible not to pull for. All those affiliated with the ABA — from players and coaches to owners, managers and, most of all, the fans — have sought vindication for our love of and investment in the ABA.

"I always felt that vindication occurred most obviously at the 1977 All-Star game after the leagues merged — 18 NBA teams and four ABA teams and a smattering of ABA players from the teams that didn't merge. So roughly 20 percent of the new league was from the ABA. Yet ABA players made up over 40 percent of the all stars that year. By the end of the season, about 40 percent of the league's top 20 players in each statistics category (scoring, rebounds, assists, steals and blocked shots) were ABA players. And, let's be honest, they were a heckuva lot more fun to watch them play. Those of us who grew up with the ABA have been waiting 45 years for the respect our league deserved and are still waiting. We know how special the league was. But it sure would be nice if a major production formally and eloquently explained it to the rest of world.

"I remember (former ABA player and NBA coach) George Karl well and got to meet Dr. J (superstar Julius Erving) several times. One funny story and I'll wrap this up. I was a ball boy at the 1976 ABA All Star game in San Antonio. In the fourth quarter, I got to give Dr. J a paper cup with water. As he reached for it, it spilled on him. I was mortified. He just smiled and said, 'What I'd really like is champagne.' He made it all okay for a nervous young boy. Always a class act. I met a young man last week who works for the Brooklyn Nets. I asked him who the most significant player in the franchise's history was. Without missing a beat, he said, 'Dr. J.' I said, 'You are exactly right!' Dr. J was the precursor to Jordan, Kobe, Magic and LeBron. But Dr. J was the original who transformed and modernized the game probably more than any other player and who more players have tried to imitate without even knowing it.

"Of course, I'm biased. All ABA fans are. But we had good reason for that bias and hope the full ABA story finally and fittingly gets told by you and your team. You won't regret it ... and you'll be hard-pressed to find a more fun project in your lifetime." After the ABA folded, Brown Jr. reportedly paid $1 million for partial ownership in the NBA's Buffalo Braves (now Los Angeles Clippers). He wanted to move the Braves to Louisville but was blocked by a court ruling. So Brown and a partner then exchanged the Braves for the Boston Celtics in the first trade of pro sports teams.

*Ellie Brown, who became the nation's first woman to own a professional basketball franchise, the Kentucky Colonels, in 1973, posed with her children — John Y. Brown III, Sandy Steier and Sissy Brown. (Brown Family Photo Collection)*

On Colonels' failure to join the NBA, Brown III recalled, "I was deeply saddened but not as shocked or upset as when I was told about the unexpected sale over three years earlier. This time it was more of a slow grieving process. Years later, I joked with Dan Issel that many in my generation remembered where they were when John F. Kennedy was shot, and for those of us who were Kentucky Colonels fans, we remembered where we were when we heard Dan Issel had been traded. Dan smiled and with a deadpan response quipped, 'I remember where I was, too, John.'

"It was an awful time when my father traded Dan to the Baltimore Claws to try to keep the team financially afloat. Later on, the New York Nets would have to do the same thing with Dr. J. Trading Dan Issel was, in many ways, the beginning of the end of the Colonels. The corporate community in Louisville specifically and Kentucky generally just weren't willing to step up to save the Colonels. Despite all the successes, the team was still losing significant money annually, and it had become too much for one person or one family to try to support. Adjusted for inflation, the NBA was asking for about $20 million in today's dollars for expansion fees with the only guarantee being that we'd probably continue to lose money annually.

"I don't think our city or state leaders recognized how much was at stake and how great a vacuum losing the Colonels would create. Many of our city leaders back then were galvanized around growing the city's commitment to the arts and looked at sports vs. the arts as an either/or decision and opted for the latter. Despite all of the challenges, my father tried a backdoor approach to getting an NBA team to Louisville by purchasing the Buffalo Braves with the money he received for the Colonels' dispersal draft. He had hopes of eventually bringing the Braves to Louisville but hit some unexpected challenges that thwarted that effort and eventually traded the Braves for the Boston Celtics, and then sold his share of the (Boston) Celtics to run for governor.

"Even had the Braves somehow made it to Louisville as our NBA team, it wouldn't have been the same. It would have been without the former UK and U of L players or other longtime beloved players that fans had become attached to and loved cheering on. They wouldn't have been the Colonels. You may ask, so how did it feel when your father ended up with the Boston Celtics? Honestly, I felt we had traded down. I met Red Auerbach a few times, and he was all business and didn't seem comfortable around kids. Sure,

I was aware of the storied history of the Celtics and their NBA dynasty. But that was with a brown ball and they didn't have Louie Dampier, Dan Issel, Artis Gilmore, Bird Averitt, Joe Hamilton, Wendell Ladner, Maurice Lucas, Will Jones, Ted McClain, Hubie Brown, or my mom, Ellie Brown.

"Hubie Brown said of the 1975 Colonels, they were probably the best basketball team ever to take the hardwood. The Colonels were better than the Celtics. They also personified the love of the game and were all good people who cared about their community. It was a special team and a special time. The Boston Celtics — or any team for that matter — just couldn't compare."

## Mike Casey

In the 1970 ABA draft, the Kentucky Colonels drafted three Wild-cats — Issel, Pratt and Casey. While Issel and Pratt signed big pro contracts, Casey chose to finish up his career at UK, earning All-SEC honors during his senior year. Casey was eligible for the draft because he was a member of the graduating class (fourth year in college). Also, he was picked by Chicago in the eighth round of the NBA draft. But in the following season, Casey had to try out for a spot on the Colonels roster even though he was a big-name Wildcat star. The ABA club also had another high-profile rookie — All-American Artis Gilmore from Jacksonsville — along with other first-year players. But unlike Casey, Gilmore had a no-cut contract reportedly worth $2.4 million. (It has been reported that Gilmore's total compensation package, however, was much less than $2.4 million.) According to Casey, he signed a one-year contract for $125,000, but it was not guaranteed. He would have to make the team, and it wouldn't be a cakewalk as Kentucky was already loaded with outside shooters — Louie Dampier, Darel Carrier and Issel. New Colonels floor boss Joe Mullaney also was looking for someone with quick hands to play defense.

"I went through six weeks of summer camp — Artis Gilmore and myself," Casey said. "As a matter of fact, I averaged 27 points a game during that time. We played about 12 games — we played Carolina, Indiana and Virginia. Gilmore was the only one that had a no-cut contract, which I understood. But I never will forget that night he (Mullaney) had to go in and make the final cut (in eliminating Casey from the squad). We had beaten Indiana with (star rookie) George McGinnis and his bunch."

So Casey's pro hopes dashed. That meant he wouldn't play with his college teammates in the ABA. He was very downhearted. He had thought his chances with the Colonels were good. "That was one of the hardest things I had to endure because everybody thought (I would make it) after 27 points and we were undefeated (in the preseason)," Casey said. "I remember I had to walk out and tell my mom and dad that I got cut. Nobody could believe it. It all boiled down to one (factor or two). I had $125,000-a-year contract and Mike Gale had a $17,500 (pact), which was the minimum at that time. And Mike Gale was a real good defensive specialist. They had Dampier, Carrier and Issel, and Gilmore was a rookie that year. So, they had enough scorers.

"But it was hard. (I was cut) even though we had about 400 season tickets sold in Shelby County because one of the guys who helped represent me had 400 signed up. That was part of his deal to get so many people — season ticket holders. But it got down to just basic business, dollars and cents. You know it was disappointing. It was a business decision, but it is cold how they do it. That's, you know, part of life and you have to go on."

One year later, in 1972, Casey went to Memphis in hopes of playing pro basketball. He wanted another chance. Casey was going to the struggling Memphis franchise, which had underwent major changes with new ownership and management, and he agreed to a one-year contract for $17,500 if he made the squad. The new owner was none other than controversial Charles O. Finley (who also owned the three-time World Series champion

Oakland A's during the early 1970s). And the owner himself wanted someone with a big name. So he hired Adolph Rupp to be the team's new president. Plus Finley wanted Memphis to have new colors and a new nickname, changing from the Pros to Tams. The green-and-gold Tams represented the tri-state area of Tennessee, Arkansas and Mississippi. "I had been to Mexico and playing down there for about a month and then got a call from Coach Rupp, asking that I come and try out for them," explained Casey of his Memphis stint. "Johnny Neumann (All-American from Ole Miss) was there, and I stayed around for about a month there, but got cut." On the team's sparklingly new uniforms, Casey said, "I remember they gave us all a green-and-gold 'Tams' to wear. It had the 'Tams' on it. It was cute."

While in Memphis, Casey didn't see much of Rupp, who traded stories and discussed basketball with the squad's new coach Bob Bass. "He was down there to make a personal appearance or something, and he would stay a day or two and then leave," commented Casey. "We were practicing twice a day so he didn't stay around too long. They used him more as a consultant. I enjoyed my stay in Memphis. We stayed right in downtown at Howard Johnson's, and we would walk over to the old (arena). It was quite an experience." The ex-Wildcat also added that he never had a conversation with Finley.

After two unsuccessful attempts in pro basketball, Casey decided that was enough. "I never did go to the NBA because I thought my chances were better in Louisville being in the proximity to the Colonels and Shelby County and all that," said Casey, who also conducted summer basketball camps with Issel, Pratt and Rupp in the early 1970s. "But as I look back now and got drafted by the (Chicago) Bulls and the Cleveland Cavaliers (in 1971), I probably should have followed those (players) who had gone up there (in the NBA) and tried out."

## Kentucky Sportswriters

"I would have to say my favorite ABA memory came on the night of May 22, 1975, when the Kentucky Colonels won their first and only ABA championship," said Jim Kurk, now retired after many years of sportswriting with Somerset's *Commonealth Journal* and Henderson's *The Gleaner*. "With first-year coach Hubie Brown at the helm, they beat their rival, the Indiana Pacers, 110-105 in Game 5 of the ABA Finals at Freedom Hall. Superstar center Artis Gilmore led the way with 28 points and an astounding 31 rebounds. I was lucky enough to have a press credential for that game and watched it from an end zone courtside seat. It was great to see the Colonels' two longtime stars, former Wildcats Louie Dampier and Dan Issel, finally win a championship after so many seasons of heartbreak.

"I was a big Colonels fan for all nine of their seasons and saw more games, mostly from the stands, than I could count. It was fun watching those powerhouse Colonels teams go up against the ABA greats such as Julius 'Dr. J' Erving, Rick Barry, George 'Ice Man' Gervin, Moses Malone and David Thompson, to name a few. Some other games I saw that stand out: An exhibition game against the Milwaukee Bucks featuring Kareem Abdul-Jabbar and Oscar Robertson. The 1972 ABA All-Star Game — Dan Issel was the MVP. A game against the San Diego Conquistadors (or the Q's) coached by Wilt Chamberlain. And the infamous Wendell Ladner water cooler game. It's a shame that it all came crashing down not long after the championship season. The Colonels folded and faded into history. I still miss them." Kurk also mentioned other Wildcats like Tommy Kron (a Rupp's Runts standout of 1965-66 who played for the Colonels in 1969-70 after three NBA seasons) and Jimmy Dan Conner.

John P. Herndon is another Kentucky sportswriter who has fond memories of the Colonels when he was a youngster. "I was a huge Colonels fan from Day One. I grew up in northern Anderson

County, about 50 miles from Louisville, so I could sometimes pick up the Colonels games on WAVE Radio in the first few years," recalled Herndon, who has been writing sports for over 40 years. "I had just started watching basketball about the time of Rupp's Runts at UK, and Louie Dampier was my favorite Wildcat. So, obviously from the beginning, he was my favorite Colonel. I can remember seeing an ad in the *Courier-Journal*, which we took at home, about some car dealership giving away tickets to a Colonels game if you test drove a car. In addition, some of the Colonels would be at the dealership that day.

"So, my parents drove to that dealership, and I met Goose Ligon and Howard Bayne. I was only nine years old but remembered Howard Bayne from his days at Tennessee. I remember being blown away that he could talk about the farm with me. I guess the little kid in me still remembers things like that.

"I remember that first game my family went to see was against New Orleans at Convention Center. The Colonels won 110-105. I remember that, believe it or not. When the games switched to WHAS, everything changed. I listened to Van Vance every game I could. The fact that Dan Issel had become a part of the Colonels was even bigger. I mean, how much better could it get for a Wildcat fan than having Dampier and Issel in the starting lineup? Having Mike Pratt come off the bench was even better.

"When the Colonels orchestrated the move to get Artis Gilmore, I thought they would have a dynasty. Obviously, he'd broken my heart when Jacksonville beat Kentucky in the 1970 NCAA Tournament, but I knew just how good he was and thought that a front line that included Gilmore and Issel would be practically unstoppable.

"The Colonels were not on TV much, but every time they were, I did all within my power to make sure I was home to watch the games. Seems kind of strange to think that way now with wall-to-wall sports (on many channels) and DVRs but in the '70s, if you didn't see the game when it was broadcast, you just missed out."

Herndon also has other favorite stories about the Colonels. "The biggest memory I have is being able to be a part of one of those 'High-Pro' doubleheaders. I think that was the official name. The Colonels would invite high school teams to come in and play before their game. It was a real doubleheader with the high school game as a preliminary to the Colonels' game. I was the manager at Anderson County High School, and in my junior year, we were ranked in the state's Top 10. We were invited to play Louisville Butler in the preliminary game, which was a huge deal to play on the Freedom Hall floor. Our dressing room was right next to the Spurs' locker room and seeing guys like James Silas, George Gervin and Swen Nater — guys you'd heard Van Vance talk about — was a huge thrill.

"The other big memory I have of the Colonels and the ABA was just how exciting the league was. You'd see the NBA on TV and it was good basketball, but it was largely 'a pound the ball to the post' league. But watching the ABA, you'd see little guys like Louie Dampier or Darel Carrier or the Pacers' Freddie Lewis light it up from downtown for three, it was exciting. And seeing guys like Dr. J bring a style of play to the game that I'd never seen before was just amazing. If you saw Dr. J play for the Virginia Squires — I did — you saw the true trailblazer. When I got my driver's license, he'd been traded to New York, so I made it a point to get to Freedom Hall every time the Nets were in town. It was worth the price of admission to watch his dunking show in warmups."

As the 1975-76 season approached, things began to fall apart in the ABA. "John Y. Brown Jr. had sent Dan Issel to Baltimore, then had to orchestrate another trade of Issel to Denver. Issel was a fan favorite, the blue-collar guy who had played at UK and was highly visible in Louisville and across the state. When he was traded, some fan enthusiasm left too. I think I was like most fans who loved Louie Dampier and Artis Gilmore but were tired of the constant roster flux in 1975-76. You never knew who was going to be on the team from one game to the next, then with the Utah and San Diego franchises folding in mid-season and the constant rumors that the Squires were done too, the schedule was constantly changing. I think everyone knew the ABA was in big trouble, but just assumed the Colonels would live on if there was a merger. How could the Colonels not live on? Even though interest had declined that final season, the Colonels were still one of the best draws in pro basketball. So, yes, even 50 years later, I still miss the Colonels."

## Frank Ramsey

In fall of 1970, Ramsey returned to pro basketball after a six-year hiatus. No, he didn't go back to Boston where he previously helped the Celtics win eight NBA titles. A three-time All-American at UK, Ramsey went to Louisville where he was hired to coach the Colonels. While aging Rupp, nearing retirement, was still coaching the Wildcats in Lexington — one hour away from Louisville on I-64 — the 39-year-old Ramsey was persuaded to leave Madisonville, his hometown, where he found business success. Shortly after Colonels President Mike Storen announced the appointment of Ramsey as the new floor boss of the Colonels, many of Ramsey's basketball friends sent telegrams. Sending congratulations were several big-name folks like Rupp, Red Auerbach, Bill Sharman and Cliff Hagan (who at the time had just retired from ABA's Dallas team as player-coach).

"A guy that I had known for sometime, Mike Storen, contacted me," Ramsey said. "He said that he was going to make a coaching change. I had just sold a business in Madisonville, and I had some spare time. But I told him that I wasn't interested. He asked me again and I said no. Finally, he said why don't you give it a try so I did. That year we went to the finals of the ABA (against the

Utah Stars, coached by Sharman, a former Celtics teammate of Ramsey's)."

Before Ramsey took the job, the Colonels were already 17 games into the season. The team was doing all right with a 10-5 mark, but Storen and popular coach Gene Rhodes reportedly had a personality conflict and Rhodes was dismissed after 15 games. And former UK All-American and Colonels business manager Alex Groza took over the coaching duties for a couple of games — both victories — on an interim basis.

Ramsey's coaching record for the 1970-71 regular season wasn't spectacular. He compiled a 32-35 mark. But his team bounced back and did well in the playoffs, winning the first two rounds against the Floridians from Miami and a strong Virginia Squires club before losing to Utah in seven games in the championship series. One of the highlights of the Colonels season featured Dan Issel's blazing success as a pro rookie. Issel captured the league's scoring title with an average of nearly 30 points a game. Issel and Charlie Scott of Virginia shared ABA's Rookie of the Year honors. (The Squires were coached by Al Bianchi, a former boss of ex-UK coach Rick Pitino when they worked at New York in the NBA. Bianchi served as the Knicks general manager during Pitino's two years with the Knicks in late 1980s.)

But Ramsey didn't stay in the coaching business very long as he quit his post after the season. He would not be around to watch the Colonels and the league grow the following season. "At the end of the year, I had to decide whether to stay in coaching or in business," he explained. "It was very difficult. I was having to drive and fly, drive and fly. I couldn't coach with my business interests (in Madisonville). My family was still in Madisonville. I only had a hotel room in Louisville. It got to be too much. So, with my children and the ages they were, and my businesses, I decided to stay in Madisonville. I've never regretted it." He was replaced by ex-Los Angeles Laker coach Joe Mullaney.

On his one-year coaching experience with the Colonels, Ramsey said, "It was interesting. I enjoyed coaching and working with the players. I had a wonderful group of players — Issel, Pratt, (Cincy) Powell, Walt Simon, Darel Carrier and Louie Dampier. I enjoyed being associated with them. It was a very enjoyable experience. I'm glad I had it. My life then was not totally basketball like when I was in Boston. My life in Boston was totally basketball."

In 1981, Ramsey received the highest honor a player or coach can have when he was named to the Naismith Basketball Hall of Fame in Springfield, Mass. At that time, he became the third representative from UK to receive the Hall of Fame honor, joining Rupp, who was inducted in 1969, and Hagan, inducted in 1977. But when he first received a notification that he was chosen for the honor, he didn't believe it. A Hall of Famer? No way, he thought. "The first thing I thought it was a joke because the words were misspelled," Ramsey said. "I got the letter in my mailbox. I read it, but I didn't think that it would ever be possible that I would be elected to the Hall of Fame. My wife was on a tour, I believe in Italy, and I thought it was a joke so I didn't say anything to anybody. Finally, I told her and then it was announced in the paper. It was extremely difficult to believe that a substitute, particularly a boy from a community of 5,000, could be elected to the Hall of Fame. It was thrilling. Unbelievable. I didn't deserve it. I'm just honored to be included in such a group. (Clarence) 'Big House' Gaines who coaches in North Carolina, Hal Greer and Willis Reed were elected that year."

## Jimmy Dan Conner

A former Mr. Kentucky Basketball in 1971 from Anderson County High School, the 6-foot-4 Conner was among the four standouts from UK's 1975 national runner-up team who was drafted by the

NBA.  The Phoenix Suns picked Conner, a two-time All-SEC performer, in the second round as the 36th selection overall in the 1975 Draft. (UK All-American Kevin Grevey was a first-round pick — 18th overall — by the Washington Bullets while Bob Guyette and Mike Flynn were picked in the third and seventh round, respectively.)  Conner opted to play for the Kentucky Colonels who obtained him from the Virginia Squires in a trade.  The Squires had selected in Conner in the second round of the ABA Draft. (Flynn also played in the ABA, signing with the Colonels' rival, Indiana Pacers.)

Conner made his pro debut in late October of 1975 when he helped the Colonels to an 130-112 victory over visiting Virginia at Freedom Hall, scoring nine points in eight minutes. Overall, Conner saw action in 24 games during the 1975-76 season, averaging 10 minutes and 4.4 points while hitting 48.8 percent of his field goals.

Conner said he will always remember playing against sensational Julius "Dr. J" Erving and his New York Nets for the first time as a Colonel.  It was Erving who captured the first-ever Slam Dunk contest at the 1976 ABA All-Star Game. Conner marveled at Dr. J's spectacular play against the Colonels.  Said Conner, "Dr. J got the ball at the hash mark directly in front of me sitting on the bench. He drove to the baseline and took off outside the pro free throw lane. Awaiting him on defense was 7-foot-2 Artis Gilmore along with 6-foot-8 Will Jones and 6-foot-11 Caldwell Jones. Looking at the basket, all you saw were outstretched arms two feet above the rim. As Dr. J headed to the basket, he held the ball behind the backboard as he was flying to the basket. At the last second, he pulled the ball back out and slammed the ball landing beyond the pro free throw lane. Eighteen thousand fans rose to their feet as did our entire bench for a standing ovation. In all my years of basketball, I had never witnessed anything like that. What I really appreciate about Kentucky people is how they appreciate basketball at its core. What makes the event even greater is what a fantastic gentleman Dr. J is."

*Author with ex-UK standouts Kevin Grevey, Steve Lochmueller and Jimmy Dan Conner at Rupp Arena in 2012. Grevey and Conner, the team's top two scorers, helped coach Joe B. Hall's Wildcats reach the 1975 NCAA championship contest before losing to UCLA. (Vaught Family Photo Collection)*

On Conner's days with the Colonels, Anderson County native and sportswriter John P. Herndon, who shared some of his ABA memories earlier in the chapter, said, "I remember thinking how cool it was for a guy who lived not far from me going to play for my favorite pro team. I didn't know Jimmy Dan well growing up. I remember meeting him while he was in high school and also when he came back to Lawrenceburg while at UK and with the Colonels. I never really got to talk with him much until ᴵ writing sports for *The Anderson News*. Every time I wanted to talk with him for a story, he was extremely gracious with his time.

"Jimmy Dan was a bit older than me, so he was one of my childhood heroes. I went to all of his home games and a lot of his away games at Anderson County. Every single game, the gym was packed, regardless of where the Bearcats played. What Jimmy Dan taught me was the importance of being a team player on a championship team. In high school, he could have scored many more points, but he got his team involved. But when the team needed him to take over, he did." During his senior year, Conner, averaging 24.7 points and 14 rebounds, helped Anderson County reach the state tournament finals before dropping to Louisville Male 83-66 in 1971.

Herndon added Conner "was never the big scorer at UK, but his passing and defense were incredible. And when they needed a bucket, he could get it. To this day, I believe that 1975 team would have won it all had (UCLA coach) John Wooden not announced his retirement the day before the championship game."

## Mike Pratt

In a 2001 interview with the author, when Pratt was asked about the Colonels' big announcement that he and Issel had signed fat contracts, he said he actually didn't get a $400,000 contract that was reported by the media, including Louisville's *Courier-Journal* which ran a big front-page article.

"First of all, none of the dollar figures that were in the newspapers in those days about the two leagues' (bidding war) were correct dollar figures," said Pratt. "In talking with everybody involved at that time, all those numbers were inflated and that was part of the hype — the battle between the two leagues. The money wasn't there then. Only a few guys made $100,000 and they were the guys who were already playing. So, none of those numbers were real numbers."

When the duo of Pratt and Issel, along with their agent, had reached the final agreement with the Colonels, they were vacationing on a spring break in Florida, just days after their disappointing season-ending loss to Jacksonville. Pratt said the Colonels were practically the only pro team that he and Issel had negotiated with. With the verbal deal with the ABA franchise nearly finalized, Pratt said the Colonels "put us in John Y. Brown's jet, the fried chicken jet, and took us to Florida (on spring break) and paid for everything — my wife, myself, my daughter, Dan and his wife. We were in Florida, and (we) got back and forth on the phone (during contractual talks) and agreed to it. Then they brought us back (to Louisville) on Eastern Airlines first class, picked us up and took us to the hotel. A couple of hours later, we had a press conference and announced the signing.

"They kind of hid us out (in Florida) from the NBA people before we signed the contracts. My dad (Pete) got a couple of calls from agents that represented NBA people wanting to know where we were and wanted to talk to us. My dad was told not to tell anybody where we were, and he didn't know where we were, but my mom knew where we were. But they were told not to tell anybody. So, basically the deal was cut and dried."

According to Pratt, a 6-foot-4 forward who was a three-time All-SEC selection, Armand "Mondo" Angelucci did a lot of contract negotiating with the Colonels, representing the former Wildcats. "He was a friend of Coach Rupp," said Pratt. "He represented both Dan and I. He got us down to Louisville to talk to the owners of the Colonels. Mondo cut the deal with them and never let us talk to any of the NBA people and it was a done deal. He really wasn't an agent. He represented us as an attorney, and obviously he was very good." The first Monday after the signing, Pratt had to go back to Lexington and do some student teaching. His anxious students obviously knew about Pratt's new status as a pro player, asking him about his big contract. "I just told everybody, 'Don't believe everything you read in the paper,' " recalled Pratt, who grew up in Dayton, Ohio. "Having grown up as a blue-collar, middle American back then, money was never (a big influence). We never had a lot. (But the pact) certainly gave me a good start on life."

*Former Wildcat star Mike Pratt (UK Athletics Photo)*

While he played in the ABA for only two years, Pratt shared some thoughts and entertaining stories about the pro league. "It was quite a league," said Pratt, who compiled an ABA career average of 5.6 points in 143 games. "The ABA was a very talented league. What we didn't have then, compared to NBA, was television (coverage). Having played forward in college, I had to move to the guard spot. We had some talented guards, quick guys who were smaller than me. They were really good. It was not a power (league). It was a quickness league. The NBA was a power league. They had power centers. We didn't have that many centers in the ABA."

On one particular weekend during his rookie season of 1970-71, Pratt remembered an unusual game, which included big promotional giveaways at halftime, in Pittsburgh's 13,500-seat Civic Arena. Kentucky was facing the red-and-gold Condors, one of the league's weakest franchises in home attendance, in the last game of the regular season. Pittsburgh was very lucky if they drew 3,000 fans to a contest. "We showed up there and the dang gone place was full," said Pratt, whose team later lost 149-132 in a high-scoring affair. "We couldn't believe it. The place probably sat 15,000 and there were like 10 or 12,000 people. We found out (later) because at halftime they were giving things away. They had everything from washing machines to (whatever) you name it. They had advertised this giveaway.

"So they had a delayed halftime and they had this drawing with the ticket stubs. If you had a ticket stub, you had to be present to get something, and they gave all this stuff away. Frank Ramsey is coaching us and he said, 'Guys, just relax. It is going to be a long halftime.' We came back out to warm up for the second half, and you could have shot a cannon through there. There was nobody left. Once they gave all the prizes away, everybody left. People just came in to have a chance to win a prize."

Another memorable incident involved Pratt's teammate, 6-foot-7 Cincy Powell, and others in Game Five of the 1971 ABA championship series with the Utah Stars at the Salt Palace. Said Pratt, "I'm in the game, and I'll never forget it because I was looking. There was a fast break situation and a foul was called. All of a sudden a lady runs out of the end zone, right on the floor, and takes an umbrella and hits Cincy Powell on top of the head. Cincy had his back to her. And pretty soon the Utah bench empties, our bench empties. There were people pulling people out of the way. There was a huge, huge fight (among the players), and it all started because a lady ran out of the end zone and popped Cincy." When the emotionally-charged game ended, the Stars were the victors, winning 137-127 behind the outstanding backcourt play of Ron Boone, Merv Jackson and Kentuckian Glen Combs.

Utah center and ex-NBA star Zelmo Beaty also put in a superb performance, pumping in 32 points and snatching 22 rebounds with the victory giving Utah a 3-2 series advantage. Leading the Colonels was Dan Issel, who had a game-high 33 points and 16 rebounds. In a reserve role, Pratt played 22 minutes, scoring 10 points and grabbing five rebounds. As record books will show, Utah eventually defeated Kentucky for the league crown in seven games.

One of the meanest guys in the ABA, if not the meanest, was John Brisker of Pittsburgh. A 6-foot-5, 230-pound high-scoring performer, he played three years in the ABA. He was a superstar, earning All-ABA honors in 1971, but he was very mean, scaring his opponents and teammates alike. The Utah Stars once staged "John Brisker Intimidation Night" when Brisker and the Condors visited Salt Lake City. After the league folded the Pittsburgh franchise, Brisker then went to NBA's Seattle Supersonics in 1972. "The last I heard Brisker was a mercenary back in the '80s or '70s in Uganda or someplace, and (he) has never been heard from since," Pratt said. "He was a tough guy. I never saw him get in a fight but he sure looked tough. He had that look about him — that mean look in his face. But he could shoot the ball. He could score points.

"But In the ABA there are a lot of stories about bounced checks and a lot of things. It was a lot of fun. It was basketball. It was up and down the floor. It was tough. You know people would fight because this was better than digging ditches or teaching school for a living. Guys would fight you (for the ball). On that floor, it wasn't millionaires taking care of millionaires. It was guys making $12, 15, 20 or 25,000 trying to hold on to their job."

4

---

# Shot Heard Around Kentucky

(Paul Andrews)

In May 2025, several days after a horrifying tornado in London, Ky., had destroyed nearly everything in its path, receiving nationwide attention, including cable television networks and streaming platforms as well as major outlets like the *New York Times* which did a feature story, former Kentucky Wildcat basketball player Paul Andrews and I had an interview at his medical clinic office. We discussed the storm damage in his original hometown of London where he starred at Laurel County High School during the early 1980s. According to London mayor's office, 280 homes were completely destroyed in Laurel County with nearly 200 homes having major damage.

"It has affected me because this is my hometown, and I've been very fortunate that I didn't have a lot of family that was affected, but I've got a lot of friends that have been affected," Andrews said. "I've got some friends who have lost everything. Being back here in London, I've bought into as a part owner of the Kentucky Family Practice, and we've got patients that have lost everything. I've been here this week taking donations and giving things back to the community. It is just devastating.  I had an opportunity to go yesterday, and over the last couple of days, and drive through some of the affected areas, and I've never seen anything like it. It's heartbreaking just to see what the families have gone through. You've got families have lost their homes; they've lost loved ones.

"But what's very encouraging is to see the community come together. You've got everybody that's rallying around London and Laurel County from throughout the state of Kentucky and even outside of the state of Kentucky that are coming to this community to help. That's been very encouraging to me. I don't know that there's one person in London or that's from London that has not been impacted by the storms. I know it went through Somerset, too. (Former UK standout) Reggie Hanson and I are really good friends and very close. He and I communicated too, and then just checking to see how things were in Somerset. But it's just very disheartening and heartbreaking to see kind of what some of these families are going through."

A two-time All-Stater, Andrews is probably best-known for hitting his famous 45-foot basket at the buzzer in leading his fifth-ranked high school team to the 1982 state tournament crown with a 53-51 victory over No. 2 North Hardin before over 13,000 fans at Rupp Arena. Over 40 years later, folks are still talking about this memorable moment. "It is still hard to believe that special moment happened to me and my great high school basketball team," said Andrews, who was a junior when he made that shot. "You dream of making a game-winning shot and play the scenario over and over while playing basketball at the park or in the gym. Every kid who plays basketball in the state of Kentucky grows up wanting to someday play in the state tournament and hopefully be blessed with an opportunity to win it. I was very fortunate to be in the right spot at the right time and was able to live out a dream. We were well-coached by Chuck Broughton. We had great players and strong senior leadership in Joe Karr, Jamie Maxey, Norm Bowling, Teel Bruner, Jamie Ross, etc. The one regret that I have about the shot is that it somewhat took away from the outstanding year that we had as a team. It was truly a team effort that put us in a position to capture the state title." The Cardinals finished the season with a remarkable 33-3 mark. A year later, Andrews was the runner-up in 1983 Kentucky's Mr. Basketball honors, placing behind winner Winston Bennett, a future UK teammate.

*Former Kentucky Wildcat Paul Andrews in 2025 (Photo by Jamie H. Vaught)*

# Tennessee Vols & Charles Barkley

Before signing with Kentucky, Andrews considered several major schools. Where should he play basketball? "Coming out of high school, I was being recruited by quite a lot of teams," he recalled. "I narrowed my choices down to Kentucky, Tennessee, Auburn, Virginia Tech, and Purdue. Those were the teams that I visited. Not a lot of people know this story, but I actually committed to Tennessee early on, and then I changed my mind and signed with Kentucky. But (Tennessee coach) Don DeVoe recruited me really hard. (Auburn's) Sonny Smith recruited me really hard. Probably my most memorable recruiting trip was at Auburn. I went to visit Auburn, and one of my hosts was (future NBA star) Charles Barkley. Coach Smith was having an ice cream social at his house. Charles came and picked me up at the hotel, and we were on our way to Coach Smith's house. Charles said, 'Hey, I want to stop at this grocery store.' So he stopped at the grocery store and said, 'I'll be right back.' So I sit in the car. He comes back out and he's got a bag, and it's all Reese cups. So, from the time we left the grocery store parking lot to the time we got to Coach Smith's house, he had eaten, I'd say, probably 30 Reese cups and we were going to an ice cream social. Then, he had a bunch of ice cream there, too. That was a very memorable trip.

"My host at Virginia Tech was Dell Curry, Stephen Curry's dad now, and he was a freshman at the time and a great player, but he was my host there. When I went to visit Tennessee, their big star was Dale Ellis. But back then, the movie, *An Officer And A Gentleman* (starring Richard Gere), had just come out and was a pretty popular movie. Well, one of the stars in the movie was a graduate of the University of Tennessee. I got to meet him (David Keith) at one of the practices. When we went to a football game, it was Alabama versus Tennessee. It was Bear Bryant's last game as coach of Alabama in Knoxville and Neyland Stadium (in 1982). I got to meet Bear Bryant. That was my first time meeting Bear

Bryant. So, after that trip, I came back and I told my high school coach, 'I think I'm going to Tennessee.' But being from Kentucky, I grew up watching Tennessee, too because all of the local (TV) stations here in London came out of Knoxville. I didn't have cable. So I grew up watching Ernie Grunfeld. I grew up watching Bernard King. I grew up watching Tennessee as much as I did Kentucky. But it came down to I love Kentucky, and I love Coach (Joe B.) Hall.

"I wanted my parents to be able to see me play any time, even though Knoxville was not that far away from London. One of the things that really made me make my decision was I kind of looked at the future. I wanted to look at where I saw myself after basketball. I love Lexington and I saw myself in Lexington. After basketball, I spent a lot of years living in Lexington, and I just loved it.

"My mom and dad really never tried to influence me in any way, and we met a lot of good coaches. Coach Gene Keady came down to London when he was head coach at Purdue. My mom really liked Coach Keady and had a good visit with him. Bobby Cremins came down and visited with us, and that was when Coach Cremins was at Georgia Tech. My dad really liked Bobby Cremins, but they both liked Coach Hall. They liked Don DeVoe, but it just came down to Kentucky basketball. I mean, as a kid growing up in the state of Kentucky and being a high school kid here, who would not want to go represent their state and go play for the University of Kentucky? I was just very fortunate that I had that opportunity and that a lot of kids would love to have."

Speaking of Coach Smith, a native of Roan Mountain, Tennessee, he once coached at the old Pine Knot High School in McCreary County during his early days. In late 2024, the popular Smith announced his retirement as radio analyst for Auburn men's basketball games.

Asked which college coach did Andrews enjoy the most during the recruiting process, he said, "Probably Coach DeVoe. Yeah.

I really enjoyed Coach DeVoe and I got to spend a lot of time with him. Again, I grew up watching Tennessee as well. When I went to Knoxville, I got to see the campus. At that time, they were still playing at the old Stokely Athletic Center, but they were already in the process of building the new arena. When they were recruiting me, they told me that the arena would be done by the end of my sophomore year. But it really wasn't even done before I graduated from Kentucky. So it did not get done until after I already graduated. But I really enjoyed Coach DeVoe, and I liked their style of basketball." During his 11 years at Tennessee, DeVoe's teams posted an overall mark of 204-137, including six trips to the NCAA Tournament. His Vols beat the surprising Wildcats 75-69 in overtime in the championship game of the 1979 SEC Tournament. In 1982, DeVoe, who once served as an assistant to legendary Bobby Knight at Army, guided Tennessee to the co-SEC regular season crown (with Kentucky).

## Wildcat Sub

Even though he started several games during his career at UK, Andrews didn't see lots of action on the floor. He was mostly a 6-foot-3 backup guard. How tough was it for him to stay motivated? "It was a challenge going from high school where you were the star," said Andrews, who in 1984 hit a career-high eight points against eighth-ranked Southern Methodist University. "Even at Laurel County, I played with some great high school players, and a lot of those guys I played with ended up having great playing careers as well. But you go from being this high profile player in high school to where you're recruited by a lot of college teams to going to Kentucky where you're playing with all these All-Americans. I always kept that in the back of my mind as I'm playing for the University of Kentucky. I'm representing my home state. I have an opportunity to play for (one of the) winningest college basketball programs in the country. My family and my friends get to see me play every game. I'm getting a great college education at a great university. That was really all that mattered to me.

"There were times when it got discouraging when I wasn't getting to play. You're right, I did start several games. One of the games that really sticks out for me is my sophomore year. I got to start against University of Louisville in Freedom Hall, and that was one of the highlights for me. But I played with a lot of great players, and I played with guards James Blackmon, Roger Hardin, Dicky Beal, and Ed Davender. They were just great guards.

"I didn't have the talent that a lot of my teammates had, but I was very fortunate to be in the situation that I was. I never let it get me down if I wasn't playing as much as I thought I would be playing. I knew I was there representing my state, and I was still going to give it everything I had. I was going to leave the university, and I wanted fans to be proud of me as a person, as a good teammate, and as someone that when he was on the floor, he gave it every thing he had and regardless of how many minutes that I played."

Had Andrews played at a different school, he would have seen more minutes on the floor. "I do think I could have probably gone to some other schools and probably started and played a lot," he said. "That stuck out in the back of my head, too. But growing up in Kentucky, I always wanted to play for University of Kentucky. When I got the call from Coach Hall about an offer at the University of Kentucky, there's just no way a kid from Laurel County would say no to that. The year before I started there, I've watched Derrick Hord and he was a senior, Charles Hurt was a senior. Those were the guys that I watched. The individual who got me first really interested in possibly playing for Kentucky was Larry Johnson and he just passed away. I was a big Larry Johnson fan, and I wanted my game to be after Larry Johnson, but I have no regrets. I could have probably gone somewhere else and played more, but the friendships that I made at the University of Kentucky and the connections that I made that have helped me throughout my professional career after basketball, I wouldn't trade it for anything."

Asked when Hall was recruiting Andrews, did the coach warn him about not having a lot of playing time? At the time, the Wildcats were loaded with talented stars like Sam Bowie, Melvin Turpin, Kenny Walker, Jim Master and Winston Bennett. "No, he didn't," said Andrews. "Coach Hall's philosophy was every player comes in and brings something different. Coach Hall saw me as a defensive player, and he made it very clear from day one. He said, 'I want you to focus on defense. I know you can shoot, but I want you to focus on defense.' That's what I did. The playing time I got my freshman year (in 1983-84) I was so excited because I was a freshman right out of high school, and I'm playing on this team that's No. 1 in the country with Sam Bowie and these guys, and I'm still getting to play some minutes.

"I remember we were playing in the SEC Tournament in Nashville, and we were playing against Georgia. Something happened. I don't know if it was Jim Master or somebody who made a mistake on a defensive end. Coach Hall came down and he said, 'Paul, get in and get him out.' So I was excited because I got in to the game. I was in for defense, and I had an opportunity. I made a basket, and then we came down the defensive end, and I made a mistake. I turned around and somebody was coming to get me out, but I was all excited. I got in for the SEC Tournament as a freshman."

## 1984 NCAA Final Four & Joe B. Hall

While at UK, Andrews was a rookie member of the 1984 NCAA Final Four team which boasted a strong frontline of 7-foot-1 Bowie, 6-foot-11 Turpin and 6-foot-8 Walker. And it was UK's first Final Four appearance since the 1978 team, led by All-Americans Jack

Givens and Rick Robey, both seniors, won the whole thing in St. Louis.

That 1983-84 Wildcat squad, however, lost to 7-foot star Patrick Ewing and eventual national champion Georgetown 53-40 in a disappointing and shocking performance which saw UK hit only a paltry 24.5 percent of its field goals (9.1 percent in the second half) in the national semifinals in Seattle. Said Andrews, "Although the outcome wasn't what we anticipated, the experience of being there and participating at that level was great."

*Former Kentucky coach Joe B. Hall chats with Paul Andrews at a reunion for Hall's former players held in Lexington during the 2010s. (Andrews Family Photo Collection)*

Before Hall retired from coaching in 1985, Andrews got to play for him for two years. What is Andrews' favorite Joe B. Hall story? "There were so many stories in my time playing for Coach Hall," he commented. "One that sticks out was early in my freshman year at one of my first practices as a Kentucky Wildcat in Rupp

Arena. I believe I messed up a defensive assignment, and Coach Hall stopped practice and instructed me to run the stairs at Rupp. I was under the impression that I needed to run to the top of Rupp Arena. Coach Hall noticed that I was all the way up to top and began yelling, 'What the hell are you doing? Just half way up and back.' That was an eye opener for a little freshman from London, Ky."

A disciplinarian, Hall was tough to play for but the players respected him. If one of his players did something Coach Hall didn't like, he would get some form of punishment. "Now one of the things that Coach Hall would do is if we did something wrong in practice or if we missed curfew or whatever, he would have a manager wake us up at five o'clock in the morning, put us in a van and drive us way out at the Athens Boonseboro exit (at I-75), drop us off, and we'd have to run back to the Wildcat Lodge. So, that was the punishment for missing class or any type of disciplinary issues that we had."

Other than occasional mistakes during team practices, Andrews said, "I never did (get punished). I was always on good behavior."

"There are stories like Melvin Turpin having his girlfriend throw food up into the window so he can have food and he was supposed to have been on a diet," added Andrews. "There were times Kenny and I would go visit some friends of ours, and we had curfew that night. We came back and we'd be back one minute before curfew. We walk in at (Wildcat) Lodge and Coach Hall is sitting in the chair just waiting. It's like one minute before curfew. He's just looking at his watch, and we're like, 'Well, we're here.' He was watching. He was just sitting in a chair just waiting for us and to watch everybody (come in). He didn't do it that often but did that night.

"We always had breakfast. All the players had to be up for breakfast check. That's how they made sure that we were up and then we were going to class. We always had a place where we would always go for breakfast. Then one of the managers had to sit and check off everybody's name. Make sure they were at breakfast, and make sure they were in class. They will always have somebody checking class to make sure we were in class."

Andrews, then a freshman, remembers when Hall called a team meeting in the locker room at Memorial Coliseum. "One of the first meetings that I had as a team member for the University of Kentucky was right after summer," he said. "He starts going around and he starts pointing out, 'Sam Bowie, I know what you did this summer. I know you worked hard. I know you worked out.' Just started going around. Then he got to me and he said, 'Paul, by the time I get done with you, you're going to call your mom and dad, and tell them to come pick you up, you're ready to come home.' So I thought, 'Oh, what have I got myself into.'

"Coach Hall was just a very intimidating coach. He demanded a lot. He was a very disciplinarian coach. But one thing I remember him telling us during one meeting early on in my career, he said, 'The one thing that you'll get out of playing for me is that it will make you become a man quicker than you probably would have.' I can say that a lot of things I went through at the University of Kentucky, it really molded my personality and my professional career after basketball."

Andrews said Hall often had summer cookouts — pork chop lunches or dinners — for the team at his farm in Harrison County.

Hall's 13-year record at UK was 297-100, including three trips to the Final Four with one NCAA championship in 1978. A member of the College Basketball Hall of Fame, Hall captured national coach of the year honors in 1978 and four SEC Coach of the Year awards. He passed away in 2022 at the age of 93.

## Toughest Road Environment

During his playing days, Andrews was asked which school had the most hostile environment when the Wildcats played on the road? "I'd say probably the toughest place I played in the SEC was probably LSU," he recalled. "LSU fans are just hardcore. I remember the night before the game, we would get to the arena for practice. So, where the bus would pull up, it let everybody off and you had to walk down this little tunnel into the arena where there would be students and fans standing there, and they were just yelling, 'Tiger Bait.' This is the night before the game. And then they were just very rowdy during the game. In my opinion, LSU was probably the toughest place that I've ever had to play at. Kansas was right up there, too. I played at Kansas a couple of years, and Kansas had a tough crowd. Back then, we played Indiana every year, and Bloomington was another challenging place to play."

## Wildcat Teammates

Some of Andrews' closest teammates included Cedric Jenkins, Leroy Byrd and Irving Thomas. They spent a lot of time together outside of basketball. "The three of us always went to the SEC Tournament together after we stopped playing," said Andrews. "Irving, he's a scout for the Lakers, and so we would always meet him. He would have to work the SEC Tournament, so Cedric and Leroy and I would meet wherever the SEC Tournament was, whether it was Atlanta or in Nashville. That was kind of our time to stay connected. But Cedric passed away a couple of years ago. Leroy, Irv and I are still close. We talk at least once or twice a week, so we're still really close. My family and I go out to Los Angeles at least once a year. Irving gets us tickets for a Lakers game, and we go out and watch the Lakers play at least one or two games a year.

"In my freshman year, my roommate was Kenny Walker. Kenny and I had a great time together. One of the stories I remember I brought Kenny down to London after after we were conditioning one day. The season had started, we had a Saturday off, and I brought him down for a high school football game at Laurel County High School. We left the game and went to a Jerry's restaurant here. So, we go there and we're sitting down eating. My cousin, Charlie Andrews, whom I'm really close with, like a brother to me, was with us as well. We're sitting down. And this man comes up and just sits down but we don't know him. He starts eating the food. That's one of the funny stories we had, but with Cedric and Leroy, we were always teasing each other. We were always talking about where are we going to go eat?"

## Eddie Sutton

In 1985, after Joe B. Hall retired from coaching at the age of 56, Eddie Sutton, 49, was named the head coach at UK the day after Villanova upset Georgetown in the championship game during the NCAA Final Four in Lexington. Sutton, who led Arkansas to 1978 Final Four, famously made a statement at his introductory press conference, saying, "It's the only job I'd leave the University of Arkansas for. When (UK president) Dr. (Otis) Singletary and (athletics director) Cliff Hagan and the rest of the committee called me, believe me, I would have crawled all the way to Lexington. I just happened to be here because of the NABC board meetings and the rules committee meeting. I'm really excited."

Coming off his sophmore year when the struggling Wildcats surprisingly finished the campaign with an 18-13 mark while making the Sweet Sixteen, Andrews had a new coach who would be a future member of the Naismith Basketball Hall of Fame. "Coach Sutton and Coach Hall were, in my opinion, very different coaches," he said. "When Coach Sutton came in, I didn't know what to expect. I remember my first meeting with Coach Sutton, and I'm sitting in his office and he's kind of going through his philosophy. He's going through kind of what he expects from the players. At the end of the conversation, I looked at him and I said, 'I just have one question, Coach. Obviously you're coming in from Arkansas. I'm from the state of Kentucky. What can I do to ensure that I get some playing time?' He said, 'I'll let you know after the first day of practice. I'll tell by then if you're somebody that we're going to be able to use.'

"But one of the things he said, 'Look, we know that you can shoot.' He said his teams have been known as defensive teams. He said 'We need you to be a defensive stopper, and we want you to be a zone buster and a defensive stopper on the defensive end. I'm going to work your butt off on the defensive end.' He did. I think that's probably my favorite story with Coach Sutton.

"I would have to say that having played two years under both (coaches), Coach Sutton was more of a player's coach. What I liked about Coach Sutton's style of basketball was that you were able to be a little bit freer and a little bit more loose on the offensive end. Coach Hall was more of a structured offensive mind coach where he had set plays, and he expected you to run the play the way it's supposed to be run. Coach Sutton let you freelance a little bit more with the basketball.

"Coach Hall was more of a screamer and yeller. (As for) Coach Sutton, he at times would yell and scream, but Coach Hall did more of that. Coach Sutton brought a brand of basketball that I felt like the players really enjoyed playing. When he came to Kentucky, the college game was changing a little bit because if you think about it, it was my senior year was when the three-point line was introduced into college basketball. So the game of basketball for college was changing at that time, and I think his style of play was more suited for what the players were looking for coming out of high school.

"The one thing I can say about Coach Sutton, when I graduated in '87, my summer job was working at a bank. I worked at First National Bank of Nicholasville every summer except for one. My freshman year I worked on a horse farm outside of Lexington, but I really wanted to go into banking. Then I graduated and I thought, 'I may want to try the coaching thing. Coach Sutton actually had me an assistant coaching job lined up at, I think, Southeastern Louisiana State. I remember I went there and visited with the coach at the time, but I decided that I did not want to go to coaching route. I wanted to go into business world. I ended up leaving the banking business, and I started working for the state. Then I went into healthcare, and I've been in healthcare ever since. Coach Sutton got me my first college coaching offer. Then my girlfriend and I were trying to buy our first home. I called Coach Hall (who was working at Central Bank), and he actually helped me get my first home loan. So, that's the type of relationship that those two coaches had with their players, even after basketball.

On Sutton, Andrews added, "I remember going out and spending Thanksgiving out on his farm and his wife would fix Thanksgiving dinner. Then we took the trip to Japan the summer after my junior year. I think that was a nice bonding trip for, not only the players, but for the coaches and the players. At that time, Coach Sutton had just completed his first year at Kentucky. Even though we had a great year his first year, we were still in that honeymoon phase where we were still trying to figure out how he wanted, his expectations of playing. It was a great trip for us to be able to bond with the coaching staff as well as the players. Both Coach Hall and Coach Sutton were somebody that you could pick up the phone and call and say, 'Hey, I'm struggling. Can you help me out?'

It is a well-known fact that likeable Sutton, who passed away in 2020 at the age of 84, had struggled with his drinking problem over the years. While he was coaching the Wildcats, Sutton quietly entered the Betty Ford Center in 1987 for treatment of his alcoholism. Andrews has said the team knew of Sutton's problems but the assistants did a nice job of keeping things going. Rex Chapman also discussed Sutton's struggles in his 2024 memoir, *It's Hard for Me to Live with Me.* Chapman wrote that Sutton, who was named to the Naismith Basketball Hall of Fame less than two months before he passed away, is a decent man who can coach but the veteran coach wasn't in a great shape mentally when the future NBA standout first arrived on UK campus.

## 1985-86 Wildcats

Speaking of Sutton's first year at Kentucky, the 1985-86 Wildcats, led by 6-foot-8 All-American Kenny Walker, were one of the nation's top teams and a strong Final Four contender. They ended up with a trip to the NCAA Southeast Regional finals, dropping to LSU 59-57 in Atlanta. It was the fourth game UK played against LSU that season after beating the Tigers three times. Also, it was the year the Wildcats faced Coach Wimp Sanderson's Alabama teams four times and won all of them. Third-ranked Kentucky, which captured both the SEC regular season and tournament titles, finished with an overall mark of 32-4, including 17-1 in the SEC.

"We had a really good year, and there was excitement about Coach Sutton coming in," said Andrews of his junior year in 1985-86. "We were coming off of a subpar year the year before where we ended up making it to the NCAA Tournament. We had lost a lot the year before that because we lost Sam Bowie. We lost Melvin Turpin; we lost Dicky Beal and Jim Master. So it was kind of rebuilding year, but we ended up making it to the tournament and did pretty well and (it was) Coach Hall's last year. So, we were excited about Coach Sutton coming in and had a great year, and unfortunately (we had) to try to beat a team four times in one year, and that's a challenge. That's kind of what we were tasked with.

"We ended up having to play Alabama four times, and we ended up beating them four times. Then we had to play LSU for a fourth time and had beat them three. Unfortunately, we fell a little bit short in the regional championship game. They had a heck of a team that year, but it was just hard to beat a team four times in one year. I think because of what happened to us, the NCAA changed some of their rules as far as how they pair teams and when they do the announcements of the tournament. I think a lot of that was done because of what happened to us, having to play Alabama and LSU four times in one year."

On LSU, Andrews commented, "They played us tough every game we had. We played them two times in the regular season. We played them in the SEC Tournament, which was in Lexington that year, and then we had to play them again in the NCAA Tournament. There is some of that revenge factor. When you beat a team three times, they're going to look at the film; they're going to look at every game. They're going to dissect every possession and try to figure out what they can do to make sure that they don't get beat this time. I think that's what they did. And they were well coached by Dale Brown. They had a good team, but I still think that we should have been in a situation where we would've been in the Final Four that year. You think about what would've happened if we'd won that game, then we would've played Louisville in the first game of the Final Four. That would've been something for the state of Kentucky."

*Paul Andrews (UK Athletics Photo)*

redshirt that year. We had a bunch of injuries in the beginning of the season. Cedric Jenkins had a stress fracture in his foot and was out five or six games. I had a sprain of my knee, and I missed four or five games. I had to wear a big brace on my knee.

"We played a lot with the three-guard lineup, and the starters at guard were Rex, James Blackmon and Ed Davender. Rex was probably the tallest of the three at 6-foot-5. Then I was the backup coming in. We relied a lot on our outside game because we just didn't have the beef inside with Cedric and Winston being out."

"So, Winston, Blackmon and I came in together to Kentucky. We were freshmen together. We had some challenges that year. We were a young team. Rex was just an unbelievable talent. We struggled with a big man. Rob Lock, who was from California, was our starting center. We had another individual that came in from Greenup County. He was a 6-foot-11 kid who was at Wake Forest. Mike Scott came in after Christmas, but we struggled on the inside and it was a very, very challenging year for us. But we won some games that we probably shouldn't have won, and then we lost some games we probably shouldn't have lost. Rex had a great year. We beat Louisville in Freedom Hall by over 30 points (85-51), and that was Rex's coming out year." (For the record, Chapman gunned in 26 points, including five three-pointers against the Cardinals.)

"We didn't know that we would get an invite to the NCAA Tournament but we did. Unfortunately, we played Ohio State in the first round in Atlanta. They ended up beating us."

Andrews remembers a rare two-game stretch at the end of the regular season when the Cats played for two straight days at Rupp Arena. "We played Mississippi and that was on a Saturday afternoon, and then Senior Day was the next day. That was the Oklahoma game," he said. "So, my last game in Rupp Arena was the Oklahoma game. We ended up winning both of those games, barely. Both of them by one point. Those were my last two games in Rupp Arena."

## Leonard Hamilton

One of Andrews' assistant coaches at Kentucky was Leonard Hamilton, a longtime Joe B. Hall assistant who also stayed another year at the university when Eddie Sutton took over the program. In 1974, Hamilton became the first Black assistant coach in UK hoops history, joining other assistants Dick Parsons and Lynn Nance on Hall's staff. The well-respected Hamilton had the reputation of being one of the nation's top recruiters. He later became the head coach at other universities, including a successful stint at Florida State. And it was Hamilton who hired current Kansas boss Bill Self, then 23 years old, in 1986 as an asisstant at Oklahoma State. Andrews said he and Hamilton shared a good relationship.

"Coach Hamilton was great, and he recruited me to Kentucky out of high school," said Andrews. "I really enjoyed my relationship with Coach Hamilton, and to this day, we have a good relationship. I communicated with him several times. Actually, when one of my teammates, Cedric Jenkins, passed away, he and I spoke at Cedric's funeral. He actually drove over from Tallahassee and was there with a lot of the former players. (He) actually took a lot of the former players who were there out to dinner, and it was great to connect. He was always that coach that when you were having a bad game or you were down about something, you could go to Coach Hamilton and just talk to him.

"He was always recruiting. I didn't see much of Coach Hamilton. But during the season, he was always there for the players and someone that we could always go to under Coach Hall as well as under Coach Sutton. He had that way of just making you feel better about the situation whatever it was. He was a very unique individual, and he's going to be a Hall of Fame coach, and you look at what he's done at Kentucky and since he left Kentucky. But we've always had a really good relationship. I think he has that with the majority of the players who played at the University of Kentucky, Oklahoma State, Miami and Florida State. He had one year where he was with the Washington Wizards (in the NBA)."

A three-time Atlantic Coast Conference Coach of the Year while at Florida State, the 76-year-old Hamilton retired after the 2024-25 season.

## Fishing

Growing up in Laurel County, Andrews enjoyed fishing at Laurel Lake. While at UK, he also would return home and fish during the summer months. "I actually grew up on Laurel Lake," he said. "I had a lot of friends that had houseboats there, and I would go and have the opportunity to go and spend some time there riding jet skis, fishing. I was there a lot on the weekends. Laurel Lake has a special place in my heart. I spent a lot of time fishing on Laurel Lake."

He often would take his teammates for a weekend trip to the lake. He remembers a time during his sophomore year when he took freshman Ed Davender, who is from Brooklyn in New York City, and others. "(For Davender), it was a little bit of a culture shock coming from New York City to Kentucky," said Andrews. "I was taking some of the teammates, bringing them down to London to spend the weekend on the lake. So we're driving down on I-75, and we had to pull the car over. Ed's like, 'Pull the car over.' So, we pulled over, and Ed had never seen a cow before. There was a cow in a field, so Ed wanted to see this cow."

After his playing days at UK ended, Andrews graduated with a bachelor's degree in General Studies and found success as an executive in the healthcare industry over the years.

# 5

# From Hyden to Hall of Fame

(Tim Couch)

1998.

It was one of the most exciting football seasons Kentucky has ever had in a long time. The long-suffering Wildcat football fans had seen so many disappointments and losing seasons over the years, but they got to see the offensive-minded Cats, led by the nation's top quarterback, Tim Couch, make a rare New Year's Day appearance at the Outback Bowl. It was the first time Kentucky had posted a winning season (7-5) since Coach Jerry Claiborne's 6-5 team in 1989. It was a very exciting time in the Big Blue Nation, who several months earlier also saw first-year coach Tubby Smith and his basketball team capture the national championship.

The football Wildcats, through coach Hal Mumme's "Air Raid" offense, were wild, scoring points like crazy and setting school records for total offense (5,876 yards) and scoring (417 points). They scored 68 points against Louisville, 52 vs. Eastern Kentucky,

39 vs. LSU and 55 vs Vanderbilt. For the season, the Cats, who were on national or regional television eight times during the pre-SEC Network days, ranked No. 2 in the country in passing offense and third in total offense.

And it was junior QB Tim Couch, arguably the most decorated football player in UK history, who sparked the Wildcats to new heights. With his pinpoint passing, Couch became a first-team All-American, breaking several NCAA, SEC and school records. In addition, he was a finalist for the Heisman Trophy in 1998 before leaving for the National Football League.

On playing in the Outback Bowl, Couch said, "It was just being there as my favorite moment because Kentucky hadn't played in a New Year's Day bowl game in 46 years. So, it'd been a long time since Kentucky had played in a big bowl game at that level. Then obviously getting to go and play against such a legendary coach in Joe Paterno and Penn State. It was a very, very good experience for us all. I knew that it was going to be my last game ever at Kentucky, so I was just soaking in every moment with my teammates.

"We got to Tampa early, maybe a week or a week and a half early before the game. Just got to spend a lot of quality time around those guys that I knew I was never going to get to play with again. And it was a special week. It really was. Even though we didn't win the game (a 26-14 loss), we played pretty well. We got off to a good start. We just didn't finish the game like we wanted to, but I just remember knowing it was going to be my last run with those guys and with Coach and all the people that had meant so much to me. So, it was an emotional time, and it was a special time and one that I look back on with great memories."

## Growing up in the Mountains

Tim Couch grew up in Hyden, the county seat of Leslie County with a population of less than 500 citizens (according to 1980 census). This little-known town got some national attention during the 1970s. In 1970, nearly 40 coal miners were killed in the Hurricane Creek mine disaster. In 1978, when Couch was a one-year-old baby, President Richard Nixon made his first public speech since he resigned from the White House in 1974 due to the Watergate scandal. Nixon visited the area as the new recreation center was dedicated and named after him. Hyden is not a real easy place to reach. It's a one-hour drive from I-75 in London. Also, it's a 30-minute drive from Hazard, primarily through the Hal Rogers Parkway. Even President Bill Clinton, during a 1999 visit to Hazard, praised UK basketball along with Couch, saying, "Since I've been in office, UK basketball has had the most successful six years since Adolph Rupp was the coach. And Tim Couch hasn't done badly, either."

One of Couch's close friends and future wide receiver at Leslie County High School is Landry Collett, who spent a lot of time at Couch's home, near the Rockhouse Creek. "When Tim was around 12 years old, Tim's brother, Greg, and I were upstairs at his home in Leslie County at Rockhouse, playing Tecmo Bowl (a video game)," Landry recalled. "We were getting ready to go outside and throw football in the yard. Tim and Greg had a large bag with 12 footballs in it. As I watched Tim from the upstairs window, Tim opened the bag of balls and started throwing the footballs at a telephone pole that was about 30 yards away that ran right beside U.S. 421 (highway). Tim took all 12 balls out of the bag and started throwing and hit that pole every time. If he had missed that pole one time, the ball would've gone into the highway.

"The first time I ever met Tim, I was 12 playing church league basketball at the old high school gym on a Saturday. It was the church league championship game for 12 and under. I thought I'd had a great game. I scored 63 points that game and my team won the game, but there was a tall long lanky kid that played for the other team and he had scored 73 points against my team. After the game, out of respect, I went up to him because of elementary school ball. I wanted to know who this kid was because I would probably be playing against him again during the elementary school season. When I asked Tim how old he was, he said nine years old. I couldn't believe it."

Added Couch, a highly-recruited quarterback who was named the 1995 National Player of the Year by *Parade* magazine during his senior year at Leslie County High, "Landry and I grew up super close. We were very much like brothers almost. He was older than me. He's three years older, so he played with my brother Greg mainly. He was with Greg for three years. I only had him for one year. He was a senior when I was a freshman. We've known each other our whole lives. He was just a great player. He was a heck of a high school athlete. He was fast and strong, had great hands. He was everything you want in a wide receiver. He was tough and he was competitive, so he was very fun to play with."

A four-year starter, Couch led the Eagles to a four-year mark of 38-13 and appearances in the state Class 3A playoff semifinals his junior and senior years.  He also was named Kentucky's Mr. Football in 1995.

Looking back, Couch said living in a small town has helped his athletics career.  "There weren't a lot of distractions growing up in a small town like that," he recalled. "Really, all I had to focus on was playing ball and getting better at football and basketball, and just always practicing, always participating in sports. So, it was a great place to grow up. It was a very supportive community, a very family-oriented community, so it was a great, great experience for me. I just loved my time growing up in eastern Kentucky and will never forget the people there that helped me get to where I'm at today and really supported me throughout my high school, college and NFL career."

*Former football stars at Leslie County High School —
Landry Collett Jr., Tim Couch and Landry Collett Sr. —
pose with the new statue of Couch near the football field at
the high school during a special statue dedication ceremony
in 2024. (Photo Submitted)*

Longtime TV sports journalist Keith Farmer, who began his career at Hazard's WYMT-TV during the early 1990s, covered Couch in high school. "I started at WYMT when Tim was just a sophomore at Leslie County," said Farmer, co-host of *BBN Tonight*. "There are a lot of memories I can share about him, but the first two are not for his play at quarterback. The first time I saw him play was on a Saturday afternoon game at home against Lloyd Memorial. He saved the win for the Eagles when he was playing safety and knocked a pass down in the end zone. I also vividly remember the defensive play he made against Highlands at Tates Creek in the Thoroughbred Bowl for his senior season. Unbelievable game on offense, but he sealed it with an interception and he knew the quarterback was going to throw it to that wide receiver. (He) jumped in front of it before anyone knew it.

"As far as his offense, that was like watching a video game because he had so many weapons at wide receiver and even running back. His coach, Mike Whitaker, was innovative with his schemes just so far ahead of most defensive minds. The fields where he played at home or away were always packed with those wanting to see this star player. I just considered it a blessing to be able to follow his career from such a young age until he was in the pros. Off the field, he was so nice to talk with about where he grew up or what schools were coming to the small town to try and lure him to their campuses."

The 6-foot-5 Couch not only played football, but also starred in basketball, his favorite sport. He played on the high school varsity team since the seventh grade and led the state in scoring as a junior, averaging 36 points, earning first team All-State honors. As a senior, he averaged 25.5 points and was chosen to the first-team All-State again.

"I think like most kids growing up in Kentucky, you grow up dreaming about playing basketball at the University of Kentucky," said Couch. "Basketball was my first love and I always considered myself a basketball player. My junior year in high school, I was averaging 36 points a game and really getting recruited heavily in basketball as well. So, I think at that point, I didn't really know if I was going to be a football or basketball player. Really, I came to Kentucky with the idea of playing both sports here at UK. But I think once I got to college, I realized that I was going to have to pick one or the other and really specialize in that. I chose football, and I think it ended up working out for me pretty well."

When he was a youngster, Couch enjoyed traveling to Lexington with his family to watch the Wildcats at Rupp Arena. "(I enjoyed) the atmosphere, the environment of being in Rupp Arena, watching those great players that we've had come through this university," said Couch, whose favorite UK player was Rex Chapman. "Just being in Rupp Arena is a great experience. It was loud. It's fun. I went to several games growing up, and it was always a treat to get to go to those games. My dad would take me. Just to be able to spend time with him and to go watch the Cats play is always exciting for a young kid to get a chance to do that, so I always loved those opportunities to go to Rupp Arena."

Couch also enjoyed attending the state high school tournaments in Louisville and Lexington, including the days when future UK standout Richie Farmer and Clay County advanced to the championship games for two straight years during the late 1980s. Clay County, coached by Bobby Keith, won the state title in 1987, beating Louisville Ballard and Allan Houston 76-73 in overtime, with Farmer gunning in 27 points before 19,000 fans at Rupp Arena. In the following season of 1988, Farmer pumped in 51 points, but Clay County lost to Coach Scott Davenport's Ballard 88-79 before a Freedom Hall crowd of 19,575. Farmer was named the Most Valuable Player in Sweet Sixteen both times.

# Football Legend Paul Hornung

If you go back and look through old newspaper or magazine articles, you will see many comments by Louisvillian Paul Hornung, the 1956 Heisman Trophy winner from Notre Dame and a pro football star best known for his days with the Green Bay Packers. He often discussed the Leslie County superstar. During the recruitment of Couch, Kentucky coach Bill Curry, who previously served as the head coach at Alabama, posting a three-year mark of 26-10, wanted help from Hornung, his former Green Bay teammate. So, in December 1995, Hornung and his wife traveled to Leslie County to visit with Couch and speak at his team's football banquet. In an article by Billy Reed in the *Lexington Herald-Leader*, Hornung said, "We went to the house, spoke to the mom and dad. Billy (Curry) was worried about him going to Tennessee. I told him, 'Don't worry about it.' I went into his bedroom, and there was nothing but blue." In a *USA Today* story by Harry Blauvelt in 1996 previewing the upcoming football season, Hornung said he was pleased to see Couch has the basketball-crazed state of Kentucky "thinking a little more about football than basketball for a change. He'll be sensational." Couch at the time was preparing for his freshman year as a backup QB.

What was Hornung like? "Paul was great," Couch recalled. "He actually came down and he spoke at my high school banquet for my senior year of high school. He presented me with the Mr. Football Award, I think, at the time. Then I got a chance to be good friends with Paul. He shared a lot of his stories with me about his days at Notre Dame and with the Green Bay Packers. A very inspirational person, just such a legend in the football world. It was such an honor for me at such a young age to be able to spend time with Paul and talk to him about his experiences and how he got to the level that he got to. It was awesome getting a chance to meet him."

## Recruiting Tales

Kentucky was not the only school that wanted Couch's arm. Major schools like Tennessee, Notre Dame, Ohio State, Penn State, Florida, among others, wanted him, too. Eventually Couch narrowed his top choices to UK and UT. Couch shared his recruiting experience with the author. "It was a very intense recruiting process," he said. "There were coaches calling every day. They were coming to visit at the high school. They were coming to watch my games. I just remember how intense it was and how it was nonstop. It was a different world back then. Recruiting is different now than it was 20 some years ago, whatever that was. But I just remember it just being very hectic, a stressful time really, because it is such a big decision on a 17, 18-year-old kid trying to decide where he wants to go play ball and go to school."

Couch is glad that he picked Kentucky over Tennessee. Beyond football, Couch is thankful for "the connections I made while I was here at UK have really been super beneficial to me and helped me grow as a businessman and do a lot of different things that I never thought I'd be able to get into."

Tennessee was a serious contender. Why? "I think I grew up just kind of about the same distance to Knoxville, Tenn., as I did to Lexington, so I was always watching Tennessee football because they were always so good, had such a great tradition. I started getting interested in Tennessee when Heath Shuler was the quarterback there. Heath was such a fun player to watch. He was a great player, one of the top five or six picks (actually No. 3 overall pick in 1994 NFL Draft) when he came out to the (Washington) Redskins. So, I started watching it then. Then obviously Peyton Manning came there and I got a chance to be really good friends with Peyton and visited Tennessee quite often.

"Because it was so close to my house, I would go there for games, for visits and just spent a lot of time around the coaching staff — (Assistant) Coach (David) Cutcliffe and Coach (Phillip) Fulmer. Really got to be close with that whole staff and the team as well. So, I felt really comfortable around those guys and it was a great environment. I was verbally committed to Tennessee during my senior year and ended up changing that last minute (on pre-Christmas announcement) and on signing day (in February.) Ended up going to Kentucky, but it was a very close call whether I was going to Tennessee or Kentucky. I think at the end of the day, my parents and family and friends wanted me to go to Kentucky pretty heavily. That influenced my decision quite a bit." Had Couch gone to Tennessee, he likely was expected to redshirt during his freshman season with then-junior Peyton Manning starting at QB.

It's not a big surprise that Couch's parents, Elbert and Janice, had a considerable influence on his collegiate decision. "My dad was a big influence on me deciding on Kentucky. I think he was thinking past the athletic career, which he ended up being correct on that," he added. "He was saying, 'If you go to Kentucky and make the connections and meet different people in the business world, you set yourself up for life after football as well,' and that's the way it ended up working out. He was definitely correct on that.

"So, I'd have to say at the end of the day, my dad was probably the biggest influence on why I had a change of heart last minute and decided to come to UK."

Couch also desired to play college basketball. Tennessee didn't like the idea of having a two-sport athlete. "They weren't very on board with playing both sports in Tennessee," he said. "They recruited me heavily in basketball there, but when I was telling them I wanted to play both sports, it wasn't going over great. They wanted me to be fully invested in one or the other, which I definitely understand. But at that point, I was just kind of a torn between football and basketball. I hadn't really made up my mind yet which direction I wanted to try to go in. But they were pretty set on me just deciding on picking one (sport) and staying with it.

"I had a lot of offers in basketball. I had Kentucky, Louisville, Tennessee, Ohio State, USC, all kinds of schools in basketball as well. I wanted to play both sports obviously in college. A lot of schools weren't on board with that. They wanted me to play one or the other, and then Kentucky came in when Coach (Rick) Pitino was there and Coach Curry. They decided they were going to let me try to play both, and that was a big selling point for me because I thought for sure that I was going to do both in college. Once I got into college, I realized how difficult that was going to be to play two sports and a full academic load as well, trying to keep up grades and go to classes and do those things. So, I knew pretty quickly I was going to have to choose one or the other and ended up deciding on football."

It helped that former hoops star Rex Chapman, who played two years under coach Eddie Sutton at Kentucky during the late 1980s, had some influence on Couch to attend UK. As mentioned previously, Chapman was Couch's favorite basketball player. "When I was getting recruited by Kentucky, they actually sent me over to meet Rex at his house (in Lexington) and he was playing in the NBA at the time. So, I got a chance to meet him and it was a great experience. We've become good friends over the years since then. Growing up, it was Rex Chapman whom I looked up to. He was doing such great things at the university at that time when I was really at the age where I was influenced by watching those games and dreaming about playing for Kentucky and aspiring to be a great athlete. So, at that time, it was definitely Rex because he was a Kentucky kid as well, playing for his home state school. I think that certainly had a big influence on me choosing Kentucky as well."

## College Freshman

When the 1996 football season began, Couch, as expected, didn't start in UK's season-opening 38-14 setback to Louisville in Lexington. But the record-breaking crowd of 59,384, which was the largest in the history of Commonwealth Stadium (now Kroger

Field) at the time, loudly cheered when Couch came on the field in the second half. Replacing starting QB Billy Jack Haskins, a Paducah native who was Kentucky's Mr. Football in 1992, Couch completed eight of 20 passes for 101 yards, including a 20-yard TD. That was his first collegiate performance.

After two straight poor seasons of 1-10 in 1994 and 4-7 in 1995, including two losses to hapless Vanderbilt, Kentucky coach Bill Curry's seat had gotten a lot warmer after his team's disappointing performance against U of L. And the demanding Big Blue Nation crowd wanted to see Couch start in place of Haskins. But Curry said no. Then, after UK's suffered a 21-point loss to host Cincinnati with Couch seeing limited action as a backup, Curry's seat got much, much hotter. A very dark cloud was hanging over the football program, and the Wildcat fans were extremely frustrated and unhappy. Well-known columnist Billy Reed wrote athletics director C.M. Newton should fire Curry.

Things weren't much better in the following weeks. The Wildcats couldn't score as they barely beat Indiana by a "baseball" score of 3-0 before dropping to Florida 65-0 in Gainesville and Alabama 35-7 in Tuscaloosa. It was Couch who engineered the drive that set up the game-winning field goal in the final seconds against the Hoosiers. Kentucky could only win three more games, defeating Georgia, Mississippi State and Vanderbilt, and Curry was fired. For the season, Couch threw 32 completions in 84 attempts for 276 yards in seven games with two starts in the option offense. When he started against Florida in a blowout loss, it turned out to be one of the low points of his life. "That was tough," Couch said. "That's when I kind of knew I'd made a bad decision as far as football-wise, because I was in the offense that didn't suit my skill set. Running the option just wasn't for me, and Florida was the national champion (that season)." Nevertheless, it was a very tough campaign for the freshman who at the time considered the possibility of transferring depending on the new coach and his offense.

Couch said C.M. Newton played a big role in encouraging him to stay at Kentucky. "He was a great person, someone I have a tremendous amount of respect for," said Couch. "He did a lot of great things in his career and he influenced a lot of people, and I was certainly one of them that he influenced. I remember during that process after the freshman season didn't go well, I was going to transfer back to Tennessee where I was originally committed to. C.M. knew that. After Coach Curry was fired, he asked me to go through the coaching process with him and just wait until the new coach was hired before I made a decision to transfer or not. So, I told him I would wait and go through the process with him.

"He went out and found Coach (Hal) Mumme who no one knew at the time. Coach was at Valdosta State and no one really knew who he was or what type of offense that he was going to be bringing in. Once C.M. told me who he'd hired and I got a chance to meet with Coach Mumme, I knew it was going to be a great fit. The (pass-happy) offense was very similar to what I was doing in high school and had so much success with. So, I felt pretty confident I was going to be able to do great things in that offense, so that's ultimately why I ended up staying at Kentucky."

After the football season ended, Couch focused on basketball but it didn't last long. "I actually went over to practice with the basketball team a couple of times my freshman year after football," he said. "I went over, practiced with Coach Pitino and those guys. I realized pretty quickly at that time — that was in 1996 when they won the national championship — they had guys like Jeff Sheppard, Ron Mercer and Derek Anderson, and about 10 other NBA players on that team. So, I realized pretty quickly when I got over there and practiced with those guys that I wasn't going to be able to play football half a year and just show up over there and get up and down the court with those guys. I knew it would have to be a full-time commitment if I wanted to compete against those guys. So, I knew pretty quickly that my take was going to be playing football. I remember just going over there and scrimmaging with those guys. I remember how good they were. Everybody seemed so big, athletic, and fast. That was a heck of a team they had. I was at Kentucky in '96, '97, '98, and they went to three straight national championship (games) during those years and won two of them. So, it was a heck of a program. Coach Pitino and then Coach Tubby Smith had the program rolling, and it was in a great spot at that time."

## Hal Mumme

With Kentucky's new pass-happy offense, popularly known as the "Air Raid," Couch flourished in the next two years under Mumme's leadership. Asked about his favorite games or moments, Couch said, "There were several games that jump out, but it was probably the game against Alabama where Kentucky hadn't beaten Alabama in 75 years. We got to play them here in Lexington. It was my sophomore year (1997). The game went into overtime, and I was able to throw a (winning) touchdown pass to Craig Yeast. The fans rushed the field and tore the goal posts down. It was one of those moments that you live for as a college quarterback and one that I'll never forget. It was a great moment for me, my teammates, and for Coach Mumme, Coach (Mike) Leach and that whole staff. They did such great things. That was kind of the moment that kind of got the ball rolling for us and let everyone know that we were going to be very, very competitive in the SEC. Kentucky hadn't been (competitive) in recent years, so that kind of showed everyone that we could play with the big guys, and it was a great upset victory for us."

For the record, the Wildcats stopped the Crimson Tide 40-34 with Couch passing for 355 yards and four TDs. C.M. Newton, 67, quipped, "If I weren't so old, I'd have torn them (goal posts) down myself." And Kentucky finished with a 5-6 mark, including a season-opening victory over Louisville. In that first game of the

1997 season, Couch threw for a then-UK record 398 yards against the Cardinals. In a 49-7 victory over Indiana in Bloomington, he passed for a school-record seven TD tosses. A second-team All-SEC (behind Tennessee's first-team All-SEC QB Peyton Manning), Couch finished in the Top 10 in voting for the Heisman Trophy.

*Record-setting quarterback Tim Couch during his UK days in late 1990s. (UK Athletics Photo)*

What was Coach Mumme like? Was he strict with the team? "He was," said Couch. "He was very laid back at times as well, but he had his moments where he could get on guys. I think he had a very good balance of being laid back where he made the game fun, but he also held guys accountable and he made sure guys were doing what they needed to do, putting in the work that they needed to put in in the film room and the weight room. I would say, out on the practice field, he would get on guys, for sure. Coach Leach would as well, but they were also very fun at times.

"I really enjoyed being around them, spending time with them. And they were innovators. They were way ahead of their time as far as offensive football goes. They really did change the game with the 'Air Raid' offense that we started in 1997. It's still very, very relevant in college football even today. So, there's a lot of teams still run a version of it. It's made its way into the NFL as well. So, it was a game changing thing and certainly something I'm very, very proud of that I was able to be a part of."

After the Outback Bowl, Couch completed his UK career on a high note, setting numerous NCAA, SEC and school records. Named 1998 SEC Player of the Year, he was chosen first-team All-American by a couple of outlets. He also a finalist for the Heisman Trophy again, finishing No. 4 in the balloting.

## Highly-Publicized Tragedy

On a Sunday morning in 1998, the day after Kentucky crushed Vanderbilt 55-17, a tragedy took place in Pulaski County when a pickup truck carrying three young men went out of control and flipped over on a highway, killing two and injuring one. They were on a deer hunting trip. Wildcat player Artie Steinmetz, who transferred from Michigan State, and EKU student Scott Brock passed away. Jason Watts, UK's starting center who was the driver, survived with injuries. The accident made the national news for several days, and the blood alcohol tests revealed all three men were legally drunk. Watts was charged and later sentenced to 10 years before being released on shock probation after four months.

The tragedy hit the football team hard, especially Couch, who had just lost his best friend, Scott Brock, a former player at Leslie County High. The team canceled practice on Monday, and the players attended two funerals during that week. Couch traveled to Hyden to attend Brock's funeral and served as a pallbearer. "When you lose your best friend, it puts everything into perspective," said Couch several months later in a 1999 article by Mary Kay Cabot in Cleveland's *Plain Dealer*. "Football is important, but it's not No. 1. Family and friends are."

Added Couch in 2025, "That was probably the hardest time of my life, just being what was the 19, 20-year-old kid at the time and having to deal with that and going back down to my hometown for the funeral and spending time with his family, being a pallbearer in the funeral. It was just a gut-wrenching moment. It's tough on anyone no matter what age you are, but when somebody passes away so young like that, when life is cut short at 19 years old, it's just there's an extra sadness involved in that. I think that he was such a good person and such a good friend. All of a sudden, he's gone. It's such a change of way of life. Not having him around was a big adjustment for me, and it took a long time for me to heal from that, but I'm very thankful for all the time we got to spend together and still miss him every day.

"Scott and I grew up (together). We were very, very close. We went to even preschool, kindergarten all the way through high school together. He lived right down the street from me as well, so we spent more time together than I did with my own family. He was either at my house spending the night or I was at his house spending the night. It was one of those relationships where I'd go to his house and I wouldn't even have to knock on the door. I would just walk right in like I was part of the family. And his parents accepted me as part of the family and my family accepted him as part of the family. We were just very, very close. We played all the way through kindergarten to high school together. He was a running back and linebacker, played a little bit of receiver as well. He was a good football player, very tough, hard-nosed guy. He was one of those guys that gave 100 percent effort in practice and games. He was just one speed, just always full go, nonstop all the time. He was a great teammate. The accident happened. Obviously two of my teammates at UK were in the car as well, and one of them passed away. One of them survived."

With the tragedy hanging over the Kentucky program on campus during the emotional week, the Cats, who were 7-3 at the time, were not able to focus and missed some practice time in preparation for the season finale with the Vols in Knoxville. "We probably shouldn't even have played that game (won by Tennessee in a 59-21 blowout) because that whole week we didn't even really get to practice because the whole team went to the funeral of Scott down in Hyden, and then we went to my other UK teammate. We all went to his funeral as well in northern Kentucky. Artie Steinmetz was his name. So, it was a very, very, very emotional week for our football team. We were just drained. Like I said, we didn't have much time on the practice field. We certainly didn't have anything emotionally to put into it.

"We ran out on the field in Knoxville against a great Tennessee team, and we were just as flat as can be. We had no chance of winning that game. The Tennessee game was one that I'll never forget. Our minds were anywhere but the game, I should say. A big game like that, normally you come out and you're completely locked in and laser focused and excited. It was the exact opposite of that. I remember guys sitting in the locker room before the game, dead silence. There's no one trying to get people excited, get people hyped up. It was just people. We were all just sitting there at our lockers with our heads down and didn't really want to be there, to be honest."

Over a month later, the Cats arrived in Tampa for the Outback Bowl. "We played a little better in the Outback Bowl," said Couch. "A little time had passed. It'd been a month or so, so we were able to get back into a normal routine of practice and just being around the facility and kind of recovering from what had happened to us a month or so before that. So we played better that game."

## 1999 NFL Draft

It was a very memorable night for Couch in New York City when NFL commissioner Paul Tagliabue announced the Cleveland Browns, an expansion franchise, had selected the Kentucky QB as the No. 1 pick of the NFL Draft. Hours before he was drafted, Couch and the Browns reached a deal on a seven-year contract. Couch was asked by the author if it was true that he signed the contract in the men's room at the Madison Squre Garden where the draft was held.

"That is true," he said with a smile. "The Browns were adamant about (getting an agreement). They didn't want me to be a training camp holdout with negotiating contracts and stuff like that. They said, 'If we take you, we want the contract done and signed and you're on board. There's going to be no holdout. We want you to camp on day one.' Literally, when I say last minute, it was last minute. My agent, Tom Condon, had been negotiating all throughout the night before with the Browns, and finally that morning, they came to an agreement on the contract. As I got to Madison Square Garden, that's when I learned that the Browns were going to take me and my agent had the contract waiting for me. We went somewhere private where people wouldn't see me signing it and give away who was going to be the No. 1 pick. So, we ended up going to the men's room and getting that contract signed." Condon also represented Tennessee's Peyton Manning, who was the No. 1 pick in the 1998 NFL Draft.

What was the first thing Couch did or bought after signing the $59 million contract? "The first thing I did was I paid off all of my parents' debt and retired both of them," he said. "They had both worked very hard their whole lives. My dad was a transportation director. My mother worked at a welfare office, the social security office, so they had spent a lot of money on me and my brother growing up. It's expensive to play sports and to go to all these camps and to train and to eat the way you're supposed to as an athlete. It gets very expensive, so they had piled up some debt. I paid off all their debt and retired them so they could just travel and go to all of my (NFL) games and just be there and enjoy the moment as much as possible."

According to an *USA Today* story by Larry Weisman, Couch's hometown weekly newspaper, *Leslie County News*, couldn't afford to send reporter Sam Highton to the NFL Draft. But the reporter got to cover it with the help from churchgoers.

During their pro careers, Couch and Peyton Manning spent a lot of time together. Their friendship actually began when Couch was in high school. "We actually were very close," said Couch. "When he was at Tennessee, he was a couple years ahead of me. So when I was in high school, I'd go there to visit a lot and got to spend a lot of time with Peyton, Eli, Cooper and Archie. The whole family, I got to know really well. Peyton was the No. 1 pick the year before me in 1998. So, when I was coming out the next year as the No. 1 pick, Peyton is the one who helped me. I had a lot of questions for him about the process, and he's the one that helped me find my agent, Tom Condon. (He) just helped me a lot as far as adjusting to life as a rookie in the NFL.

"If you remember, Peyton had a really tough rookie year (at Indianapolis). I think he broke the record for most interceptions thrown in a season, and he was just telling me how tough the adjustment is and how it's so different than college. We actually ended up talking a whole lot during my career. We would actually catch up usually at the beginning of the week on Monday or

Tuesday, just on the phone. We would talk about our game we just had. If we had a common opponent, if I had just played the Bears or whoever it was, and Peyton had them the next week, he would call me and ask me questions about what'd you see? What type of defense? Are they aggressive? Are they man to man? Are they zone? Do they blitz a lot? Just things that quarterbacks talk about and I would do the same with him, obviously bouncing questions off of him about preparation and what he does to get ready for a game throughout the week and play on Sunday. We had a really good relationship and very thankful for everything that Peyton helped me out with along the way."

Couch is the only UK football player in school history who has been selected No. 1 overall in the NFL Draft. He was asked how he felt about that honor. "Very proud," Couch commented. "I think it's something that's rare. There's not many guys that can say they've been the No. 1 pick in the NFL draft and certainly very, very proud of that. Still, even to this day, I remember that moment just like it was yesterday. It's one of those moments when your kids are born or just some big event in your life happens to you. You never forget how you felt in that moment, where you were. You kind of remember everything in vivid detail, so it was a very, very special moment for me coming from a small town in eastern Kentucky all the way up through the University of Kentucky and ending up being No. 1 pick in the draft. It was an unbelievable run for me as far as an athlete. It was a special moment and one that I'll never forget."

Kentucky has had other players who were drafted very high in the first round, but not the No. 1 selection overall. UK's only No. 2 overall picks were quarterback Rick Norton (in 1966 American Football League draft) and defensive end Art Still (1978 NFL Draft). The No. 4 overall picks in the first round include QB Babe Parilli (1952), defensive tackle Lou Michaels (1958), and defensive tackle Dewayne Robertson (2003).

## Pro Football Days

"I think I was excited to go to the Browns even though they were an expansion team. I knew it was going to be tough because we were literally starting from the ground up with that organization. Because in 1996, I believe it was, the Browns left (Cleveland) to move to Baltimore and become the Baltimore Ravens. So, they'd been out of the league for three years. When they came back in the league in 1999, I was the No. 1 pick in their brand new franchise. It came with a lot of pressure, certainly a lot of expectations from the fans.

"Obviously with the contract and everything, there's a lot of pressure on the No. 1 pick in the draft. Going to the worst team in the league, it's kind of the deal. You may be the No. 1 pick, but you have to go to the worst team because they get to pick first. So, for me, it was something that I embraced. I felt like it was something that I went through at Kentucky. They weren't very good when I got there (at UK), and we were able to turn that thing around and get it going in the right direction. I really felt that I could do it in Cleveland as well. But it was definitely a tough experience. The first couple of years were rough. I got sacked a lot. I got hit a lot. I got to start as a rookie and played a lot of football, and it was a good experience."

On his best memory or game as a QB in the NFL?

"Oh, man. Probably the first win stands out," said Couch, whose Browns at the time began the season with an 0-7 mark. "We were playing the New Orleans Saints in New Orleans in the Superdome, and we hadn't had a win yet. We were struggling as an expansion team, and we were winning that whole game. All of a sudden, the Saints came down and kicked the field goal to take the lead with just 20 seconds to go or something like that. So, we thought we're going to lose another close game. (But) I was able to throw a 'Hail

Mary' (pass) to win the game, about a 60-yard (actually 56-yard) Hail Mary that Kevin Johnson caught in the corner of the end zone. Just to get your first win as an NFL quarterback and get it on a Hail Mary of all things like that (is a great feeling). To win a game that way, a walk-off touchdown was something that you never forget, for sure."

After coach Mike Ditka's Saints came out with a 16-14 lead on a late field goal with 21 seconds left, Couch managed to guide Cleveland to thrilling 21-16 victory, marching 75 yards in three plays, including a "Hail Mary" pass to Johnson, a rookie. For the contest, Couch completed 11 of 19 passes for 193 yards and three TDs. When the 1999 season ended, the Browns posted a 2-14 record with the other victory taking place at Three Rivers Stadium in Pittsburgh, defeating the Steelers 16-15. Couch finished his rookie year with 2,447 passing yards, including 15 TDs, in 15 games with 13 interceptions.

Couch perhaps had his most emotional moment of his sports career while with the Browns. It was the year Cleveland made the playoffs in 2002 as a wild-card entry with an 8-6 mark. "It was my fourth year when we went to the playoffs," he recalled. "We'd had a really good season. In the last game of the year, we had to win to get into the playoffs. We were playing the Atlanta Falcons and Michael Vick at home in Cleveland. We got off to a good start in that game. Unfortunately, I broke my leg in the second quarter of the game. So, for me, coming into that franchise from day one as expansion team and getting beat up the first couple years and then getting to the point where we were about to make the playoffs, and I broke my leg in the game we had to win to go. We ended up winning the game, but I didn't get to play in the playoff game.

"That was probably the most emotional moment for me just because I wanted to be out there so bad with my teammates. I kind of started from day one with that organization and to not get to play in the playoff game was pretty tough on me." In the playoffs, the Browns dropped to the Pittsburgh Steelers 36-33.

Couch, who has done some TV broadcasting work in recent years, struggled with some injuries and eventually retired after five NFL seasons, passing for a career total of 11,131 yards and 64 TDs in 62 games.

## Media Folks

Award-winning sportswriter Rick Bozich, recently retired from Louisville-based WDRB.com, has seen Couch play football. "Tim Couch changed the course of Kentucky football, entertaining crowds, winning games and setting records," said Bozich, who covered Couch's playing days while at Louisville's *Courier-Journal*. "He could have gone anywhere in the country, but his love for UK brought him to Lexington, where he thrived over his final two seasons. I was always worried that Couch would not be able to live up to the hype he generated in high school. He more than lived up to it. He exceeded it — and remained remarkably comfortable and accessible despite all the demands on his time. Tim Couch remains one of my favorite players that I had the privilege to watch at Kentucky."

Sports columnist Mark Story of the *Lexington Herald-Leader* remembers a particular play on a November night at then-called Commonwealth Stadium in 1998 when Couch's Cats faced a good Mississippi State team coached by Jackie Sherrill, a Bear Bryant disciple who played at Alabama.

"Tim Couch threw what I consider the most remarkable pass I've ever seen thrown by a Kentucky quarterback," said Story. "UK was clinging to a 30-29 lead over Mississippi State in the fourth quarter when Couch took a shot gun snap and received the ball around the MSU 11-yard line. As Couch dropped back, the pocket collapsed and the Mississippi State pass rush broke through. Buying time, Couch just kept backpedaling. By the time Couch had dropped back to around the MSU 21-yard line, three

Bulldogs defenders had broken clear and had an unimpeded path to the Kentucky quarterback. Couch was literally falling backwards to the ground when he lofted a pass toward the left side of the Mississippi State end zone. The ball hung in the air for what seemed like forever — then dropped from the night sky into the hands of a leaping Craig Yeast for a Kentucky touchdown. It was a near miracle that Couch got the throw away, but to throw it while under such duress to a location where Yeast was able to run under the football was beyond amazing. That play put Kentucky ahead 37-29 with 8:21 left in the game and turned out to be the decisive score in a game UK won 37-35 over an MSU team that would go on to win the SEC West."

Sports anchor Keith Farmer of WLEX-TV, whose family has close connections with Couch and his folks in Hyden, recalled several moments. "After high school, I remember most games like many others. That first game he got in and ran the (ill-suited) option, oh my. The win over Alabama was magical. The game in the Outback Bowl felt like he had gotten us on the path to being a special football program.

"After he was drafted, our sports director at the time, Gary Johnson, had put in for (media) passes to the Browns opening game that season against the Pittsburgh Steelers. He decided he wasn't going and asked if I wanted to cover it. With my connection to Tim, I felt like I had to go. It was special to be on the field listening to the Cleveland fans cheering for him to come in the game and, while it was not spectacular at all (as Pittsburgh blanked the Browns 43-0), it was awesome to see his dream coming true at the professional level.

"I just hate the turn that his career took with all of the injuries. And most of that started with the Browns not giving him a good enough offensive line to start with in his NFL career. I believe he's never really dwelled on that and always had a positive attitude that he's going to find something to get involved with whether that's business related or maybe spending time traveling or on a golf course. I will also say, it was special to cover him in high school playing basketball. Man, he could score, and his jump shot was so pure because he almost didn't have any arc on his shot. Just one of the special athletes I've covered."

## Reaching Hall of Fame

Couch, who lives in Lexington, discussed the day when he learned that he was voted into the College Football Hall of Fame in 2024. "It was a fun day," he said. "My family came over and surprised me with the news. We were having a dinner, and they just handed me a piece of paper and asked me to read it, and it said that I was selected to the 2024 Class of College Football Hall of Fame, and it was a great night to celebrate with my family and one of those special nights I'll never forget.

"They (National Football Foundation & College Hall of Fame) wrote a letter. They sent it to my family just so they could surprise me with it. I'm honored and humbled. This is an unbelievable honor; I'm blown away by it."

Couch, who is co-owner of Meridian Wealth Management with his older brother and former EKU football standout Greg Couch, joins several other former UK standouts in the College Football Hall of Fame, including coach Paul "Bear" Bryant, tackle Bob Gain, QB Vito "Babe" Parilli, end Steve Meilinger, tackle Lou Michaels, defensive end Art Still and Jerry Claiborne, who was the head coach at three schools, including UK. Bernie Shively, who was athletics director at UK, was inducted into the Hall of Fame in recognition of his playing days at Illinois. Couch and Claiborne are the only two native Kentuckians in the College Football Hall of Fame.

After UK dismissed coach Joker Phillips, a former wide receiver who starred for the Cats during the early 1980s, for his team's poor performance with a 2-10 mark in 2012, Couch served as an advisor to athletics director Mitch Barnhart during the coaching search that eventually selected Mark Stoops.

## Post-Playing Days

Couch still follows the Wildcats closely. "I've had season tickets there for a long time," he said. "I've been going to games since I got done playing in the NFL. I've been living back in Lexington and try to go to almost every home game. I go to the basketball games as well."

After leaving UK for pro football, Couch didn't finish his college education. "Once I left after my junior year, I didn't go back and finish," he said. "But thankfully, I was able to make a lot of the connections that kind of helped me get started in the business world. My brother and I started a financial business that we own called Meridian Wealth Management, and we've had that for about 13 years now. That's off and running really well. We've got a bourbon company called Limestone Farms now, and I've got several other things as well that we are invested in. So we kind of diversify quite a bit and get into quite a few different things."

Couch and his brother, Greg, have been very close since their early days at Leslie County. "He's been my No. 1 supporter and inspiration. He was a quarterback (in high school and college) as well. He was four years older than me, so he was a senior when I was in eighth grade. I was his backup on the varsity (team). So then he went to play football at Eastern Kentucky University for Coach Roy Kidd, had a great career there. And then he started working for me when I got drafted, working with my financial people and learning that business that way. Then we ended up starting our own business, the financial business that I mentioned earlier. So, we do everything together now. We do all of our business stuff together. We're 50/50 on everything pretty much, and we're as close as brothers can be as far as that goes."

Couch was asked to tell something about himself that not many people know. "Oh, man. That's a tough one. I really don't know," he smiled. "I think it's pretty much what you see is what you get. I'm obviously a big UK supporter, and I'm still a big fan of the Cleveland Browns. I love being a father (of two sons). I play a lot of golf. I'm always working out and very into fitness and those kinds of things, but I think most people know those things about me. I don't have anything behind the scenes that I like to do that people don't know about."

# 6

## From London to NBA

### (Reed Sheppard)

When Reed Sheppard was a youngster growing up in the London, Ky., area, he had dreams of playing for UK, his parents' alma mater. That dream came true in November 2022 as he officially signed a letter of intent with Kentucky. Sheppard, who had committed to the Wildcats a year earlier, said it was an easy decision as he chose UK over schools like Louisville and Indiana. "Ever since I've been a little kid, I'd wanted to go to the University of Kentucky and play basketball," Sheppard told the author. "Being able to follow after my mom and dad's footsteps, it was something I definitely could not pass up on, and I was super thankful for the opportunity and the experience."

Added then-UK coach John Calipari, "I know playing for Kentucky has been a dream of Reed's ever since he was a child. But Reed isn't here because he wanted to be here. He's here because he's a really good player who can help this team win. He has terrific fundamentals and is the kind of player who can excel on or off the ball. I love his work ethic and the fact that he wants to be pushed on the biggest of stages to reach his full potential."

*North Laurel High School's Reed Sheppard, shown in action during the 13th Region Tournament, received numerous prep honors, including McDonald's All-American in 2023. (Photo by Danny Vaughn)*

Sheppard's signing ceremony at North Laurel High School auditorium took place nearly three weeks before he started playing his senior year in high school. One of the nation's Top 25 prospects, Sheppard didn't miss a beat in the season opener as the 6-foot-3 guard hit 23 points and grabbed eight rebounds in leading the host Jaguars to a 77-65 victory over Lexington Catholic.

One memorable showdown took place in January 2023 when North Laurel and Lyon County clashed in Lexington, featuring the state's No. 1 player in their respective classes with Sheppard in

2023 and Travis Perry in 2024. Both star players didn't disappoint the crowd, scoring a combined 77 points as Lyon County prevailed with a 90-83 victory. Sheppard came up with a triple double with 32 points, 10 rebounds and 13 assists. Perry, a 6-foot-2 junior who hit 10 of 16 three-pointers, finished with 45 points.

As it turned out, Sheppard and Perry were named Kentucky's Mr. Basketball for 2023 and 2024, respectively. North Laurel, which posted an unbeaten mark of 16-0 in the 13th Region, would go on to win the regional tourney in Corbin, clinching a spot in the state tournament for the second straight year. Sheppard's Jaguars, coached by Nate Valentine, finished the year with a 25-11 record.

Before his senior year began, Sheppard, a 2023 McDonald's All-American, had many great performances which attracted national attention from many big-name schools. Les Dixon, a longtime Kentucky sportswriter who writes for the 13th Region Media Network, had followed Sheppard's five-year high school career, including eighth grade. Dixon has a favorite memory. "Easily my favorite story about Reed is his quadruple-double he recorded during his freshman season against Jackson County," he said. "You'll never meet a more humble athlete than Reed. It was awesome seeing him come out of the locker room after the game and being greeted by a lot of kids and adults alike waiting to congratulate him and asking for his autograph. He stayed out there greeting everyone and signing everything until everyone had left. He continued to do this throughout his high school career and at the University of Kentucky. His actions as a freshman told me he understood not only the game but what with being a star player."

When he was an eighth-grader, Sheppard was very excited to get a dunk after many unsuccessful attempts. "My first dunk came after practice one day," he smiled. "I was trying all day, and I finally got one at the end of practice, and so that was a pretty cool moment just because I had been trying for a long time and finally got one."

Sheppard usually takes a nap before every game. What if he overslept and missed the pregame warmups? "I have never missed a game or a pregame meal," he said. "I always take a nap to get my mind off the game for a little bit and just rest and have about an hour or so just to relax. Try and take a quick little nap to get you ready for the game."

Sheppard and his parents are not the only athletes in the immediate family. His older sister, Madison, starred at North Laurel High before playing at Campbellsville University as a 5-foot-7 guard. In addition, his first cousin, Maci Morris, is one of UK women's all-time leading scorers. "I think that is unbelievable," Sheppard said of his athletic relatives. "I think it's really cool to have family that played at Kentucky and even family that didn't play at Kentucky. Everyone in my family plays a sport or plays basketball, so it's really cool. We're a really competitive family, so anytime we get together we're always playing games or trying to do something that's competitive. It's really fun being able to get together with all the family and compete."

## COVID-19 Pandemic

In March 2020, a few days after then-freshman Sheppard hit 25 points and snatched seven rebounds during North Laurel's 66-64 setback to Knox Central in the 13th Region tournament, the U.S. and the entire world began to implement shutdowns in order to prevent the spread of worldwide COVID-19 virus. Many establishments closed, and the schools from K-12 to college moved to online learning. In Kentucky, the state basketball tournaments for boys and girls were canceled.

But Sheppard found ways to continue playing basketball during the shutdown in his hometown of London. It was when Sheppard's basketball stock went up dramatically in becoming one of the state's top players in the following season, which was delayed until January 2021. During the shutdown, Sheppard practiced with a couple of NCAA Division I players KK Curry and (former North Laurel standout) Adam Sizemore, both of South Alabama. Added ex-Wildcat Jeff Sheppard, Reed's father, "Being able to play ball during COVID was a huge advantage for Reed." The elder Sheppard said several NAIA players also worked out with Reed and his high school teammates in a private gym.

Former Wildcat Cameron Mills said it helped that Reed Sheppard was a gym rat. "It's a lesson I learned when I got to Kentucky, that you can't be a great player unless you're a gym rat," said Mills. "I wasn't a gym rat, which again, is one of those things where I think, how much better could I have been if I had been a gym rat? Reed is a gym rat. Reed's dad was a gym rat. Reed's mom was a gym rat.

"But this guy comes in who's not his mom and his dad, and he starts teaching Reed and he would take Reed through Division I workouts. Pretty much the next year, after that summer, that's when Reed made leaps. He went from a great player to one of the best players in the state because he spent, I'm going to guess, six months or longer just working out (that summer). His workouts were no longer high school workouts. They were Division I college workouts. When you get someone else, a friend who's not your mom and your dad, who comes in and shows you, 'Hey, this is what we do here. This is what individual instruction is here.' Reed took that to heart and started doing it every day with this guy and without this guy. What Shep has told me is that that's when Reed went from good to great. Actually that's probably not even fair because he was a great player before. Because COVID shut everything down, he had nothing to do but spend time in the gym, and that's what he did."

## College Days

While he stayed at UK for only one season before playing in the NBA, Sheppard had some good moments on the hardwood floor and enjoyed his time as a freshman student-athlete in Lexington. He got to wear his father's Wildcat jersey number —15 — when Jeff Sheppard starred during the mid-1990s. On the academic side, the younger Sheppard said he took online and face-to-face classes. "I ended with a 3.6 GPA and my toughest class was probably one of my math classes in the summer, but school was a lot of fun and it was a neat experience being able to do it," he said. Sheppard said taking online classes while in the NBA is a possibility after settling down his pro career.

*Kentucky's Reed Sheppard looks for an open teammate during a game against Ole Miss. (Photo by Wayne Mason)*

In his first UK game, a season-opener with New Mexico State, Sheppard saw backup action in 21 minutes while hitting 12 points and grabbing five rebounds in UK's 86-46 win. It was an experience he will never forget. "It was awesome. Putting on the jersey for the first time and running out with my teammates, running out to the best fans in the nation hollering," he said. "It was really, really cool and something that I have dreamed of my whole life. It was a dream come true; it was unbelievable. On his dunk, "First point (as a Wildcat) so it was really cool that I could do that. D.J. (Wagner) made a great save and pass."

Calipari liked what he saw from his freshman guards — Sheppard and Rob Dillingham — who played solid defense. "We guard the ball pretty good but those two are really disruptive," said Coach Cal in the postgame press conference, who added Wagner played good defense but wasn't as disruptive. "Reed played great, did great stuff."

As the season progressed, Sheppard began to improve, and the NBA scouts started discussing his pro potential more than ever, ranking him very high on the draft list. Toward the end of the season, Sheppard was hot in a matchup that took place in late February at Humphrey Coliseum in Starkville where the then-No. 16 Cats faced the Bulldogs from Mississippi State. It was a long night as the Wildcats struggled and fell behind by 13 points in the early second half. However, Sheppard sparked his team with his 23 second-half points to lead UK's comeback. And it was the London native who hit a game-winning 15-foot jumper as Kentucky won 91-89. The red-hot Sheppard finished with a career-high 32 points along with seven assists.

Said Sheppard, "I think the most memorable moment (at UK) for me was my game-winning shot at Mississippi State. That was just a really fun, fun game and being able to celebrate it with my teammates after was a lot of fun." He added that winning field goal may be the most thrilling moment of all during his pre-NBA days.

Even though Kentucky finished the regular season on high note with five consecutive victories over SEC teams, including an impressive road win at fourth-ranked Tennessee in the season finale, the Cats didn't last long in the postseason action. After dropping the first game of the SEC Tournament, the No. 3 seed Cats lost to No. 14 seed Oakland in a first-round NCAA Tournament shocker in Pittsburgh. It took one little-known player from a little-known school in Michigan to beat the mighty Kentucky Wildcats. Starring for Oakland, rated No. 126 according to NCAA's NET rankings (compared to UK's No. 18), was sixth-year senior Jack Gohlke, a backup guard who gunned in 10 of 20 three-pointers for a game-high 32 points to stun Kentucky 80-76.

"Oakland played a heck of a game," said a dejected UK coach John Calipari, whose Cats finished at 23-10. "They made some unbelievable shots." When UK's locker room was made available to the media, Sheppard, surrounded by reporters, was in tears and emotionally struggled to speak. As it turned out, it was Reed's and Calipari's last game at Kentucky.

Sheppard, who averaged 12.5 points, 4.5 assists and 4.1 rebounds, finished his collegiate career with numerous honors. He was chosen National Freshman of the Year by a couple of outlets. He was also SEC Freshman of the Year as well as All-SEC Second Team. Sheppard, who led the team with 148 assists, made five starts while shooting a nation-best 52.1 percent of his three-point field goals.

Was Calipari an easy or a difficult coach to play for? "Coach Cal, to me, is an unbelievable coach," said Sheppard. "I think he's the best coach in the world, and he means so much to me and my family, and I can never thank him enough for all that he has done for me and and my life outside of basketball, but basketball as well. He is someone that I can always count on, so I really appreciate him and I loved being able to play for him."

*Reed Sheppard answers a question during a
postgame news conference at the SEC Tournament
in Nashville after the Wildcats lost to Texas A&M.
(Photo by Jamie H. Vaught)*

Calipari said Sheppard thinks like a coach. "He's got a coach's mentality," he commented. "He will come to me with stuff on different players. He's the greatest in that. 'Just give it to Robert (Dillingham), and we will get away from it.' Think about that."

Coach Cal added Sheppard was a great teammate and a terrific player with an unbelievable feel.

Calipari, though, got a little frustrated at times when Sheppard made mistakes, especially in late second half. "I said to him, 'You are better than what you are playing at the end of games. You are turning it over and leaving three-point shooters (open). You're too good of a player.' I love coaching him because he's an unbelievable teammate. The guys know they can count on him."

What former UK player does Sheppard remind you of? The author asked former UK All-American Jack Givens about that, and he had trouble answering the question. "I haven't really found a player to compare Reed to," said Givens. "I think the player that comes to mind is possibly Derek Anderson because he, like Reed, can do some of everything on the court at a high-level basketball IQ. He has qualities of several other players such as Dirk Minniefield, SGA (Shai Gilgeous-Alexander) and Jodie Meeks because of how well he shoots from distance. But maybe Derek Anderson is closest."

Oscar Combs, the founder of *The Cats' Pause* magazine, said Sheppard and Anthony Davis, the consensus National Player of the Year in 2012, were the two most exciting Wildcat freshmen he has seen in his lifetime. "They were in a league of their own," he said.

## On Mark Pope and Leaving UK Early

Asked if she had expected her son to stay at UK for at least two years or more, Sheppard's mother, Stacey, said she didn't have any expectations for him. "The most important thing for me was that Reed continued to be himself, have fun, and work his tail off to be the best version of himself. Ignore all the critics and outside noise," said Stacey, a two-time All-SEC performer who starred for UK women's basketball team during the early 1990s.

"However, never in my wildest dreams could I have imagined the season Reed had at UK (in 2023-24)."

Sportswriter Les Dixon had expected Sheppard to stay at UK for more than one season. "I honestly thought Reed would be a four-year player at UK," he said. "Of course, he was the best high school player that I ever covered, but I thought for him to be successful, his outside shot had to improve once graduating from high school. Boy, was I wrong! His outside shot as a freshman was unbelievable along with his shooting percentage. As the season progressed, the more and more I was thinking, he's going to be a lottery pick."

When Mark Pope became the new coach at Kentucky, did Sheppard think about staying for another season to play for his father's college roommate at UK? Many observers were expecting a high NBA draft pick for the youngster. "Reed actually had already made his decision privately to go to the NBA before Mark was named the new head coach," said Sheppard's father, Jeff. "Mark still gave his very best effort to get Reed to change his mind multiple times."

Reed Sheppard met with Pope, adding the new coach was very understanding of the situation. "He was my dad's roommate at Kentucky. When Coach and I talked, it was a very easy and short conversation," said the younger Sheppard. "He was just reaching out saying he was proud of me and he was going to be pulling for me no matter what decision I made. He would love to have me back, but if not, he completely understood, and I've known Coach and his family my whole life, so I'm excited for him and I think he's going to do great things."

The elder Sheppard has a fun fact. Jeff Sheppard, who was named the Most Outstanding Player of the 1998 NCAA Final Four, pointed out that "Pope was the first college coach to recruit Reed and the last college coach to recruit Reed. When Reed was six years old, Pope was an assistant coach at the University of Georgia, and he and his family decided to stop by our home for a visit. Mark called it recruiting! And the last coach to try to recruit Reed before he announced his decision to go to the NBA was Mark Pope."

Reed remembered that visit Pope and his family had made. "I would say my favorite memory is just when him and his family came over," he said. "I was probably like, I don't know, maybe six or so, and him and his girls and his wife were all over at the house, and they just spent the day with us so that was pretty cool."

Reed said he began considering his possible NBA career after the Wildcats lost to Oakland in the Big Dance. "I never thought about the NBA during the season," he said. "I was just focused on just the season and helping the team and being the best player that I could be, but after the season, I was able to talk to my family about it and we just thought that that was the right thing to do at the right time, so that's what we did."

## 2024 NBA Draft

Kentucky had three stars who were selected in the 2024 NBA Draft, which was held at New York City, with Sheppard getting drafted at No. 3 overall by the Houston Rockets. Rob Dillingham was chosen at No. 8 overall, while Antonio Reeves went to the second round as he was picked at No. 47 overall. Asked how he felt when the NBA Commissioner Adam Silver announced his name at the NBA Draft, Sheppard said, "It was unbelievable. It was a dream come true. It's something that I've been dreaming of since I've been a little kid. Having my family with me at the table, my coach, my agent, having my family in the crowd, I couldn't ask for anything else. It was my mom's birthday, so that's an awesome thing to celebrate as well. I'm at a loss for words. I'm super happy to be here and super thankful."

Sheppard, who had just celebrated his 20th birthday a couple of days earlier, was glad to see Dillingham, his college roommate at

UK's Wildcat Coal Lodge, chosen among the Top 10 draft picks. (Sheppard's UK roommate on the road was Tre Mitchell.) And Dillingham was excited, too. "It's crazy. It just shows you a lot of things work in ways you never think because we came in and we were roommates and we were really in the same position," said Dillingham. "We didn't know if we were going to get past our first year. We were just playing basketball. Seeing Reed, my roommate, he's a great dude. He always pushed me, and he always helped me. Me seeing him and we going together, it's just crazy to even see, and I'm thankful."

On the day before, Sheppard and the family rode the subway to Queens and visited the Citi Field, the home of the New York Mets. Wearing a Mets City Connect jersey, Sheppard threw a ceremonial first pitch to his mom, who served as a catcher, jokingly telling him not to knock her down. Asked if he was going to become a Mets fan, Sheppard commented, "I never had a baseball team because there was no baseball team close to Kentucky, but I think I'm going to be a (Houston) Astros fan now." For Sheppard, his closest MLB team, the Cincinnati Reds, is nearly 2.5 hours from his hometown of London.

His first cousin, Maci Morris, a Bell County native who is now a physician assistant in London, and her family also attended the NBA Draft to support Reed. "It was a special experience to be there and watch Reed be drafted, and at No. 3 made it even more exciting," she said. "It was fun to be a part of his big day and see him be surrounded by so many of his close family and friends to celebrate his hard work and dedication. It was also nice getting to spend time with family exploring NYC. It was my first time visiting there so I got to sightsee and do tourist things as well."

Added Morris, "I've obviously always been a big UK fan, but you cheer a little harder when you have someone in your family playing. I was not surprised in how well he did (at Kentucky). I know he's a great guy and he is very disciplined. Knowing how much time and effort he puts into the game and knowing how his parents, sister, and other family members helped prepare him to be successful, it's not surprising to me. Reed is a great athlete and he took advantage of the opportunities given to have a great year at UK, and he now gets to extend that into the NBA."

A former Kentucky's Miss Basketball while at Bell County High School, Morris, certainly didn't disappoint the Big Blue Nation during her four productive years at Kentucky with her hot shooting prowess. Playing for then-coach Matthew Mitchell, the two-time All-SEC performer was fun to watch in becoming one of UK's all-time scoring leaders with a four-year average of 13.1 points before graduating in 2019.

When 6-foot Morris signed with UK, Coach Mitchell said, "When you watch her play, you can just see her basketball IQ's very high and she just makes what I call winning plays." The ex-Wildcat boss even began to call her 'Coach Morris' for her strong understanding of basketball while helping her teammates.

*One of Reed Sheppard's relatives is former Wildcat star Maci Morris (Photo by Jamie H. Vaught)*

Before Morris was born, her parents were struggling to find a good name for their baby. Her dad suggested the main character who was portrayed by actor Clint Eastwood in a 1976 western movie, *The Outlaw Josey Wales.* That character — a Missouri farmer by the name of Josey Wales — decided to join a Confederate unit, seeking revenge after seeing his family killed by the Union Army. "My parents were trying to figure out what to name me," recalled Morris. "My dad first wanted to name me Josey after *The Outlaw Josey Wales*. My mom was like 'absolutely not.' So, he said, 'Well, Kyle Macy's one of my favorite UK basketball players. So what about Macy?' And they agreed on that."

On Sheppard being a No. 3 draft pick in the NBA, sportswriter Les Dixon said, "What an accomplishment! Reed going as the No. 3 pick overall is something that we just don't see in our area in southeastern Kentucky. I'm a North Laurel graduate, actually graduated as the first class there, and to have Reed accomplish the feat is just unbelievable and makes me proud to be a Jaguar. To have someone from London, Ky., to get picked as third overall, is something myself nor other folks would have dreamed we'd see happen.

"You could tell Reed was going to be something special way before he even started playing elementary basketball at Bush. I'd be covering games, and he'd come out on the gym floor at North Laurel High School during halftime and shoot with other kids, and even at that young age, you could tell Reed had 'it.' The sky was the limit for him. And, in time, he proved just that. He will always be remembered as one of the greatest to play basketball in the state."

Sheppard's parents have done a very nice job of raising their son. "Reed is a winner on and off the court," said Dixon. "Any time I asked him if I could interview him, it was, 'Yes, sir.' I covered him from elementary on, and he never displayed or thought he was above anyone. Total class act. Jeff and Stacey have to be proud of the young man that he is."

Former Wildcat Cameron Mills is a huge fan of Sheppard. "I was rooting for Reed harder than I was any (UK) player that's played here in the last 20 years," he said. "But what's funny is I remember all the UK fans thinking that because Reed's a Kentucky boy and because Cal offered a Kentucky boy a scholarship, he's going to be here (at Kentucky) four years. And I kept telling people he might, but don't be surprised if he's not because of his work ethic, his pedigree, and his basketball IQ. Those three things add up to I think what we see now (in the NBA). I didn't expect him to be here one year and then be the third overall draft pick. I didn't expect that, but I sure am and was thrilled about it and happy about it."

During his NBA rookie season of 2024-25, Sheppard showed a lot of promise even though he didn't see a lot of action. That was because a very good Houston team, which finished with a 52-30 mark, had outstanding guards ahead of him. Sheppard averaged 4.4 points and 12.6 minutes in 52 games. In the latter part of the season, he had several outstanding performances, including 25 points with five assists against eventual champion Oklahoma City in his first NBA start and 20 points against the Los Angeles Clippers.

## Faith

On a terrifying night in May 2025, the Kentucky cities of Somerset and London were hit by a deadly tornado, destroying everything in its stormy path and killing nearly 20 victims. And Sheppard was one of many volunteers who helped his hometown of London clean up the debris and recover, less than two weeks after his Houston Rockets lost the opening round series against the Golden State Warriors in the 2025 NBA playoffs.

He posted his feelings about the ordeal on a social media post. "Kentucky will always be home. Seeing the devastation from the tornadoes has been heartbreaking," wrote Sheppard on Instagram. "These are the streets I grew up on, the people who raised me, the community that shaped me. I was so thankful to be able to spend some time at home recently, it reminded me just how special this place really is. I've always been proud to be from London, but watching how hardworking, selfless, and strong this community is in the face of tragedy makes me even prouder. You are the true heroes. My heart is with every family, every neighbor, and every friend who's been impacted. If you're able to donate, volunteer, or send supplies please do." Even Kentucky coach Mark Pope and his two daughters came to London to help.

Sheppard said his faith is very important to him. "I've grown up in a church my whole life, and we never missed a Sunday or a Wednesday growing up," he told the author. "Every time we would go to church, we would have family dinner after, so being able to go to church every week and being able to spend time with my family there and knowing that that's what we do is just really special to me, and it's an unbelievable place to be able to go to every week."

On when he first understood the meaning of God and Jesus, "I think when I first started understanding it was really when I got baptized. It was around sixth grade, so I was probably 13 or so. I'm not exactly sure my age, but it was a very easy decision for me growing up in church my whole life, being able to have conversations with my parents and the rest of my family about everything."

Sheppard's home church is in London. "I've went to Faith Assembly of God my whole life, and we are still going every Sunday," he said shortly before his NBA career began.

On handling the most difficult or frustrating moment of his career, Sheppard said, "There's a lot of things that are hard with being a basketball player and being an athlete in general. There's just a lot of things that you have to do that maybe that you don't really want to do. You got to get up, you got to go work out, you got to lift, you got to eat right. You can't do certain things with your friends and your family sometimes. You got to stay away from certain things, but at the end of the day, it's all about staying positive and having that relationship with God and knowing what is good for you and what is not good for you, and at the end of the day, just staying true to yourself and knowing what you need to do."

*Former Wildcat standout Stacey Reed Sheppard speaks at a special ceremony held at the London-Laurel County Wellness Park in August 2024, honoring the Sheppard family and history of Laurel County high school basketball. The basketball courts at the park were renamed in honor of the Sheppard family. Also pictured, from left, are Jeff, Reed and Madison. (Photo by Jamie H. Vaught)*

On getting his best life or career advice from his family — his father, mother and sister — Sheppard commented, "They all three mean the world to me. My family is very close and I'm very thankful for them and the relationships that I have with them. Their biggest thing is just with basketball, it's just have fun, enjoy it. Never let anyone outwork you. Just every time you go onto the court, play as hard as you can and just enjoy every minute of it. It goes by super fast and then off the court, just be yourself, treat others the way you want to be treated. Just be the best person that you can be. Everybody that comes in contact with you, make their day better, just make them smile. Just be a great person in general."

Sheppard was asked if he could tell us something that many folks don't know about him. "I would say I don't play video games, and I just love to be outside and hang out with my friends and my family," said the former Wildcat, who also enjoys fishing.

# 7

# Aussie Superstar

(Georgia Amoore)

Over the years, Kentucky women's basketball program has produced a handful of stars who were drafted in the Women's National Basketball Association (WNBA), which was established in 1996. They include Rhyne Howard (1st pick overall in 2022), Evelyn Akhator (3rd pick overall, 2017), Makayla Epps (33rd pick overall, 2017), DeNesha Stallworth (25th pick overall, 2014), A'dia Mathies (10th pick overall, 2013), Victoria Dunlap (11th pick overall, 2011), Shantia Owens (53rd pick overall, 2000). And don't forget UK's all-time leading scorer (men's or women's) and Hall of Famer Valerie Still, who starred in the Italian Professional League, American Basketball League for Women, and WNBA during the 1980s and 1990s before retiring.

And you can add UK All-American Georgia Amoore to that impressive list. The year after the Indiana Fever of WNBA had chosen college basketball sensation Caitlin Clark as the overall No. 1 draft selection, Amoore, the 5-foot-6 graduate student, was selected as the No. 6 pick overall in the 2025 WNBA Draft, which was held before the bright lights of New York City and ESPN audience. Amoore's family from Ballarat, Victoria in Australia was there. Her parents, Kelly and Phil Amoore, and her younger sister, Jemma, who had just completed her freshman year as a basketball player at Sacramento State, attended the extravaganza affair. (Her brother, Toby, remained in Australia, taking college classes.) It was a very memorable night for the Amoores, and it was their first trip to NYC.

*Georgia Amoore smiles with her parents at the 2025 WNBA Draft in New York City. (UK Athletics Photo)*

As the national television audience saw at the WNBA Draft on a June night of 2025, Amoore wore a custom-designed outfit — a cropped blazer and a skirt — created by NBA star Russell Westbrook. Shortly after being drafted by the Washington Mystics, Amoore was asked about her fashionable outfit. "I can't even find the words, so if you can help me, because it's phenomenal," said a pleased Amoore. "He's done such a good job, and it didn't feel like just to put his name on something. When we talked about the fit, it was very collaborative. He spent hours with me at the hotel today fitting it, trying it on. He's been very active in the process, and I can't thank him enough because even the little bits of advice he's given me along the way, to have a contact like that now as someone I can try and lean on or lean into. It's amazing and I think it's the start (of a trend). You're going to see this happen more often, and I think it's just a blessing to be the first one to do it."

In addition to Amoore, the Washington Mystics also had top draft picks overall at No. 3 and No. 4. The Mystics selected Sonia Citron of Notre Dame with the No. 3 overall pick and Kiki Iriafen of Southern California at No. 4. It is very unusual to see a team getting three top players among the Top 6 in the draft. While at Virginia Tech before transferring to Kentucky in 2024, Amoore faced Citron and Notre Dame as both played in the Atlantic Coast Conference. Amoore and Citron were named to the All-ACC teams in 2023 and 2024. Like Amoore and Citron, Iriafen earned All-American honors.

"It feels amazing," said Amoore of her new teammates during the Draft Night. "I've always said playing against Sonia for the past four years when she was at Notre Dame and I was at Tech that I wanted to play with her one day. Now, I didn't think it would be in a situation like this. I've told her that. I'm pretty sure I've told her mom that. So I'm super excited to be with her and through this. And I love Kiki, her personality and her demeanor, but when she gets on court, it's wraps, and I think I've had good experience with the both of them, playing against them, but even going to camps. I went to camps with Kiki. So I'm just super excited to be with both of them. They're great people, great players, and I'm just thrilled to be a part of that."

*Kentucky coach Kenny Brooks and Georgia Amoore pose at the 2025 WNBA Draft in New York City. (UK Athletics Photo)*

Several days later, the trio of Mystics' top three picks — Citron, Iriafen and Amoore — also enjoyed a special evening at the Nationals Park. They threw the ceremonial first pitch and watched the Washington Nationals face the Baltimore Orioles.

As for playing in the WNBA, Amoore said she has the mental capabilities and confidence to meet the new challenge. "A part about me that might surprise people; I haven't felt like I've shown the ability to be that pesky, annoying defender," said Amoore, who unfortunately suffered a season-ending knee injury during a Mystics preseason practice in 2025. "I think just being a little bit conservative, knowing I had to be on the court during my times at Kentucky and Virginia Tech, I'm excited to kind of be able to go ahead and do that."

While recovering from her surgery, Amoore had a solo press conference in mid-June 2025 in Washington, discussing several topics. She was smiling and in good spirits. During the recovery process, spending time with her teammates and learning the plays while sitting on the bench have been very beneficial to Amoore. "Going into your rookie year, injured or not, you always want to be a sponge," she said. "I still have that ability to do that. I'm making the most of it, and obviously being around practice helps that, but I guess my role is to be that sponge."

On playing and living in Washington, D.C., Amoore commented, "It's different than college, obviously, but I think the coolest thing about DC is I'm getting noticed the same as I did in Kentucky. It's kind of crazy to think of a college campus vs. a big city, but that's how much DC loves sports. I'm not going to classes, but it hasn't changed with the feeling and support, and the just love for all the teams."

Amoore played for Coach Kenny Brooks at Virginia Tech (four years) and Kentucky. She said Brooks has given her valuable advice as far as hoops career is concerned. "He's always told me to stop and smell the roses, not to get too ahead of yourself or live too far in the past and just be super present with what's happening, and it helped me tonight (at the draft) and it's going to help me going forward," Amoore said.

While at Kentucky, Amoore started in 31 games during the 2024-25 season, averaging career-highs in points (19.6), assists (6.9), and assist-turnover ratio (2.2) along with a team-high 32 steals. She also established the school record for most assists in a single season (213). In addition, her 78 three-pointers made in a single season marked the third most in program history, passing Maci Morris who had 75. Rhyne Howard and Sara Potts had 84 and 81 three-pointers, respectively. A three-time All-American, Amoore was also named the SEC Newcomer of the Year and earned All-SEC First Team honors. At UK's annual CATSPY Awards, Amoore earned the school's Female Athlete of the Year honors along with Brooklyn DeLeye (SEC volleyball player of the year).

Speaking of WNBA, Amoore's college coach loves the pro league. "I'm a big fan of the WNBA," said Brooks, who has coached at least nine WNBA Draft picks in his tenure. "I think it's growing the way that it should. There have been so many great players that haven't had the opportunity to play in the WNBA because there were limited spots. Now with the growth of women's basketball, the expansion with the WNBA, I think it's continuing to be seen. I think we're in a very unique situation with it. It almost mirrors back when Larry Bird and Magic Johnson came out (in 1979 when NBA began its explosive growth). With the rivalries that they had, there have been comparisons with Caitlin (Clark) and Angel (Reese) scenarios. It's something that if we as women's basketball people can embrace it and market it the right way, I think the boom can happen like it did back in the days.

"The brand of basketball is continuing to get great. The games are unbelievable. The New York Liberty and (Minnesota) Lynx game the other night had me on my seat. You're watching it, and it's pure entertainment. I think we have a responsibility not only as women's basketball, WNBA coaches, but college coaches, to continue that growth. We can do that by the entertainment value. If we go out there now because you have eyes on the game that really haven't been on the game. There is entertainment value to it. If we put out a product that will make people want to continue to come back and watch and watch and watch, it's a golden time to watch it explode.

"I'm excited to be a part of it. We want to do our part. But it's also a great thing for our kids to come in. My kids are basketball junkies. They're texting me, Are you watching this game? Did you see Napheesa Collier do it? Georgia talks about it all the time. Now they're becoming fans where five, six, seven, ten years ago, kids didn't even watch the WNBA. That's no offense, but it wasn't as accessible. Now it's all over the place. They find it. They tell me what channel it's on. The accessibility of it is helping as well. We as women's basketball coaches have to do our part and, if we can continue to do that, this is a golden opportunity to watch it boom. I take that very seriously. We want to put a product out there that is going to bring in the common fan. I want the person that hasn't been to a women's basketball game, they come, and they're like, 'I'm coming back because that was very enjoyable to watch.' I take that responsibility very seriously."

## Leaving the Land Down Under

Georgia's first year of living in the United States was really tough when she enrolled at Virginia Tech in January of 2020 and practiced with the team. She was very far away from home. "When I first got here, I obviously had no friends and no one, really," said Amoore, who didn't have a lot of confidence.

Added Amoore's mother, Kelly, in an interview for this book. "When she left in January, we were trying to keep a positive mind set, comforting each other by saying, "It won't be long as we will see you in May when you're home for your summer break. There was excitement and anticipation to see what was next for Georgia."

And Amoore eventually became close with teammate Elizabeth Kitley, a 6-foot-5 freshman center from Summerfield, N.C. Amoore was impressed Kitley's special relationship with her older half-sister, Raven, who is autistic. "She's so caring, and she's learned to, like, be passionate and empathetic towards people and their situations," Amoore said of Kitley, a future WNBA player. "So she just really reached out to me and helped me get comfortable with Virginia Tech and America." And the duo often would travel around the local area in Kitley's car.

*Virginia Tech stars Elizabeth Kitley and Georgia Amoore smile during an interview as they prepare for the 2023-24 season. (Virginia Tech Athletics Photo)*

In mid-March of 2020, when the COVID-19 pandemic arrived, forcing numerous countries to issue travel restrictions, Amoore had a tough decision to make. Stay in the U.S. or go back to her home country. But she chose to stay because she wasn't sure if she could return to the U.S. during the pandemic. Amoore ended up staying with Kitley at the latter's hometown in North Carolina for several months. "I got accepted into her home. That was so comforting and welcoming," she said.

Added Kitley, a three-time ACC Player of the Year, "It was kind of by force because she just got immersed into all my family issues and whatever, like she was just surrounded by it. So she had to learn me really well, and then in turn, I think, she felt more comfortable confiding in me. So, I think that just helped us get really close."

Commented Kelly Amoore, "The only reassurance and comfort we had when the world shut down was from Coach Brooks and his coaching staff from Virginia Tech. Coach Brooks spoke to me on the phone and guaranteed me that Georgia was in the best of hands and he will treat her like one of his daughters. I had no option but to trust him and take his word."

During this difficult period, her mother pointed out Georgia missed many family gatherings and events in Austraila. "The passing of my father was one of the saddest moments in my life, and she wasn't able to come to his funeral due to her loyalties and commitment to Virginia Tech," Kelly said.

On playing for Virginia Tech and Coach Brooks, which included a trip to the 2023 NCAA Final Four, Georgia said, "My story was definitely different because I was international, and I never met Coach Brooks in person until I was in his office pretty much committing. I think he did a really good job recruiting, selling his vision online. I had a lot of other coaches recruiting me, and I didn't feel that connection or that vibe. Coach Brooks is always so genuine. Him and his staff, his whole coaching staff, had that vision. I could just tell that it was a family. For me to come all the way over here, I had to have that. So a huge part of that was just the family feeling and the vision that came along with that. Sitting in his office, I committed on the spot. So, he sold it pretty well."

Before her commitment to Virginia Tech over her second choice, the University of Portland where her cousin played basketball on the women's team, Amoore and her parents also spent the previous evening at Coach Brooks' house. "It was a very relaxed atmosphere, and we felt very welcomed," said her mother. "Nothing felt forced or fake, and we had lots of laughs. I got on well with (Brooks' wife) Chrissy and met the girls." Then they flew back home in Australia, feeling good and optimistic about Georgia's future plans.

During her early days in the U.S., Georgia Amoore got homesick at times, recalled her mother. She also had to adjust to many aspects of life, including basketball, the colder weather and the American-style food. "I remember at Christmas time her having a bit of a whine," said Kelly Amoore. "She was trying to adjust to the playing style in the U.S. She was getting into foul trouble and was thrown into the deep end as the starting point guard. The challenges were big. She had to adjust and had a lot of pressure on her. I think I made the comment something like, 'If it's all too hard, well just come home.' That got her back up, and I knew that wasn't an option she would take. The challenge was ahead of her, and she wasn't going to quit."

As a freshman in 2020-21, Amoore got off to a good start with Virginia Tech in the Atlantic Coast Conference (ACC). The point guard was impressive as she started in 23 of 25 games while averaging 11.8 points and 4.6 assists per game. She also finished fourth in assists overall in the conference and earned ACC Freshman of the Week honors in Feburary of 2021.

Before coming to the U.S., Amoore began playing basketball at the age of five and played for the Australian National Team at different youth levels, winning a gold medal at the FIBA Under-16 Women's Basketball Asian Cup in 2017 and a bronze medal at the FIBA U-17 World Cup in 2018. She also played for Ballarat Rush and earned the Rising Star Award in 2019.

## Trip to Belarus

Located in Eastern Europe on the border with close ally Russia, Belarus is where Coach Brooks, on a scouting trip, saw Amoore play in person for the first time. She was representing her country, playing in the 2018 FIBA U-17 World Cup. But the coach almost didn't make it. Added Brooks, "I went all the way there to watch her play, and then that trip alone sold me, and it's changed my life because I was able to coach the best player that I've ever had, and it was sparked because of that trip, going there. Sometimes I wonder, what if I (didn't go). I almost turned around because we had difficulties with the travel. I almost got to Paris, and they said that I couldn't get on the flight to go there, and I almost went home. I often wonder what would've happened if I didn't persevere through it and get there."

Coach Brooks, who also saw Amoore at a talent camp in the U.S., liked her potential and eventually got in touch with her, and they conversed on the phone for six months before Georgia and her parents visited the Virginia Tech campus during the fall of 2019 when the youngster made a commitment to the Hokies.

## Becoming a College Basketball Star

Some observers have had concerns with Amoore's 5-foot-6 height in playing basketball, but she remarkably has overcome her short frame with her quickness and creative playmaking while becoming a prolific scoring machine. Brooks commented that Amoore gradually built her toughness mentally and physically in becoming a dominating force in college basketball.

Her mother, Kelly, was asked if she is surprised with Georgia's remarkable success on the floor despite her short height. "Basketball needs all types of players. Short or tall," she said.

"There is no written rule to say because you're 6-foot-6 you're
going to play in the WNBA. There is also no written rule to say
because you're 5-foot-6, you're not going to play in the WNBA.
I'm surprised that's she's achieved all these things more because
she's our daughter. A young girl from Ballarat who was extremely
talented but what she has achieved is what dreams are made of.
Her height hasn't mattered to the people in the know for a long
time as she has proven time and time again it definitely doesn't."

On becoming a top scorer while at Virginia Tech, Georgia said
at the beginning of her senior year, "I think just consistency and
confidence. I think shooting is definitely more mental than anything. I say this all the time, but coming into college I was not a
shooter. I was not preferred to shoot a three. Seriously, I think
one of my teammates from Australia brought that up, and I was
reminiscing on that because now I feel not normal when I don't
attempt a three in a game. Sharing the ball is still a huge part of my
job ... to make everyone better. But I know I have to be a threat,
and I know I have to shoot. Coach Brooks has placed stress on
me that everything I'm able to do comes from me being a threat
from three. I can't be a good pass without being a threat. I can't
drive without being a threat from three. So just remembering that
is my No. 1 priority, and keeping up with that is going to help me
on every other aspect."

Added Brooks on Amoore's commanding presence on the court
and her development, "(When) she came here (at VT), and immediately I knew we had something special, and I told everyone
we stole one, and not just because of her basketball ability, but
because of her work ethic, her demeanor. She came over here
in a very tough time. COVID hit two months into her being here.
Then the very next year, the season was cut short, and she had five
nonconference games before we threw her into the ACC battles.

"I knew she was going to be special, and I challenged her, and I
coached her like that. If you had watched my practices (at Virginia
Tech) with her, you might have thought it was child abuse because

I was really going after her because I knew the toughness level that she needed. She handled every bit of it. Her demeanor is one of confidence. The kids will follow her. She's like the Pied Piper. If she said, 'let's do this,' the kids will do it. She's the funniest kid on the team. She's the most quick-witted kid on the team. And she's our leader."

*Georgia Amoore celebrates after Virginia Tech advanced to the 2023 NCAA Final Four, defeating Ohio State 84-74 in Elite Eight in Seattle. (Virginia Tech Athletics Photo)*

When Georgia was a small child, she played nearly every sport and often against boys, including swimming, track and field, netball, Australian rules football, cricket and taekwondo (martial arts). Sports have helped Georgia develop a toughness that she needed to play college basketball. "When I used to play football,

I used to be really fast, and boys would grab my ponytail to stop me," she said. "So I've definitely learned a lot from that. In terms of toughness, football is purely about tackling and dodging all those instances. It definitely helped me be tough. Definitely taught me that, when I get hit, get up, test it out, and then go out if you're really hurt."

After a memorable 2022-23 campaign when the 31-5 Hokies, who captured the ACC Tournament title, went to the Final Four in Dallas, Brooks said his two star players — Amoore and Elizabeth Kitley — were very popular and didn't have a lot of privacy in Blacksburg. "I think it's really hard for those two to go to Kroger's and just have a peaceful afternoon or evening because everyone wants a part of them," said the coach.

As it turned out, eventual national champion LSU defeated Virginia Tech 79-72 in the national semifinals with All-American Angel Reese making two critical baskets for the Tigers while finishing with 24 points and 12 rebounds. Like Reese, Kitley posted a double-double — 18 points and 12 rebounds — in the setback. Amoore, who had 17 points against LSU, established a record for the most 3-pointers made in a single NCAA Tournament with 24, but the record didn't last long as All-American sensation Caitlin Clark later tied Amoore's mark in the second national semifinal. Clark finished with a record 32 three-pointers made in a single NCAA Tourney. During that season, Amoore, the MVP of 2023 ACC Tournament, also set a program record with 118 3's made, the second-most in the nation behind Clark's 140.

In the national semifinals, Amoore faced an LSU player by the name of Last-Tear Poa, a reserve guard who is from Australia. "We're both from Victoria. She's from the metro (Melbourne), I'm from the country. We played against each other all juniors. We even went to India together as part of the national team. I'm very familiar with L.T., great family. Her mom's so cute. I'm so proud of her. She went to juco, came up, landed at LSU. I'm so proud of her because she stuck through it, and it's paying off for her."

At Kentucky, Amoore was to able to spend some time and share stories with an Australian teammate,  6-foot-3 Amelia Hassett, who is from New South Wales.

*Virginia Tech's Georgia Amoore shoots against LSU during the 2023 NCAA Final Four in Dallas. (Virginia Tech Athletics Photo)*

During her senior year of 2023-24 at VT, Amoore also helped the 25-8 Hokies to ACC regular season title, earning third team All-American honors. Virginia Tech had high hopes of making its second straight trip to the Final Four but Kitley, a fifth-year senior, suffered a serious knee injury in the regular season finale and was forced to miss the postseason action.

Asked about her career at Virginia Tech in 2024, Amoore said, "I came here, and I was not good, couldn't shoot, probably a little too overweight, probably too slow, had too much fun, had to get reeled in. But I got here, and it was the perfect place for me to settle in and kind of not control myself, but lock in on basketball. It's a perfect place to do that.  I trusted Coach Brooks 100 percent even when I didn't trust in myself. It's paid off immensely. I couldn't be more grateful for our time together.

"I think being a foreigner, America is fun, but Blacksburg is the place where I've developed, and it's kind of like my home away from home. I couldn't be more appreciative of how it's transformed me as not only a basketball player, but a person, and it's because I surrounded myself with great people. I truly think that (when) I came out of high school, I had four offers or whatever. I took two visits, and one of them just happened to be here, and that's a blessing in disguise. I didn't know at that time how it would play out, but I took the chance, and I'm very, very grateful that I did because I've got him for life now. I've loved it, and I couldn't be more grateful."

## Body Language

On the basketball court, Amoore plays with joy and passion, but she doesn't show much emotion on purpose.

"It's very intentional," she said. "My freshman year Coach Brooks kind of made it known that I'm the point guard, so when the ball is in my hand, everyone is reading my body language, be it him or my team. I have to exude confidence. No matter what's going on, they're going to take on the body language of me. I carry great responsibility with that."

## Kim Mulkey on Amoore

In recent years, LSU's flamboyant coach Kim Mulkey has seen a lot of Georgia Amoore in games against Virginia Tech and Kentucky, as well as the 2025 WNBA Draft. Unfortunately for Amoore, Mulkey's LSU teams have won each time, including the 2023 Final Four battle in Dallas when the ninth-ranked Tigers prevailed over the fourth-ranked Hokies 79-72.

*LSU coach Kim Mulkey chats with Georgia Amoore after the Kentucky-LSU game at Historic Memorial Coliseum in 2025. (Photo by Jamie H. Vaught)*

Mulkey has high praise for Amoore, comparing her to superstar Caitlin Clark. "Her range is unlimited," said Mulkey of Amoore. "You could put her in the category like Caitlin Clark. She has an unbelievable step-back move which takes her even further away from the three-point line. She gets her teammates involved. A tremendous point guard who makes everybody else better. Not only can she score it, but she can get her teammates open looks. She's fun to watch if you're not competing against her."

Moments after No. 7 LSU defeated the Wildcats 65-58 on ESPN at Historic Memorial Coliseum in late February 2025, Mulkey had a question for Amoore while on the handshake line. "When are you graduating?" asked LSU coach. "Same thing I told Clark. It's like, 'I'm tired of seeing you' as a compliment. Don't take that the wrong way. She said this year, this year. What a tremendous player."

(In 2024, at the press conference following her team's loss to Iowa and Clark, who gunned in 41 points along with 12 assists, in the NCAA regional finals, Mulkey was asked about the long postgame embrace with Clark. "What did I say to her?" commented the LSU coach. "I said, 'I sure am glad you're leaving. Girl, you something else. Never seen anything like it.' ")

## Georgia's Mom & Horse Farm

Amoore's parents live on horse farm near the local race track in Victoria. The author jokingly told her that she could move to Kentucky, which is considered the horse capital in the U.S, especially in Lexington. When she visited Kentucky to watch her daughter play, she fell in love with the Bluegrass State. "Oh my God, yes! We loved the city, such a unique place," said Kelly Amoore. "What more could you want? Horses and basketball sounds like heaven to me." In February and early March, she got to see Georgia star in several games, including road trips.

Asked about her job as receptionist/administrative assistant at an equine clinic where she trains and rehabilitate horses, Kelly explained, "I rehabilitated horses in a business we started with my older sister. I also have my horse trainer certificate but I'm not active with it. Just recently I have started a new job as a receptionist at the Ballarat Equine Clinic. The hours are kinder, and I'm not outside in the freezing colder weather in Ballarat's winter."

Georgia's father, Phil, is a former athlete who is a service manager for a company that rents out and fixes fork lift trucks.

## Georgia's Final Year

On Sunday, March 23 at Historic Memorial Coliseum, when No. 13 Kentucky finished its memorable 2024-25 campaign with a one-point overtime loss to Kansas State in the second round of the NCAA Tournament, it meant Amoore's collegiate career was over — but in a nice way, as it was her fifth straight appearance in the Big Dance.

Amoore, playing as a graduate student, and her teammates tried their best to advance to the NCAA Sweet Sixteen, but things didn't work out. The Cats — who posted a final 23-8 mark, including five wins against Associated Press Top 25 teams — would have won had Amoore made the last-second jump shot near the basket just outside the paint. To her credit, Amoore didn't let her missed field goal affect her, displaying a good sportsmanship and demeanor at the end of the game. "I'm not going to let one shot affect five years; that's pretty much it," explained Amoore. "As soon as I caught it, I realized how open I was, and it's up to fate at that point."

Nevertheless, the fans who attended UK's NCAA Tournament games in Lexington definitely got their money's worth that weekend. The Wildcats had two exciting ESPN-televised games with a one-point win over Liberty (after giving up a 17-point lead in early fourth quarter) on Friday and an 80-79 setback loss to Kansas State. And Amoore was all over the floor against Liberty, entertaining the crowd while gunning in 34 points and giving out eight assists, both game-highs. Amoore now is the only player in program history to total 52 points in any two-game span in the NCAA Tournament.

Kentucky's heartbreaking loss to K-State before a crowd of 4,218 was a classic NCAA Tournament matchup that many folks won't forget. It was an evenly-fought game that you hated to see either team lose. "It was a very good basketball game," said coach Kenny Brooks. "I hope everybody was entertained. It was really fun to be a part of. It was two good basketball teams going at it. They made probably one more play than we did. So they're moving on (to the Sweet Sixteen), so congratulations to them."

I wrote a postseason column, saying, "Personally, this is the most fun UK women's basketball team that I have ever covered in my long sportswriting career since the early days of the late 1970s when I was the sports editor of the *Kentucky Kernel*, the student daily newspaper at UK. In addition to Amoore, the players, including 6-foot-5 All-SEC Clara Strack, were polite, pleasant and personable. And they were entertaining to watch. Don't forget that I also enjoyed covering the standouts and classroom stars like Maci Morris from Bell County and Blair Green from Harlan County during their days at UK. But overall, this Kentucky team has a special personality."

Amoore was asked what she will remember the most about her only season at Kentucky. "That's deep," she said, sitting with Coach Brooks and graduate guard Dazia Lawrence at the press conference. "I think in the locker room we were kind of saying that it's been such a blessing for both of us to like bring Kentucky back. Obviously, Kentucky is a name brand on the men's side. I told the girls, 'It's up to you, whatever you decide, but hang around because it's only going to go up from here.' It's an attractive style of play. Coach Brooks proves that he's a winner. So, I think it's cool to be the foundation and be the program forward. That's been the greatest thing is seeing the crowds come back game after game. Even Memorial (Coliseum), like I didn't see the old one, but I heard of it. It's been cool to play in the new one and to kind of just get things rolling back again."

Said Brooks, "This is one of the most enjoyable seasons that I've ever had in my 24 years of coaching because of the way that they came together."

Before the season began, Brooks described Amoore as "my little mini-me. We're joined at the hip. We watch film like we would watch Netflix, and we just go, and we're on the same page. It's really fun watching her bring up the younger players to get them on that same page that her and Liz (Kitley) were on."

Following UK's season-ending loss to Kansas State, Brooks added Amoore's growth and maturity "has gone through the roof this year. You get to a point where sometimes you have special players and you kind of know that it's time for them to move on because she was just so special, she was coaching us some. She was interjecting her thoughts more. This year, more so than any, they became conversations. It wasn't a lecture. It wasn't, hey, you do as I say. They became conversations. When they become conversations, you're in a special situation because not every coach gets to have that relationship with a player, and I've been blessed to be able to have that to the point where she just didn't do what I said, she wanted to know why, and it became a point where it's a two-way street, and it's fun.

"Some coaches don't ever get it. Sometimes you get it once. But when you have it, you learn to appreciate it. As she mentioned before, this year was very special for our relationship because it grew even more so when you didn't think it could grow."

Another highlight of Amoore's UK career took place in early February when she helped the No. 12 Wildcats to a 95-86 win over No. 13 Oklahoma in Norman. Against the Sooners, Amoore pumped in a career-high 43 points, including 7 of 12 three-pointers, and tying a school record for points in a game. She even had a game-high eight assists.

*Georgia Amoore warming up during a pregame practice in 2025. (Photo by Jamie H. Vaught)*

Sportswriter Jenna Lifshen, who covered UK women's basketball for the *Kentucky Kernel* during the 2024-25 season, has seen several great performances by Amoore. "It's tough to choose just one game," she said when asked about Amoore's best game as a Kentucky Wildcat. "Georgia Amoore was a one-of-a-kind player, and she is what 'brought Kentucky back,' in both her words and mine. While it may seem obvious to choose her game against No. 13 Oklahoma, I believe the best game she ever played in blue-and-white was her last one. This is probably surprising, as her last game ended in absolute heartbreak. In the last three seconds of the game, and down by one point, Georgia Amoore missed a potential game-winning shot, and Kentucky fell to Kansas State 80-79 in overtime.

"However, it was also that game that made me realize just how amazing Amoore is, not only as a player but also as a person. When she came into the postgame press conference and was asked about how she remained so composed following the loss, she made her point very clear, saying, 'I'm not going to let one shot affect five years; that's pretty much it.'

"There aren't many players who would walk through the handshake line after that with their head held high, and who would stop and congratulate every single player on the other team with sincerity. But Georgia did. Because that's who she is and that's what makes her so special. In a rebuilding season where Kentucky needed a leader, they were given something far more significant: a woman who embodied everything a player should be. Fierce, selfless, resilient, and proud.

"Her last game wasn't just the end of a season; it was the closing chapter of one of the most remarkable careers I've ever seen, and more importantly, a career built on heart, humility, and a love for the game that went beyond my comprehension. Georgia left Kentucky better than she found it, and it is something that will never be forgotten."

Lifshen also said Amoore "was the kind of player who would come up to me after a press conference and thank me for my work, even if I was the only reporter in the room. She was the kind of person who always answered every question thoughtfully and with grace. One of my favorite memories came after Senior Day against No. 7 LSU. During the postgame press conference, she was asked what message she would give to little girls watching her, especially about mental toughness. Her answer made me tear up. Growing up playing competitive soccer, I know how important it is to have a role model to look up to. I never had a Georgia Amoore. Hearing her message to young girls, about strength, resilience, and believing in themselves touched me deeply. It felt like she was speaking to my younger self as well. She said, 'Never get too high and never get too low. People are always going to talk to people or people are always going to say something.'

"After the press conference, I went to film my postgame stand-up (on the floor). That's when I saw Georgia back on the court, still in her jersey, smiling, taking pictures with fans. I'll never forget the moment I saw her kneel beside a young girl in a wheelchair for a picture. It was beautiful beyond words. It reminded me of something else she had said earlier that night: 'I hear it all the time — I'm too short, I'm not quick enough, I'm not this, I'm not that. People are going to talk, people are going to say things. I just take little wins every single day. So, if that's what you have to do, then do it. Because I'm loving life right now.' In every moment, whether in front of thousands of fans or the quiet ones after the game, Georgia Amoore showed what it means to be a role model: steady, strong, and full of heart, and it's one of the memories I'll carry with me for the rest of my career."

Lifshen admitted she was never a basketball fan growing up in Austin, Texas, let alone a fan of women's basketball. However, when she began covering the games in 2024, she realized "just what I was missing out on. Witnessing the revitalization of a program was one of the most inspiring and fulfilling experiences

I've ever had. Having a player like Georgia, who became the light at the end of the tunnel for a program at its lowest, will be one of the most special things I will ever get to experience in my career. There will never be another player like Georgia Amoore, and I will forever be grateful to have covered and watched a player as special as her. I will happily call myself an Amoore superfan for the rest of my life."

Like Amoore, Dazia Lawrence, after spending four years at Charlotte, arrived on campus as a first-year Wildcat. Both guards started every game at UK with Lawrence averaging 12.9 points. Added Lawrence, "I know for me that G has taught me to, no matter what, show up and work hard. G has had an amazing career. I followed her career since I came to college. I've always been a fan. I think, when I first committed, she texted me, and I was like, 'Oh, Georgia is texting me?' I think always just showing up and be the best version of yourself. I don't think I've seen G have a bad day in a practice or in a game or anything like that.

"She's so mentally strong, and she uplifts us every day. No matter if we just turn the ball over, took a bad shot, or anything like that, she just shows up as the best version of herself no matter what she's going through at home or outside of basketball. That's the one thing that I will forever take. And always working hard. She didn't get in this position that she's in just because she showed up. She showed up every day and worked her tail off every single day. I will always remember that and just always, because of her, show up and work no matter what."

On transferring to UK, which was coming off a very disappointing 2023-24 season with a 12-20 overall record (4-12 in SEC) under coach Kyra Elzy, Amoore said "the move to Kentucky was the best decision for me. And I'll stand by that. I threw myself into a situation, obviously, where it was brand new. I trusted Coach Brooks. I've always trusted him. He's literally never steered me wrong. I knew this was a huge responsibility coming here. And the way it played out, I got so much better in a lot of aspects of my game, my leadership, my ability to adapt to change. It's what I needed going forward for whatever my future holds.

"I couldn't be more thankful to be part of a program like this. It was kind of a blessing to have a bunch of new girls because we all had an emphasis on being great now. Like, we didn't want the excuses of being a rebuild program or getting people being like, 'Oh, that's okay, they're new; oh, it's okay, give them time.' We wanted to win now. Obviously, that's evident having the season we had."

## Mental Toughness

Shortly, after her Senior Day when LSU defeated the Wildcats 65-58, Amoore, as mentioned earlier, had a message for little girls who are watching her play as well as her mental toughness.

"I just try to make lessons out of silver linings and little things, that kind of helps me," Amoore said. "It's an honor that I get the defensive pressure I get. It's an honor that they scout me the way they scout me. It's an honor that I get grabbed and face-guarded when they pass the ball in. It's an honor that I came over here, and I got stuck during COVID because if I didn't have that, I wouldn't have the relationships I had.

"Every single thing that I've been through basketball-wise, it has shaped me into the player I am, and I think I hear it all the time. I'm too short, I'm not quick enough, I'm not this, I'm not that. I don't know if it's just being Australian or the mentality that we grow up having. Never get too high and never get too low. People are always going to talk to people, or people are always going to say something. And there's going to be days where you feel it, there's going to be days where you disagree, there's going to be days where you agree, but I'm this. I'm solid. I'm enjoying what I have. You call it what you know, what's on the other side, you know, the grass is not always greener. It may look like that, but it's not.

"I love what I have, I love the experience I've had. I've loved the staff, the guidance, the coaching. I've squeezed every single ounce of whatever orange juice was in that orange, that has been my college career, I take pride in that, and I just take little wins every single day. So, if that's what you have to do, then do it, because I'm loving my life right now."

## Coaching Career for Georgia?

Amoore has a bright future in coaching, according to Coach Brooks. "Yeah, and it goes back to my coach (legendary Lefty Driesell at James Madison), and the year I told him that I wanted to be a coach, he started coaching me differently," said Brooks. "He started teaching me how to be a coach. So she expressed to me that she wants to coach when her career is over with, and I started coaching her differently. I included her in on some coaches' meetings so she could see the behind the scenes. We even got to the point where we would ask her input, and so definitely started grooming her to become a coach. There's no doubt in my mind that she's going to be.

"The only bad part is, I think she's going to have a really long basketball career so I'm just hoping that I'm still coaching and we can be together again on my staff. But she's going to make a phenomenal coach because she just has an understanding of people and how to relate to people and how to get the best out of people, so I think she's going to be a terrific coach one day."

## Mom's Favorite Memory

Kelly Amoore was asked about her favorite memory of Georgia as a basketball player.

"Just seeing this wide-eyed undersized player bamboozle her opponents and people getting a giggle out of her tenacious spirit," she said. "She would draw a crowd at a young age as people were amazed at her skills and her size. She played with passion, flair and loved to entertain."

Outside of basketball, Kelly also commented, "Georgia is a great dancer and a lover of music."

# 8

# First Lady

(Lee Anne Pope)

Since 1931, when 30-year-old newly-married Adolph Rupp was begining his second season as the head basketball coach at UK, his wife, Esther, unofficially served as the "First Lady of UK Basketball." She would do many things for Rupp and the team, even hosting holiday dinners for the players. During the early days, she would host social events like "candlelight tea table" for the students on campus, among others. In 1998, Mrs. Rupp, who had been a widow for two decades, passed away at the age of 95 on the night before UK won the NCAA championship, beating Utah.

After Coach Rupp was forced to retire in 1972, new boss Joe B. Hall's wife, Katharine, became the new First Lady, a role she held for 13 years. Then Patsy Sutton, wife of coach Eddie Sutton, assumed the role for four years. And coach Rick Pitino's wife, Joanne, took over in 1989, a role she had for eight years. From 1997 to 2007, Tubby Smith's wife, Donna, served as the program's First Lady. Then came along a rising coach by the name of Billy

Gillispie from Texas A&M. He was divorced with no children. After the controversial two-year Gillispie era during the late 2000s, coach John Calipari came to Lexington from Memphis in 2009 and his wife, Ellen, became the First Lady for 15 years, and she often baked brownies for the players on their birthday.

And in mid-April 2024, Lee Anne Pope took over the role of "First Lady of UK Basketball" when Mark Pope left his Brigham Young post to become the new coach at Kentucky. Lee Anne Pope loves her position. "I have loved meeting Big Blue Nation wherever we go," she said in a 2025 book interview at Joe Craft Center on UK campus. "The kindness that people have shown me personally and our family has been super humbling and super kind. I mean, that title is fun, but I love meeting the people. I love playing a small role with these players that we get to coach. To me, it will always be about the players. And when it's not about them, it gets kind of silly. So I really, really value the relationship with the players and their families and their significant others.

"Last year (in 2024-25), our team, they all had serious girlfriends, and those relationships all really matter to me. I love meeting the fans, and I hope they feel our love for them because their kindness towards us has been so wonderful. So, when you say that I just think about the people. That's the best part."

She is the mom of the basketball team. She loves being the coach's wife. "I love it. I love it. I love doing this with Mark. We do it together," added Lee Anne, whose father was the head basketball coach at Idaho State and Utah. "It's the only lifestyle I know. I grew up a coach's kiddo, right? I get there's a lot of things about it that aren't for everybody, but it's for us, and I couldn't do it without Mark. I couldn't. And he feels the same way. So we're a good team, and we do it together, and I think we fill in the gaps for each other. I'm super grateful. It's a great life."

Unlike many wives of the head coaches, Lee Anne certainly has a wealth of deep basketball knowledge. And she likely could have coached had she chosen a different career. With Lee Anne's genuine, thoughtful and cheerful personality, Coach Pope has repeatedly said his wife does so many little tidbits to keep the program running in the right direction. Former BYU standout Travis Hansen has described Lee Anne as a perfect coach's wife with a score of 9.9 (out of 10), according to an article in Salt Lake City-based *Deseret News* in 2020.

## Leaving BYU

How tough was it for the Pope family to leave the state of Utah for the Kentucky job? The family had lived in Utah for 13 years, beginning in 2011 when Mark became an assistant under Coach Dave Rose at Brigham Young, a post he held for four years before taking his first head coaching job at Utah Valley. After four years at UV, he returned to BYU where he became the head coach. And BYU is also her home university where Mrs. Pope has a degree in journalism.

"We loved every minute we were at BYU, and it was not hard to leave," said Lee Anne, the mother of four daughters. "So I graduated from BYU and Arizona State. I went to both universities. We loved BYU. The relationships we built there were awesome, and they will continue. Those players will always be our boys, and I'm so happy that the university is doing great. And it was absolutely a no-brainer to leave for Kentucky. We've talked about it. We took a family vote, but it was pretty quick. And who gets to do this? It feels super special to do it as a family, to do it all together. So, it wasn't hard.

"And Shay, my youngest, has had the biggest adjustment because she's still in high school. So, it's definitely been an adjustment. An adjustment is progress, you know what I mean? It's temporary. So definitely an adjustment for everybody. We had to find a new house. But those are just logistics, and we've done that so many times, we're really good at it."

Commented Mark Pope at his introductory press conference at Rupp Arena, "This is 100 percent a true story. When Mitch (Barnhart) offered us a job, he gave us a couple of hours to consult our family. We didn't need it. He knew I would walk here to take this job. But as we gathered the girls from all of the various places, Layla Pope walks in the door, and I kid you not, her first words were, she knows the deal, 'Tell me who is in the house tonight, UK.' She did exactly that. True story."

Pope added Avery and Shay "went down in the basement in storage and both came up with '96 "Untouchable" vintage T-shirts. Ella is my oldest daughter, and she knows me the best and my history the best. Her only question was: 'Dad, when are we going?'"

"And we sat around the table and got everybody's reaction and with all of the burden, with all of the grace and courage and elegance you can imagine, Lee Anne looked across the table and said, 'Let's go.' You don't need to know this, but I will say it anyway because I can, I'm madly in love with this woman. She makes sense of my life. I'm so grateful for her. And you will quickly find out, she will get to know every single one of you and love you like crazy. It will be really special, okay?"

At BYU, Pope won 20 or more games in four of his five seasons in Provo, including two 24-victory seasons, with a pair of NCAA Tournament appearances. Pope went 110-52 during his tenure at BYU, including a remarkable 66-12 record (84.6 percent) at the 18,000-seat Marriott Center. Over the years, BYU has drawn well, ranking among the nation's top leaders in game attendance.

## Lee Anne's Early Days

During the late 1970s and 1980s in the Far West, Lee Anne grew up in an athletic family with her father coaching, and she had two siblings, Damon and Beau. "I have an older brother and a younger brother," said Lee Anne. "(Later), they both played college basketball." The family didn't stay at one place very long as her father, Lynn Archibald, had a promising career in college basketball. At her young age, she had to study the game so she could keep up with them. She played basketball with her brothers, often getting rebounds for them. She was a tomboy. "I didn't know I was a girl for a long time," she said. "I thought I was just one of the boys for most of my upbringing. Total tomboy growing up."

*The families of Lynn Archibald (left) and Jerry Tarkanian were very good friends with each other and stayed in touch over the years. (Lee Anne Pope Family Photo Collection)*

Archibald, born in Logan, Utah, but lived in Oregon and California, began his coaching career at a couple of high schools (Los Amigos High and Sierra Vista High) in California where he taught math. On the collegiate level, his first coaching job was as an assistant at Long Beach State under Jerry Tarkanian, with whom he became close friends for life. It is the same Tarkanian, a Naismith Basketball Hall of Famer, popularly known as "Tark the Shark," who battled NCAA while at Nevada-Las Vegas. When Archibald was coaching in high school, he attend many coaching clinics in California, and that's where he met Tarkanian. Archibald also had brief stints with Cal Poly, Nevada Las Vegas and Southern Cal (under future Mississippi State coach Bob Boyd) before becoming the head coach at Idaho State for five years (1977-82) and later at Utah for six years (1983-89), including a conference regular season title in 1986 with a trip to the NCAA Tournament. His overall head coaching record was 163-152. He later also served as assistant at Arizona State (five years) and Brigham Young (two years).

Speaking of Tarkanian, who was coaching at Fresno State at the time, he was very emotional about Archibald's illness with cancer during an interview with Mike Sando of Spokane's *The Spokesman-Review*. In the 1997 article, Tarkanian said, "I've known Lynn as well as anybody. One of the finest men I've ever known in my whole life. And his family is just wonderful. I can't even talk to him without crying. Every time I call him, I start crying."

Lee Anne's father took her on numerous trips while he was coaching or scouting. She has fond memories. "We went on a daddy-daughter trip multiple years," she recalled. "Every year (while) in high school. I think pretty much from junior high, seventh, eighth, ninth, 10th, all the way through high school, he took me on one trip. And sometimes it was in the summer. One year, I went to the Maui Invitational (in Hawaii) with my dad because my brothers had tournaments because they were playing high school basketball. So my mom (Anne) stayed with them, and I went with my dad to Maui, so that was one of our daddy-daughter trips.

"And with my dad passing away (in 1997), I think about those times. Those just pop out. There were so many great moments with my dad. I just think of those moments when I had him all to myself, and it was just he and I. And whether it's room service or going for an early morning run together, those things that we did just he and I just really stand out in my heart."

*Lee Anne and her father, Lynn Archibald during the early days.*
*(Lee Anne Pope Family Photo Collection)*

Asked if she as a teenager got bored watching the players play while he evaluated them during the hot summer months, Lee Anne said no. "You know why? Because he made it so interesting to me, and I just cared. I cared about my dad. So, when he would talk to me about players, I loved it. I enjoyed it. I enjoyed being around my brothers and my dad, and they talked basketball all the time. I enjoyed it. I enjoyed with my dad when he was with his coaching friends or assistant coaches, and they talked because it was always about the players.  Those are people and stories and families. And so many of those boys that were my dad's players are still in our lives today.  So, I always found it interesting and fun, because it was about people. You know what I mean? It's about jump shots and it's about rebounding and all those things, but there's always the story behind all of that, which gives it all meaning."

Through her dad's coaching career, Lee Anne has met all kinds of sports personalties.  "Because I would go to the Final Fours with my dad (at coaches convention), we've met lots and lots of people through the years. As far as friends that we spent time with, Jerry Tarkanian (is one of them). We recently just lost Lois, his wife. Their family was extremely special to our family and still is. And Lute Olson (who once was a top candidate for the UK job in 1985 to replace Joe B. Hall) was a great friend of my dad's. Bobbi Olson, his wife, was so kind to me at a young age. John Wooden was so great to dad. Also, (when) my dad passed, he wrote a really beautiful letter to my mom.

"You go to the (NABC) Coaches Convention and you see friends, and there are Nike events. At the Nike trips, we met Charles Barkley, we met Michael Jordan, and we met Magic Johnson. My dad had recruited Magic Johnson. So there's all these moments throughout the years where we met people, but as far as friends and people that you spent time with, it's a different list."

What were her favorite teams growing up?  Said Lee Anne, "Well, we were (the Los Angeles) Lakers fans. We loved the Lakers and we loved Michael Jordan and the (Chicago) Bulls.  In the early eighties, it was Magic Johnson and then we were die-hard Michael Jordan fans. I think my brothers kind of ruled the roost. They just liked players, you know what I mean? And then as far as college basketball, it was wherever my dad was coaching and then wherever our friends were coaching. So we always cheered for UNLV. We always cheered for University of Arizona. Wherever my dad's friends were coaching, that's who we cheered for. So it was more about the people than the school."

During her high school years, she lived in Arizona where she played volleyball at Corona Del Sol High in Tempe. "We were undefeated, 25 and zero. We won the state championship my senior year," Lee Anne said. "We had a great team. It was great." Then she went to Arizona State where her father was an assistant with coach Bill Frieder, who had been forced to leave Michigan during the 1989 NCAA Tournament. "I played everything (including track) growing up, and then once I hit high school, ninth grade, I just did volleyball because then I started a club. Club was kind of new then but you played year round. I just focused on volleyball."

*Lee Anne Pope (in middle) is shown with her parents and two brothers when her father, Lynn Archibald, was the head coach at Utah during the 1980s. (Lee Anne Pope Family Photo Collection)*

She didn't continue playing volleyball on the collegiate level, so she focused on sports journalism. "I had some opportunities to play at smaller schools, and then I had a couple of walk-on opportunities at bigger schools," Lee Anne commented. "But I did not love volleyball like my brothers loved basketball, and I did not want that to be my path. So I had some opportunities, but I didn't want to do that in college. I had a great college experience. I did internships, and I really loved what I was studying.

"I just didn't love basketball. My brothers would shovel the driveway in the winter so they could shoot because we didn't have an indoor hoop. Then my dad put an indoor hoop inside the garage, but it wasn't quite high enough for them to get full arc on it. But I did not love volleyball like that. And so I knew what it took and it was just not what I wanted at that time in my life. It was the right decision for me."

On her father, who was a man of strong Mormon faith. He was an active member of The Church of Jesus Christ of Latter-day Saints. "My dad was nice," she said. "He was kind and he cared a lot about people, and his faith was a huge part of that. I think it was just a part of who he was and his love for people of all backgrounds and beliefs. I think it's just super special. Some people said that he was too nice to coach, but he was wonderful. I don't think he thought that they (faith and coaching) were separate. It was altogether. It was just who he was. He was a God-fearing, believing human being, and that was part of how he coached and how he treated people and how he saw people.

"And I grew up with just a real attitude of gratitude. We just are so grateful that you get to do this. And you know what? Mark and I are the same way. There's not this separation. It's who you are. So, when you say time, he did make time to take care of our neighbors and do things to serve people. He was very much a servant leader. It was about people, and it was about serving and giving back and making people a part of it. It's very similar to how Mark and I see it as well."

Lee Anne said her parents were the big influence on her growing up years. "Both of them were a team," she said. "I'm so much like my mom, and I'm so much my dad. I think there's just a lot of characteristics that I see in myself that are equally from my mom and my dad. And being the only girl, I had both. I was my dad's only daughter and my mom's only daughter. They say your same-sex parent is your most influential person. There's probably a lot of things I got from my mom that actually I even didn't realize because she was such an example to me, and my mom has such a strong personality and I'm a lot like my dad probably naturally. But I learned a lot of things from my mom, a lot of things that make me capable of doing some of the things that I've chosen to do. My mom was tough and she was bold, but my dad was kind. They were both very fun-loving. Both my parents loved to laugh and have a good time and enjoyed being with people."

It was tough on Lee Anne's mother, Anne, when her son-in-law, Mark Pope, took the coaching job at UK in 2024. That meant the Popes wouldn't be living in Provo anymore, and Anne would not get to see her only daughter and four granddaughters very much. "I think the hardest move was for was my mom because we left Utah," said Lee Anne. "She had always gone to the games and been there, and so she misses us terribly."

Anne still follows basketball today, especially the Wildcats. "My mom's great. My mom remarried," added Lee Anne. "My dad passed away in 1997, and then my mom remarried about 10 years later to John and they have a great life. They come out to (UK) games. They came to a handful of games here at Rupp, and they met us on the road. They went to the Gonzaga game (in Seattle). They went to the SEC Tournament."

After playing college basketball, her brothers eventually went into coaching on the college level. Damon Archibald has made several stops and is working as an assistant coach at Green Bay as of 2025. Like his brother, Beau Archibald has coached at several schools, including UConn.

## ESPN and TV Host David Letterman

Lee Anne was asked about her experience working at ESPN on college internship for three months in 1996. "I graduated from BYU, and I had the opportunity to intern at ESPN in the graphics department," she said. "That's where the internship was. There used to be a show called Scholastic Sports America, and that was a show which highlighted high school athletes that usually ended up being gold medalists or Heisman Trophy winners. But Dan Debenham was the host of that, and he was super helpful to me and kind of a mentor. So, it was a very short time that I was there. But the idea was I had this internship, and it turned into a job opportunity pretty quickly.

"But all of that was still in the works when I got the opportunity to work for (David) Letterman (as a personal assistant). That was such a magical time. What an opportunity at that time in my life to be in New York City and working for the *Late Show with David Letterman*. And the people that I got to work with were the best in the business, and they still are. So, it was a dream job. We worked really hard and really long hours, and it was the chance of a lifetime. The people you got to meet, the show every night. He was wonderful to work for."

It was her roommate and close friend Heather Petersen, whom Lee Anne met at BYU, who encouraged Lee Anne to apply and get an interview at *Late Show with David Letterman*. "I was at ESPN, when Heather invited me to come interview at *The Late Show*, which led to us joining our *Late Show* family where we were Heather and Lee Anne, Lee Anne and Heather, or Mormon No. 1 Mormon No. 2 depending on who Dave liked better that day," said

Lee Anne. "We were co-workers and roommates and embarking on an adventure that would be a part of our story forever."

During the mid-1990s, they first met at a class at Brigham Young when they were students and became very good friends. Like Lee Anne, Heather majored in journalism. "We kind of always sat within a few seats of each other and chatted; then one day she came in late and I had saved her a seat and, in her words, she thought, 'Huh, I guess we're friends.' Little did I know this would lead to 26 years of one of the most special and cherished friendships of my life."

When Lee Anne and Mark Pope lived in Turkey for several months where her husband was playing pro basketball during 1999-2000, Petersen would ship the video tapes. "She was horrified when she learned that because Mark and I would be moving to Turkey for nine months, we would miss the entire fall lineup," said Lee Anne. "(It was) before internet, Netflix, Hulu and streaming. Every two weeks we received a bow box packed with a dozen VHS tapes that she had recorded all the prime time shows. She could not bear the thought that her friend didn't have access to great television. And she didn't do it because she really loved television...she did it because she loved me." Lee Anne added Petersen "loved everything about television and the television industry."

Sadly, Petersen unexpectedly passed away in 2020, and Lee Anne was one of several friends or family members who spoke, offering reflections, including some of the aforementioned stories, at Petersen's memorial service. "She has been a part of every big decision; every scary, happy or sad moment; from the births of my girls to helping me plan the perfect outfit for a special event," said a grieving Lee Anne. "She prepared me to go to the temple; I have a picture of her fixing my veil before I exited the temple on my wedding day. She is a part of who I am, part of my DNA. She is one of my greatest gifts from my father in heaven. I've made some good decisions in my life, but without a doubt, one of the best was saving that seat in 1995."

When they both worked for Letterman, people at first had go through one of his assistants — Heather or Lee Anne — if they wanted to see or contact him.

On her days at the *Late Show*, Lee Anne said, "What stands out to me are there's so many great memories with special shows when we went on the road or special guests, like musical guests, which were awesome. But it's the people I got to work with, and the people that ran the *Late Show*, the writers, the producers, and the interns. And it was a great group of people that were really wickedly smart, and really talented, and really just wonderful. And it's just like a team, just like a basketball team. Everybody bringing their talents together to make this show work.

"And David Letterman is the best to ever do it. And he was a living legend. I'm just super grateful that I got the opportunity to do that and to be in the city at that time. Ultimately, my brother set Mark and I up, but it was me going to Indianapolis to start Dave's foundation (in Letterman's home state) that led to me meeting Mark. So it worked out great for me."

A huge sports fan who at the time had mixed emotions about the possibility of leaving ESPN, Lee Anne added it was a very exciting moment when she walked into legendary Ed Sullivan Theater in NYC for that job interview. When she worked for Letterman, Lee Anne pretty much stayed away from sports for the first time. She was too busy and worked long hours.

## New York City

Living in the Big Apple where she worked for four years was a big thrill for a single young woman like Lee Anne. "New York City is my favorite place on the planet," she said. "There's, for sure, a learning curve (in living in one of the world's largest cities). I just don't remember it being hard. I loved it. It felt like I'd been there before. It felt like 'Oh, this is where I belong.' That was the feeling I had. I love everything about the city. It's not an easy city, but I love everything about it.

"Mark and I were engaged in New York. We fell in love in New York. He played for the (New York) Knicks when Avery was born. He went to medical school at Columbia, and that's where Shay was born. He won the national championship in New York (East Rutherford, N.J.) So we have a lot of ties and love for the city. And it's hard for me to even go back to when it was new to me. But I think part of the thrill was discovering the city, navigating the city, and learning the city. I loved it. I loved all of it."

Lee Anne would show Mark, then her boyfriend, the building where she worked. "(During) that whole year that we dated, he would fly in to New York, and I would fly out, and everybody knew Mark. He came to the show. So he saw everything. And I went back a handful of times after we were married. I have pictures. The girls came with me and met everybody."

What did her terminally ill father in 1996 think about his only daughter living in the big city?

"This is interesting," said Lee Anne. "My dad knew he was sick, but I didn't know he was sick. He came out to help me find an apartment. My first apartment in the city. He flew out and we were looking at apartments. Nothing was safe enough, nothing was nice enough. I was so frustrated because it's what I could afford. Heather, my roommate, and I were trying to find an apartment we could afford. But he was just like 'it's not safe enough.' And he was like 'I don't like this neighborhood.' And he was just like 'I want you on an upper floor. I don't want you on a lower floor.' And I said, 'Dad.'

"And I look back, and I didn't know it at the time, but when my dad was apartment hunting with me, he was thinking, 'I'm not going to be here in a year, and I want her to be safe.' He just had a different perspective. And I was like, 'This is just our first apartment. And when we can make more money, we'll get a bigger apartment or a safer apartment, but I just need a place.' Anyway, it's actually a very sweet memory of him and I going all over the city trying to find my first apartment.

"And then we found my first apartment, and he helped us. He didn't actually help us move in, but he helped us get all the paperwork and get everything settled, and then we moved ourselves in. So, he saw my new apartment, but he got sick right after that. Again, he was sick. I didn't know it. But I got the job in July, and it was October when I found out my dad was fatally sick. And then it was public in December. And then my dad passed in May (in 1997). So it was pretty quick.

"He didn't want us to make decisions based on him being sick. And me working for Letterman was such a fun part. My dad was sick, but he wore *Late Show's* T-shirts all the time. He wore ESPN stuff when I was at ESPN, and he'd watch the show every night. So, it was a little boost, and something fun, and a little distraction, especially when he was going through treatments. I'd call and tell him who was going to be on the show, and he'd watch the show, and we'd talk about it the next morning. It was a sweet part of it."

Lee Anne's father passed away after a long battle with prostate cancer at the age of only 52. "I lost my dad during the time that I worked for Dave, and he was extremely generous, supportive, and kind during the most difficult time in my life at that point," said Lee Anne, who helped establish the Dunk on Cancer campaign as part of her commitment to the fight against cancer. "And I will always be grateful for that and grateful for the kindness that he showed me. And I learned from the best. I mean, his team is the best in the business. And I got to be a part of that. It was super special."

Many years later, in December 2024, Mark Pope made his first official visit to the Big Apple as the Kentucky boss, taking his Wildcats to NYC for the CBS Sports Classic at famed Madison Square Garden. The night before its matchup with Ohio State, the team visited a couple of attractions — Times Square and *Hamilton* on Broadway (where the Cats went on stage after the show, meeting the cast and crew).

## Lynn Archibald and Mark Pope

Not long after Coach Archibald passed away, Lee Anne met a nervous Mark Pope, who was playing for the Indiana Pacers, in person for the first time, and she was in Indiana, handling business for Letterman. With the help of her older brother Damon, they had previously talked on the phone and wrote emails for a couple of months. So, did Coach Pope ever meet her father? Yes, as they had previously met through basketball.

"Not as my dad, but he met him as Coach Archibald because my dad recruited Mark," she recalled. "So, when my dad was at Arizona State with (Coach) Frieder, Mark was one of the top recruits and he recruited Mark. Actually, we have letters that my dad wrote to Mark during that time. So, my dad met Mark and said wonderful things about Mark. And Mark remembers meeting my dad and my brothers actually at different times, but we didn't meet until years later."

The 6-foot-10 Pope — who starred at Newport High School in Bellevue, a suburb of Seattle, receiving several Player of the Year honors in the state of Washington — began his college career at Washington where he was named the Pac-10's Freshman of the Year in 1992 and continued to start all of his team's games as a sophomore, averaging 12.2 points and 8.0 rebounds, before transferring to Kentucky.

## Journalism

Since she has media background after getting a journalism degree and working at ESPN, Lee Anne was asked if she gives her husband some advice on how to deal with the news media.

"Well, he doesn't need my help, but I critique a lot," she said. "Sometimes I'm like 'Why did you say that?' And I'm never nervous ever about Mark speaking at all. But I will say, 'You used that word seven times." And he's talked about it publicly as well. But he kept using the word breathtaking, and I was like, 'That's a weird word. Stop using it.' So yes, but more to be helpful than it is critical, hopefully."

It is obvious Pope's easy-going and friendly personality has helped in his relationship with folks in all walks of life, including the media.

*Mark Pope, then the head coach at Brigham Young University, and Lee Anne Pope pose on the hardwood floor at famed Allen Fieldhouse in 2024 when the Cougars made the first trip to Lawrence, Kansas since 1971. It was a happy night for the Popes as they saw BYU upset No. 7 Kansas. (BYU Photo)*

"And he doesn't take himself that seriously," added Lee Anne. "He's super smart, super intelligent, super comfortable with himself. So, all those things are in favor of being able to communicate and talk and be around the media because it's just who he is and he's not trying to be anybody else. Yes, he gets loving advice from me at times."

Asked if Coach Pope has had any problems with the media during his coaching career, Lee Anne said, "Not necessarily a moment, but there's been people that have been critical. That's their job to write and find stories. But we don't spend a lot of time there (as far as criticisms). There was one time at BYU (when) someone wrote an article, and it really upset the players. There was a lot of undertones in there that we did not appreciate. I think it's the only time that Mark has really addressed something with the person because it was hurtful to the players. That's when Mark had an issue because parents called, players called, and it was upsetting to people. They were upset by it, not Mark. That's the only time that Mark has had to address something because it actually was distracting. But we don't go hunt. I am super disciplined when it comes to the media. I'm super careful with what I see and subject myself to, and Mark's pretty disciplined, too."

Earlier in 1996, when Pope was a senior at Kentucky, there was a controversial article in *Sports Illustrated*. It came out about a month before the Wildcats won the national championship. The then-weekly national magazine published a cover story titled, "A Man Possessed," featuring UK coach Rick Pitino. The 12-page story, written by senior writer William Nack, described Pitino as the coach who was very fixated with winning basketball games. The article also featured several unflattering illustrations of the coach and his wife Joanne. Pitino was so upset that he asked for an apology from *Sports Illustrated*. The high-profile magazine balked, standing behind the writer and the article.

And Pope wasn't pleased with the article, either. "I was really disappointed," said Pope, who had spent nearly an hour with the writer, discussing Pitino at length. "I was disappointed by the pictures, but also just by the article. You would expect a comprehensive or at least fair-minded article. I didn't think it was fair at all. It talked about Coach's obsession with winning and losing, and with the things in his life."

While an ambitious Pitino obviously believed the one-sided article unfairly painted him as some type of maniac, he told his players not to say anything about the story. The coach, who let his own actions speak for themselves, didn't want the controversy to escalate and create unnecessary distraction for the squad. That's his problem, not the team, he said.

## First Year at Kentucky

Under the direction of new coach Mark Pope, the Wildcats surprisingly finished their memorable 2024-25 campaign with a 24-12 mark with a trip to NCAA Sweet Sixteen, including eight wins over AP Top 15 opponents. And the Wildcats managed to find success with 12 new scholarship players on the roster.

What were the highlights for Lee Anne in her first year at UK?

"There were a lot," she said. "I think of the first game at Rupp. That was super emotional for me just to walk in there and him walking on the sidelines as the head coach of Kentucky for the first time. And every time they announce, 'And the head coach of the University of Kentucky....' I get a little choked up every single time. At least this season, every home game, there's just this memento (of happiness). It's very special to me. And so that stands out to me.

"Of course, advancing in the tournament stands out to me. Big wins. Actually, just seeing the boys do what they needed to do in these moments. It's always tied to the relationship with the players. When you're on this side of it, sometimes you know someone's had a hard week, or somebody met with Mark because he's upset about something or not upset, but frustrated. Mark's worked with him, and then you see something happen on the court and you're just like, 'Yes, he needed that.' Those moments are what stand out to me. And having our girls be there.

"I just think there were so many highlights, but when I start from the beginning, I think of that first game. I think of the Duke game. I think of Gonzaga, and I was just so happy for the boys and for Big Blue Nation. (The) Duke (game) was the first time I had seen the Big Blue Nation not at Rupp. We were in Atlanta and I was like, 'This place is packed.' It was so exciting, and so the interactions with the fans and the win. Those moments are just so great. Super great." For the record, No. 19 Kentucky defeated No. 6 Duke 77-72.

Disappointing moments?

"I don't know about disappointments, but there were hard moments this season," said Lee Anne. "The injuries were hard. Lamont (Butler's) injury, Jaxson (Robinson's) injury. There were tears shed when Jaxson couldn't continue. And then to know what Lamont was doing to get on that court, how hard he was working, how much pain he was in, and how badly he wanted to do it for his guys. So hard. Andrew Carr (who struggled with back problems) and losing Kerr (Kriisa). Those moments are hard because these boys don't get another shot, and this is their time. So those are really, really hard. But that's also part of it, and injuries are part of it, too. So it's both. So when you say disappointed, I just think how hard the injuries were and how much I hurt for the boys."

For the season, Robinson, a graduate transfer, averaged 13 points, second highest on the squad, while starting all 24 games in which he appeared. Robinson had transferred from BYU where he was named Big 12 Sixth Man of the Year in 2024 under Pope's guidance. Junior Otega Oweh led the Cats with a 16.2-point average and received All-SEC second team honors. Overall, UK had a balanced scoring attack with six players averaging in double figures.

*UK coach Mark Pope hugs Jaxson Robinson during a pregame Senior Night ceremony in March 2025 at Rupp Arena as Lee Anne Pope looks on. The 6-foot-6 Robinson, who suffered a wrist injury, missed the final eight games and 12 of the last 13 games of the season. Kentucky later defeated LSU 95-64 that evening. (Photo by Jamie H. Vaught)*

## Quiet Drives & Home Life

After a Kentucky loss, does Mark Pope carry his disappointments or frustrations with him at home?

"He's great about it with the girls," said Lee Anne. "But we've been doing this a long time. So, there are quiet drives home, and it's okay. I've been doing this a long time. He's wonderful with the girls and with our family. He's sweet. He'll still help with homework. But he and I are a pretty good team. So there's quiet drives, and I know he's going to come grind it out and watch film all night. Sometimes I'm with him, and sometimes I punk out and I go to sleep. But it's part of the deal. The girls always know that he's happy to see them, and he's happy that they came to the game. And they also know too. We've been doing this a while."

Coach Pope has a very strong work ethic as a coach. But what about his home life. Does he slow down and relax?

"It's hard. I've had a ton of projects. Like every home, you have projects that you need your husband's help with and he will come home and do them," said Lee Anne. "He'll come home and help with homework, and he'll come home and put a bed together for me because he really is super handy. He can do anything. If I need a light changed, he can do all of that kind of stuff. He just works hard. And he tries to take care of his health. We try to carve out some time to get away and relax. I think it's super important. We need to get a little better at that probably."

While at Brigham Young, Pope's daughter, Avery, said her father has "a lot of energy and passion," according to a 2021 story by A. Jeff Carl in *Y Magazine,* an alumni publication at BYU. "A lot of people ask me if he's like that at home. Honestly, I think it's doubled when he comes home. He's a dad first. The dad side and the basketball side work together."

During his free time, Coach Pope said, "I love reading. We, Lee Anne and I, are early morning walkers. When we can, we try and do a 5:15 am walk. I love spending time with my girls when I can. So that's basically the sum of my free time." What about watching TV? "Yeah, we'll catch something. Usually, as soon as anybody in the family turns on the TV, I can only last two minutes before I fall asleep."

## Future Dr. Pope Becomes Coach Pope

Before Mark Pope went to the medical school at Columbia University in New York City, Lee Anne had been very concerned about her husband and his future plans after his NBA career ended. She was glad that he found a purpose in life, preparing for a medical career as a physician. "Lee Anne is just relieved that I'm doing something," Pope once said in 2006. "As we have considered retirement (from basketball) over the last few years, she has had a recurring nightmare where I'm laying on the couch at 4:00 in the afternoon, unshaven, unbathed, still in my pajamas holding a bag of potato chips, a soda, and the remote control watching Dr. Phil."

While in the NBA, after deciding to focus on a medical career, Pope took science classes at several universities, depending on where his team was located, to prepare for his medical studies. Before the online classes became popular, Pope said he had to miss a lot of class time, but the professors thankfully were cooperative. But, as it turned out, Pope didn't finish his medical school. Lee Anne supported his life-altering decision to forgo his remaining time in school. Even though Pope had already completed three years of medical study, she understood his never-ending love for basketball and his decision to become a coach.

"We made that decision together, 100 percent together," Lee Anne commented. "We talked about it inside and out. Mark will say we knew year one, but it took us two more years to get the guts to do it. I think just as long as we're together, we'll figure it out. If you don't want to be a doctor, you shouldn't be a doctor. So, that decision was totally made together, and we made it the right decision together.

"He was at Columbia, which is one of the top medical schools in the world. He was with kids who were so passionate about medicine, the medical field and changing the world. He would say, 'They feel about medicine how I felt about basketball.' And when the opportunity presented itself that it was a possibility that we could go to Georgia with Coach (Mark) Fox, that was kind of like, 'Are we doing this?' So, pretty bold."

Mark Pope jokingly said when he "dropped out of medical school, the survival rate of patients went way up." In the *Y Magazine*, Pope pointed out that, after revealing his tough decision to the dean of the medical school, "she thought I was on drugs." Pope said he couldn't wait to get started with his new coaching career, so he left the school immediately and journeyed to Georgia through the wee hours. The future UK coach also said he felt good about his future plans when he next walked on the hardwood basketball floor. "I'm the most blessed person in the world to get to do this," added Pope in the magazine.

In a 2010 email interview for my syndicated column, appearing in several newspapers in Kentucky, I asked Mark Pope, then a 38-year-old assistant coach at Wake Forest, if he had any regrets about his decision to leave medical school. "People often ask about me leaving medical school. There are two reasons why I'm sure that I made the right decision," explained Pope, who earned his bachelor's degree in English in 1996. "First, it only took me a few hours at Columbia to realize that I wasn't very smart. Second, I missed the game terribly. I enjoyed the challenge of medical school and the interaction with patients, but I love coaching. I literally can't wait to get up in the morning."

That was after Pope had spent one year at Georgia as the team's assistant director of basketball operations, doing the "dirty" work like the laundry and helping the players with coursework, among others. He couldn't resist an opportunity to coach on the floor and to recruit for the Demon Deacons. "One of the many great things about my position at Wake Forest is that I get to recruit,"

Pope said. "Recruiting can be tricky, frustrating, and exhausting, but I love it." In a brief interview with the *Athens Banner-Herald* in 2024, Pope said he made $24,000 in his first year at Georgia.

On the day he was introduced as the new coach at Brigham Young in 2019, Pope described his wife as "my No. 1 mentor, without a doubt, and there's no close second. She's the smartest person I know, she's the most beautiful person I know, and she's the funniest person I know. And she's going to be a gift to this university."

And when he accepted the Kentucky job in 2024, he reinforced those earlier statements of the gift Lee Anne would be to UK basketball.

# 9

# Growing Up in the Appalachian Mountains

(Trent Noah)

Just a few days before his graduation from Harlan County High School in May 2024, Trent Noah, who had just signed with the Wildcats earlier that month, had an interview with the author during his lunch break at the high school, just off U.S. Highway 119. That two-lane and four-lane highway actually begins in nearby Pineville, Ky. in Bell County and goes all the way through the Appalachian Mountains, ending in western Pennsylvania, not far from Pittsburgh.

In the interview held at one of the administrative offices, Noah was polite and pleasant. The four-star prospect was asked who has helped him the most over the years in becoming an outstanding basketball player. "I would say my dad (Dondi Noah)," he said. "It's been me and my dad for as long as I can remember. We just worked as hard as we could and tried to learn from other people and just kind of started from the ground up. My dad's been my rebounder and kind of my personal trainer." A retired history teacher who taught at Harlan County High, the elder Noah served as an assistant basketball coach for the Black Bears for one season, his son's senior year.

A first-team All-Stater, Noah had just finished his remarkable high school career. The 6-foot-5 Noah, who finished his prep career as the state's all-time fifth-leading scorer with 3,707 career points, helped the 34-5 Black Bears reach a state runner-up spot during his senior year. His team also became the first school from eastern Kentucky to advance to the state finals since 2011.

A lifelong Kentucky Wildcat fan, Noah is sure glad things finally worked out for him, and he is tickled to death about coming to UK after he originally signed with South Carolina. He had decommitted from the Gamecocks shortly after UK hired Mark Pope as the new coach. "It was super special," Noah said of signing with the hometown Wildcats. "It was a special moment for me and my family. It was always a dream of mine to play basketball at the University of Kentucky and then to share it with my grandfather (Charles "Perky" Bryant who played football at UK) was super cool as well. I'm just so thrilled that I'll be wearing the blue and white."

Said longtime sports journalist John Henson of Harlan County, "I couldn't tell you how many times I walked by the gym in the evenings, at any point of the year, and noticed Trent in there shooting with his dad. He put in as much time as anyone I've covered through the years. I never saw him lose his temper or composure during a game or even show a hint of being aggravated or upset with a teammate or coach. He was always focused on doing his job and whatever was needed to win. He rarely ever showed any emotion on the court, but he took his game and intensity up a level in the postseason (in 2024) with some huge plays in the regional and state tournaments. I think he knew it was up to him to make a play, and his teammates fed off that leadership and emotion when their season was on the line.

"Trent's 48-point game against Campbell County in the quarterfinals of the (2024) state tournament was the most amazing performance I've witnessed in 40 years of high school basketball coverage. He hit big shot after big shot when his team was probably one miss away from elimination. It was surreal to watch a gym full of people at Rupp Arena slowly become Harlan County and Trent Noah fans during the course of that game and week. It was very difficult for me to put into words what I had watched when it was over, and it was a tournament and performance I will never forget."

*Future Wildcat Trent Noah of Harlan County High School is shown here in the 13th Region Tournament action in Corbin when he gunned in 43 points and grabbed 15 rebounds against Clay County during his team's 66-60 victory in 2024. (Photo by Danny Vaughn)*

*Trent Noah of Harlan County High dribbles the ball past
a Clay County defender during the 13th Region
Tournament action in 2024. (Photo by Danny Vaughn)*

A valedictorian at Harlan County High, Noah, who earned a
perfect 4.0 grade point average, also took dual-credit classes at
Southeast Kentucky Community and Technical College.

Jeff Phillips, the public relations director at Harlan County Public Schools, was impressed with Noah after seeing him at a local
festival. "The highlight for me of the time I was there were the
smiles on Perky and Dolly Bryant's and Judy Noah's faces to the
awesome remarks and tribute to their grandson, Trent Noah," said
Phillips. "I must note once again what a phenomenal person he is.
If you've never seen him interact with his fans, fans of all ages, you
really don't know what a true gentleman he is.... Already a legend,
he is a tremendous role model."

Harlan County Judge-Executive Dan Mosley praised Noah's
hard work and academics. "Trent Noah is a wonderful young man,
a phenomenal athlete, and an incredible student leader," said
Mosley. "I'm thrilled this opportunity to live his dream of playing

for the Kentucky Wildcats is coming to fruition. The work he has put in on the court has made this possible. He is a role model for our youth. This is exciting for the people of Harlan County and Eastern Kentucky to have another young man to move on to UK to cheer for...."

Noah is so well-liked and popular in Harlan County and surrounding areas that his hometown medical center, Harlan ARH Hospital, is featuring him and his family in a television commercial and on social media platforms. Noah and the hospital also hosted a free basketball camp for eastern Kentucky youngsters in Harlan County in 2025. Like his teammates, Noah has partnership deals with other retail or service establishments.

## Family Support

In addition to his father, Noah said his family has encouraged him to continue playing basketball over the years from elementary school to high school, including the AAU summer circuit despite some struggles. "They've kind of always pushed me and given me the confidence and the drive," he said. "Specifically, my dad has made a ton of sacrifices for me and my mom, too. They both have driven me all over the country. My dad specifically would always do the driving. He's not a big fan of flying, so it would be harder to get him on a plane. But whenever we had to fly to the Adidas sessions, my mom would always go with me. My family has always been there for me.

"My cousin, Cameron Carmical, my mom's sister's child, went on to play basketball at Eastern Kentucky University (2017 to 2021). I was younger, and I always looked up to him. I would always go to the games and want to be like him at Harlan County. I think that he also had a big spark in my basketball interest as a kid."

Noah also has another cousin who played with him at Harlan County High. His name is Maddox Huff, a two-time All-Stater who signed to play at East Tennessee State, beginning in the fall of 2025. They were just one grade apart. "There are tons of memories with the team and with just him," smiled Huff, who averaged 29.4 points and 7.9 rebounds during his senior year of 2024-25 while leading the Black Bears to a 25-9 mark. "Going through workouts every day can get really draining and exhausting, but having somebody going through it with you is awesome, knowing that they're going for the same goals and stuff is super cool, and you push each other through that.

"But if I had to pick one story, it'd probably be one time we were going in the morning to shoot before school at about 5:30 a lot of days in a row. I think we were doing it too much and we ended up falling asleep in the locker room before even getting to shoot and woke up to the bell ringing for school. So, that'd probably be my favorite or funniest memory that I have of him (Noah)."

During his early days, Noah said he didn't really think about quitting basketball when things were tough. "I would never say I felt like quitting," he commented. "There's definitely some long days in it, but ultimately basketball is something that I love and have a passion for. But there are some hard times that come through it. In my freshman year, there was COVID. So, we had to deal with the pandemic. It messed up the high school basketball season, and then it messed up AAU. I wasn't on a national platform my freshman year.

"My sophomore year, about three-fourths of the way through the high school season, I broke my foot and that didn't allow me to play on the AAU circuit. It took a long time to heal. It was about a seven- or eight-month process so that was another obstacle.

"Then my junior year, I was thankful enough to be healthy and have a full season. Then it was one of the first AAU weekends (when) I had a grade three ankle sprain and that took a couple of months to recover. It was definitely tough. I didn't really get to have a full summer on the circuit until my last year. That was definitely tough. But at the end of the day, I knew it was all God's plan and it couldn't have worked out any better. I've just been trusting God."

*Then-freshman Trent Noah speaks with reporters in his first UK basketball Media Day festivities. (Photo by Jamie H. Vaught)*

Looking back, Noah added he and Huff "probably did way too much basketball (in high school). We would basically be there all day. We would go to the gym before school. We'd do our team stuff right after school. We'd do lifting, we'd run, we'd go back at night. Basically we just lived up there. (One time) we probably got back home from the gym maybe 11:00 that night and we were waking up probably 5:30-ish, which wasn't healthy at all. We did not get enough sleep. We were going to the gym to shoot or work out before school (began). We fell asleep in the locker room. We were there, sitting down, getting ready to lace our shoes up, and we both fell asleep in our lockers. I remember waking up to the bell ringing and people coming in and out the door.

"We actually made it to class on time. (After the first) bell went off, it kind of gives you five minutes to make your way to class.

Thankfully, that (bell ringing) was the first one. We were still on time. We definitely were groggy and tired that whole day, though."

## Early Memories

Noah's first exposure to UK was attending the football games, especially during the Coach Mark Stoops years. What was that like? "It's honestly surreal," said Noah's mother, Stacy Bryant Noah. "As a little boy, my son used to come to University of Kentucky football games just wide-eyed, taking it all in. He'd look around at the stadium, the fans, the players, and dream about what it would be like to wear Kentucky blue one day. Fast forward to now — he's not just attending games, he's playing on the court at Rupp Arena as a Kentucky Wildcat. To watch him live out the dream he had as a kid, right here at the very place where it all started, is something I still have to pinch myself about. It's been an emotional, full-circle journey for our whole family."

What about Noah's earliest UK basketball memory? "I mean a super early memory that I can barely remember is whenever they won the championship in 2012 with (Anthony) Davis," he said. "I was probably about six or seven, but I can remember it. I can remember it a little bit. I was a huge John Wall fan, too. I had a lot of John Wall shirts."

Noah was born in Corbin but has lived in Harlan his entire life. "Harlan is home," said Noah's mother. "It's where he grew up, where his roots are, and where his community has always supported him. Even though he was born in Corbin, everything about who he is was shaped in Harlan. That place means the world to him and to all of us."

He also has an older sister, Emersyn Noah, an elementary school teacher.

Stacy Noah, a former teacher and principal at Harlan Independent School System, remembers the days when Trent was playing youth basketball. "Trent wears glasses or contacts now, but when he was younger and just starting out in basketball, he wore goggles on the court," she smiled. "He was absolutely adorable in them — we still smile when we look back at pictures from those days. The goggles became a bit of his signature look for a while, and he wore them with pride. It's just one of those sweet memories from his early basketball journey that we'll always cherish."

## UK Football

Long before Noah was born, his maternal grandfather was a stand-out at Kentucky, playing football for Coach Charlie Bradshaw, a 37-year-old ex-Marine who took over the program in January 1962. But things got kind of rough in the UK camp during Bradshaw's first year. Due to brutal treatment by Bradshaw, a Bear Bryant disciple, over 50 players eventually quit the team by the time the 1962 season began. It got so bad that assistant coach Homer Rice threatened to leave the program if the head coach didn't stop or tone down his punitive workouts for the players. "Charlie had a lot of outstanding attributes as a football coach, but sometimes he let his energy go in the wrong direction," Rice once told the author.

But 5-foot-9, 190-pound Perky Bryant of Evarts in Harlan County remained on the squad, which is best remembered as "Thin Thirty," and the 1962 Wildcats finished at 3-5-2 with the junior fullback ranking at No. 9 in the SEC with 326 rushing yards. The 1962 UK football media guide, which came out during the preseason, had mentioned Bryant could be one of the SEC's best fullbacks after an outstanding spring practice. As a three-year varsity performer, he was one of the major contributors on UK's offense as a tough fullback along with blocking. During his Wildcat career, some of Bryant's teammates include future NFL standouts like QB Rick Norton, running back Rodger Bird (defensive back in pro), and tackle Sam Ball, a cousin of former UK basketball All-American Frank Ramsey.

What motivated Bryant to stay with the team after so many of his teammates left the program due to brutal workouts? "Honestly, I just didn't want to be a quitter. A lot of people poured their time, effort, and belief into me to help me get to the University of Kentucky, and I felt a deep responsibility not to let them down," he said. "I wasn't just playing for myself — I was playing for my small town, for the people who supported me from day one, and for those who believed in me when things got tough.

"One of my biggest inspirations has always been my oldest brother, James Bryant — his nickname was Banty. When I was just a kid, he earned a football scholarship to play at Hiwassee College (in Tennessee). He played one season before being called to serve in the Korean War. He went missing in action and was later declared killed in action. He never got the chance to come back home — or to college. That loss left a mark on our family and on me, personally. From that moment on, I felt like I was carrying a piece of his dream with me. Playing college football was about more than just me — it was about honoring his legacy.

"So yeah, it would've been easier to walk away at times, but I stayed because I knew who I was doing it for — and I wasn't going to quit on them."

Noah enjoys visiting with his grandpa, who was a four-sports star at old Evarts High School. They talk about sports, including Bryant's old days at Kentucky. "He's always talking about that," said Noah. "His house is full of Kentucky stuff. That's really special to see that he got to do that, and read stories and listen to stuff about him playing there." Noah's family have had season football tickets for almost six decades.

Noah said his favorite UK story as told by his grandpa was the 1962 Kentucky-Tennessee football game in Knoxville. "I would say the one that comes to my mind would be when he talks about the game at Tennessee a lot," said Noah. "That was always his favorite game. He said that it was at Knoxville. The (Wildcats) had about 18 players playing at the time. They won 12-10 and he had a run that put him in a field goal position for Clarkie Mayfield to kick the (game-winning) field goal. Quarterback Jerry Woolum had ties to Harlan and then the kicker had ties to Harlan. He talks about that game a lot. He always likes it when we beat Tennessee."

As of this writing, there were a couple of short videos of the 1962 UK-UT game on YouTube. Mayfield grew up in Harlan County where he played football at Black Star High School in Alva, Ky. Woolum was born in Pineville but played high school football in Richmond where his father was a professor at Eastern Kentucky State College (now EKU).

Added Noah's mother in 2025, "My dad is 83 now, and he's still as passionate about Kentucky athletics as ever. He played football at UK in the early 1960s, and those years meant so much to him. He often talks about his teammates, especially (star quarterback) Jerry Woolum — someone he remembers with great fondness and respect. The bond they shared and the values they built through the game have stuck with him his entire life. It's really special to see that kind of legacy now being passed down to my son, who's carrying on the Kentucky tradition in his own way on the basketball court."

Over the years, Harlan County has produced many NCAA Division I standouts who went to UK and other schools, including former Cats Wah Wah Jones and Dick Parsons. Noah was asked who is his favorite Wildcat player from Harlan County. "That's a tough one," he smiled. "I mean, there's a lot that come to my mind. I would say Freddie Maggard. I've heard a lot of stories about him. (He) played at Cumberland (High)." During the late 1980s and early 1990s, Maggard starred as a UK quarterback under coaches Jerry Claiborne and Bill Curry.

## Signing with South Carolina

While in high school, Noah was hoping coach John Calipari would be recruiting him to play at UK. But that didn't work out. He ended up signing with South Carolina in November 2023. "Obviously, I've always grown up as a UK fan, and some coaches have just different play styles, and I understand it if I don't fit that," he said. "But I was just focused on the schools that were recruiting me and the ones that were in contact with me. I had a good relationship with the coaching staff and Coach (Lamont) Paris (at South Carolina). I wanted to play big-time basketball. I mean being from SEC country, that was a huge appeal to me as well." He picked USC over Dayton, Western Kentucky, Stanford, St. Louis, Butler, among others.

Then Kentucky had a new coach in April 2024 after Calipari left for Arkansas, and Noah began to have second thoughts. On an Instagram post, he wrote, "After much thought, prayer and extensive conversation with my family, I requested and was granted a release from my national letter of intent with the University of South Carolina. I will be reopening my recruitment with hopes of pursuing basketball opportunities closer to home."

*Trent Noah in a pregame practice.*

On Mark Pope's introductory press conference, Noah said, "I didn't watch it, but I've seen some stuff about it. But that was really cool that the fan base came out for that. That many people came out for a press conference was super cool."

Pope made the announcement in early May that Noah had signed with Kentucky. "Trent Noah is one of the elite shooters in this class," Pope said in a news release. "He is a tough, hard-nosed player with a special physicality. As an eastern Kentucky native, Trent will bring a grit, toughness and determination to the program that is representative of this state. We're looking forward to Trent joining this talented group."

## Freshman Season

After struggling in preseason practices, Noah began to improve and had several outstanding performances as a key backup on Coach Mark Pope's first Kentucky team,  He appeared in 24 games, averaging 11.1 minutes and 2.7 points. In mid-February, Noah had outstanding performance in two straight games.  In No. 15 Kentucky's 75-64 victory over fifth-ranked Tennessee at Rupp Arena, Noah gunned in 11 points, which turned out to be his season-best.  He also hit 3 of 4 three-pointers in 19 minutes of action.  Several days later, the Wildcats traveled to Austin to meet the Texas Longhorns at Moody Center.  It's where Noah had seven points and grabbed six rebounds in 21 minutes as Kentucky dropped to Texas 82-78.

His performance against the Vols was extra special as he grew up watching heated Kentucky-Tennessee rivalry over the years. Asked about the old rivalry between both schools, "It's amazing, definitely one of the most fun games on the schedule," he said. "There's nothing like it growing up, watching them go down in my living room, and then crying when they lose and so happy when they win. Being able to be a part of it is so cool." Noah said he liked both UK victories over Tennessee, including the one in Knoxville, where the Wildcats also won 78-73 two weeks earlier. "They were both really special, " he said. "It's cool whenever you can do it in front of your home crowd, and it's cool whenever you can be the villain and go into Knoxville and leave with the win, so I would say it's 50/50."

"Watching my son have his best game on his home court, especially against Tennessee — a longtime border-state rival — was an incredible moment," said Noah's mother. "As a parent, you always believe in your child's potential, but to see it come to life in front of the home crowd was something else. He's put in so much work, and to have it all come together in a big game like that, in Rupp Arena, was just pure joy. It was one of those nights we'll always remember."

His parents really get nervous when they see him play on the floor. "I definitely get nervous — every single game," said Stacy Noah. "No matter how many times I've watched him play, the nerves never really go away. I just want him to do well, stay healthy, and enjoy the game he loves. My husband plays it a little cooler, but I know he gets nervous, too — he just hides it better than I do. We both feel it in our own way because we care so much and are so proud of him. It's all part of being a basketball parent."

Noah will always remember his first UK game at Rupp Arena even though it was a preseason exhibition contest against NCAA Division II Kentucky Wesleyan. It was a super special night for the Harlan County native who played well in UK's 123-52 blowout victory. Noah, who didn't see action until about the midpoint of the second half, was hot, shooting four of five three-pointers. He finished with 12 points in only nine minutes of action. "Trent is not shy. It's really great to have him on the floor," said Kentucky coach Mark Pope. "Our guys love him. Everybody on the bench was losing their mind. I thought Kerr (Kriisa) was going to start ripping his clothes off. He was so excited."

Noah was selected as one of three players UK brought out for postgame media interviews. He has said many times that playing for the Wildcats is a dream come true. On playing at Rupp Arena, Noah, who also played in the state tournament finals in the previous year at the same venue, "It was awesome. I feel like it came full circle so it's been really cool. I got to play with my guys back home (Harlan County), and now I get to play with my brothers here, so it's awesome."

Noah loves being a part of Coach Pope's system. "I really credit Coach Pope and all the coaching staff," said Noah. "They instill confidence in us — and that's what you need in a shooter — so it's a fun brand of basketball. It's fun when you can just go down and shoot threes freely and I feel like it's fun to watch too, so it's a win-win." The Wildcats, who had 32 assists with only five turnovers, hit 21 of 42 on three-point shots for 50 percent against Kentucky Wesleyan.

*Coach Mark Pope and Trent Noah at a postgame press conference following Kentucky's disappointing 82-78 loss to Texas at Moody Center in Austin during the 2024-25 season. (Photo by Jamie H. Vaught)*

Looking back at his first season as a Wildcat, Noah added there were lots of memorable moments. "This year was great. You could go many different ways with this," he said. "One specific thing that's probably the most memorable, it sucked at the time, but we had a late day (of preseason practice). Before the season, we had somebody (who came) late to film (session), so we had consequences with a lot of running. One of our rules in our program is you're on time, you're not late. Definitely that day was not fun at all, but it was one of the most memorable things. We sit around and talk about that a lot. It was terrible at the time, but now it's kind of fun to sit back and look back on it."

Noah added coach Mark Pope was not happy about the tardiness. "That's one of our standards that we kind of talked about that at the very beginning that we're showing up on time (and making sure) we're not late," he said. "But it was definitely a good learning experience. We had one late time, and then we were never late again. It was just one player. It wasn't me. I'm not going to say who it was, but there was somebody else on the team who was straggling behind. I don't know if (he) overslept or something like that."

Not surprisingly, when third-seeded Kentucky dropped to No. 2 seed Tennessee 78-65 in NCAA Sweet Sixteen in Indianapolis, Noah said that was the most disappointing moment of the season. "I feel like we were so close as a group and felt like that we had the team and the tangibles to win the whole thing," he explained. "Whenever you come up short, no matter what it is, I would say that that would have to be the most disappointing moment." In the previous two wins over Tennessee, Kentucky had made 12 three-pointers (out of 24 attempts) both times, but the Wildcats only shot six of 15 three-point field goals in the NCAA Tournament showdown. Kentucky finished the season at 24-12 with eight wins over AP Top 15 teams.

Like a typical freshman, Noah had to adjust to college basketball. "At the beginning of the freshman year, I would say the biggest adjustment was the physicality and the speed of the game," he said. "Coming from high school basketball, it's definitely a lot different being thrown into the SEC. The athletes are bigger, stronger, and faster so that's something that you have to get used to and kind of adapt to as quick as you can."

## Favorite Moment

"This basketball season was packed with unforgettable moments and incredible highlights, but without a doubt, the greatest highlight was Big Blue Madness," said Noah's mother after the 2024-25 season. "Seeing my son step into Rupp Arena for the very first time as an official Kentucky Wildcat was simply amazing. The energy in the building was electric, with over 20,000 passionate Kentucky fans cheering him on. It was something truly special. What made the moment even more meaningful was the song he chose to walk out to: 'You'll Never Leave Harlan Alive,' a powerful ode to his hometown. That song, that crowd, that night... it's something our family will never forget."

## Travis Perry

During the 2024-25 campaign, Kentucky had three freshmen on the team. In addition to Noah, the other two rookies were Collin Chandler of Farmington, Utah and Travis Perry of Eddyville, Ky. The 2024 Kentucky's Mr. Basketball who is the state's all-time scoring leader with 5,481 points, Perry was Noah's roommate. And it was Perry and his Lyon County High School which defeated Noah's Harlan County 67-58 in the state championship game in 2024.

In May 2024, I interviewed Perry, who has since transferred to Ole Miss after his freshman season, in Kuttawa in Lyon County where I stayed a couple of nights at the home of longtime friends Bill and Paula Cunningham as I had two book signings in the local area. Since Perry had his high school graduation the night before, I wasn't sure if he would show up for the 8 a.m. interview in the next morning. But he sure did, and I was very impressed. The youngster kept his word. We had our pleasant interview on

Cunningham's front porch overlooking the beautiful Lake Barkley across the street. Asked how he was feeling that morning as a newly minted high school graduate with a GPA of 4.0, Perry said, "I'm feeling pretty excited. A little bit relieved. I had to do a valedictorian speech. I was worried about that a little bit. A little bit scary with a lot of people there. But I'm mostly excited. It's been a long time at Lyon County and to be able to graduate, having done so many great things, met so many great people. It's a lot of fun."

After signing with the Wildcats in November 2023, Perry said he didn't really feel extra pressure to perform during his high school senior year. "Maybe a little bit," he said with a smile. "The Kentucky fans really, really love their players, really support their players, and so there was increased followings at our games. But still it was just playing basketball, having fun. I tried to keep it as simple as possible and just have fun. Trust the work that I put in and just try and win at all costs, and I think everything else will work itself out." Since he was a seventh grader, Perry has played basketball for Lyon County High with his father, Ryan Perry, serving as the head coach for Travis' last five seasons there. Commented Coach Perry, who was named the boys' basketball Coach of the Year by Louisville's *Courier-Journal* after guiding the Lions to a stunning 36-3 mark and a state championship, "Travis' basketball IQ is completely off the chart. He has the ability to slow the game down by using his mind. He seems to always be one step ahead of everyone else on the court, and it proves to be an equalizer for him in terms of playing against players that are much bigger, faster and more athletic than he is."

In his first and only season at Kentucky, Perry, like Noah and Chandler, was a key backup, averaging nearly 10 minutes in 31 games with four starts. The sharpshooting guard had a couple of double-figure scoring games, hitting 11 points in 30 minutes during UK's loss to Alabama in the SEC Tournament and a season-high 12 points along with four steals at Alabama.

On Perry transferring to Mississssippi, Noah said, "I was a little surprised. I knew Ole Miss recruited him a lot while in high school. I knew that he might be thinking about there, but ultimately, it was his decision and he had to do what he thought was best for him." Noah said he even encouraged him to stay at Kentucky. "I tried the best that I could," he commented. "We talked about it quite a bit and obviously I wanted him to stay here, but I get that he has to do what's best for him. He felt that entering the transfer portal and ultimately choosing Ole Miss was the best route for him. I respect it and just hope he has a good year. It definitely sucks to see him leave, and it's definitely different not having him as my roommate this (coming) year, but I'm sure that he'll have a great season and a great career wherever he ends up."

Perry, who also was a golf standout at Lyon County High, and some of his UK teammates often played golf in the Lexington area when not playing basketball. Noah was asked if he played golf. "Actually, I didn't play golf until about a couple months ago," said Noah in June 2025. "I picked it up late. We did have a lot of golfers on the team last year, and they would always try to get me to go and I never would. I just never had the drive to go with them. Then one day after the season was over, we kind of had some down time, didn't really have much to do, was taking a mental break away from basketball so I decided to go. It was a lot of fun and now I can say I'm hooked on it. But I don't think I could play the rest of my life and I still wouldn't be able to beat Travis. He's a really good golfer. His dad played college golf (at Northern Kentucky), so he's been playing it since he was young. He's definitely good at golf."

Darrell Bird of *The Cats' Pause* is one of the few Kentucky sportswriters who has followed Perry's high school and UK careers very closely. Bird even wrote a nice-looking book about tiny Lyon County High School's incredible path to the 2024 state championship, including stories about Perry and his teammates. The title of the 191-page hardcover is *Lyon Pride.* And some observers have wondered about Perry — the Sweet 16 MVP who spent his life dreaming of playing for the Wildcats, including teenage years spent making himself into a high school basketball legend — as he only lasted just one season at UK. Bird said that's really quite simple. "Perry adds a new notation to his story, though it's not one he would celebrate — a poster child for college athletics in 2025," said Bird. "Perry certainly didn't want to leave, agonizing until the deadline forced a decision, but he knew what we all knew, the kid had no choice. He is a skilled basketball player who needs to be on the court, not a glorified walk-on.

*Coach Mark Pope and his freshmen — Trent Noah, Collin Chandler and Travis Perry — discuss during the 2025 Kentucky-LSU game at Rupp Arena. (Photo by Jamie H. Vaught)*

"Welcome to the new day for college athletics, the Old West where coaches are the town's powerful business owners bankrolling hired guns to protect and advance their wealth. In olden times, less than a decade ago, Perry need only worry about beating out any new freshmen added to the roster. In this new day, however, Perry's head was on a swivel, not only looking back to incoming freshman Jasper Johnson, but ahead to a pair of hired guns — Pittsburgh junior transfer Jaland Lowe and Florida senior Denzel Aberdeen.

"Don't blame Pope. He has taken on the duty of winning NCAA championship No. 9 and is taking full advantage of the transfer portal and NIL chaos that currently rules the land. But don't blame Perry, either. One could argue he should have stayed and competed. His UK coach, Mark Pope, even said he was 'devastated' that Perry opted to leave. But let's be honest, we all knew how this story would play out next season.

"So, while Perry, the pride of Eddyville in far western Kentucky, is now at Ole Miss, he will forever be a Wildcat — the family bleeds enough blue to change the water color at Lake Barkley — but he is a gifted basketball player first and foremost. Ultimately, that is the dream that must be followed."

## Harlan County Jersey

Unlike the old days, the fans can now buy a Harlan County High School basketball jersey. It even has Noah's jersey number (No. 2) with his name on the back. How does Noah feel about that? "It's awesome," he smiled. "I've made so many great memories playing at Harlan County. It's really cool because we've had the county support throughout my five years of high school basketball, was always top-notch. I mean, they always filled the gym. They were with us on the run at the state tournament. So, being able to kind of put out a Harlan County basketball jersey was really special to me, and I wanted to make sure that I got that done because that's where I'm from and I'm super happy that that's where I grew up. I'm proud that I graduated from Harlan County."

*Trent Noah of Harlan County High drives past Jerrod Roark of Clay County in 2024 13th Region Tournament in Corbin. (Photo by Danny Vaughn)*

## Mountain Mamba

How does Noah's mom feel about her son's nickname, Mountain Mamba? Her new nickname, Mountain Mama? How did the nickname originate? "It's really humbling and special to hear my son being called the 'Mountain Mamba,' " she said. "I think the nickname actually came from a fan who called into a sports radio show and suggested it, and from there it just took off, especially on social media. To have a nickname that draws a connection to someone as legendary and respected as Kobe Bryant is truly an honor. I think it's really sweet. Being called 'Mountain Mama' feels like a loving gesture from the BBN. It reflects where our family comes from and the pride we have in our Appalachian roots. It's all in good fun and filled with heart, and I take it as a real honor."

## Freshman Classes

Toughest class that he has taken during his first year at UK? "I would say the toughest class has been a statistics class," Noah said. "That was pretty challenging, statistics and math and numbers like that. Then I also had a calculus class my freshman year. That was pretty difficult. But I would say one of those two. Thankfully I got through them both, so that's good."

## Who is Noah?

"I guess I'm just kind of an ordinary guy," said the Wildcat player. "I like to play video games; I like to hang out with my family. I like shoes, and I like clothes. So, I would say a lot of people might not know that. That's some of my hobbies that I get into." His mother pointed out Noah makes TikTok videos. "Yeah, I like to be active on social media," he added. He also enjoys chicken wings.

Noah said his faith is important. "I think that's a huge part in my life and I think that's where everything comes from," he said.

"I mean, that's the foundation. Having a relationship with God and be able to trust Him on this journey is huge. Being a college athlete, it gets brutal at times and you have long days and then you're doubting yourself and then you're anxious. Being able to have a steady foundation and a steady presence to be able to trust and lean on is huge because life gives you so many curveballs and stuff like that. To be able to have God and to be able to lean on Him and have a relationship just makes it a little easier.

"I'm a Christian. I've kind of always grown up in that kind of household and just always trust God and put Him first and His plan is bigger than ours."

Noah's home church is Harlan Christian Church in downtown Harlan. "We've been going there for a while," he said. "It's a great church there, and it's kind of been the one that I've grown up in. Whenever I'm back in town, that's where I always leave my socks out on Sundays." While in Lexington, he has been going to Southland Christian Church, adding, "They have a couple of campuses. They have one in Lexington and then their main campus is in Nicholasville. I've really liked the experience in that church and my time there."

# 10

---

# Lefty's Prize Pupil

(Kenny Brooks)

In late March of 2024, the 55-year-old Kenny Brooks had a very tough decision to make just hours after his Virgina Tech team had lost the second-round NCAA Tournament game to No. 19 Baylor. He could stay in Blacksburg where he had become the highly successful women's basketball coach at Virginia Tech of the Atlantic Coast Conference, coming off the 2024 regular season conference championship. Or he could move northwest to Lexington, Ky., — which is at least a five-hour drive — and take the same job at UK in the Southeastern Conference. He had to check with his family, including his three daughters who played basketball with their dad at Virginia Tech, and a son, and they didn't have a lot of time — less than 48 hours — to discuss and debate the pros and cons. "I think that's the nature of our business is that you don't have a whole of time to debate, " he explained.

The attractive UK job certainly appealed to Brooks. "When you think about Kentucky, to me growing up, being a big fan of Tubby

Smith, Rick Pitino, you always saw Kentucky basketball," he later commented.

*UK athletics director Mitch Barnhart and new coach Kenny Brooks at the introductory press conference held at Joe Craft Center in 2024. (Photo by Jamie H. Vaught)*

In an interview with the author, Brooks, who just a month earlier had finished a memorable campaign during his first season at Kentucky, added, "When I inherited that program (at Virginia Tech), they were in last place in the ACC and when I left that program, we were in first place in the ACC with two championships under our belt, and a Final Four appearance (in 2023). Very proud of what we did there. I know there were a lot of people there upset with the fact that we left, but this is my career. We all want challenges in life. I thought I had done a lot there, that hopefully they'll be able to enjoy because you just can't take for granted that you got to a Final Four. You can't take for granted that you won ACC championships, and so we took them places that they've never been before, so hopefully they'll understand that one day. I only have one career, and I have to get satisfaction from my career. Now, whether it means that we win a national championship, or I knew I was fighting to get to that point. That's what I want out of my career.

"I felt like UK was a sleeping giant. I felt like it's obviously in the best conference in the country, and when you think of Kentucky, you think of basketball. So to have that opportunity, to come to a basketball-crazed state that's going to really support anything and everything that you do, that was very enticing to me. I wasn't looking to leave. I was very happy at Virginia Tech. I was very comfortable at Virginia Tech. I lived in Virginia for my first 55 years of my life, so coming to UK was the first year I've ever lived outside of the state of Virginia. When this opportunity came about, I prayed about it. My family was going through a very difficult situation because my wife (Chrissy) was right in the middle of treatments for breast cancer, and we prayed upon it and everything kept saying UK is where I needed to be. Even during very difficult times like that, it spoke very clearly that this was the place I needed to be, and we decided to come.

"Through it all, I guess it's a good thing when the place that you leave is very, very upset that you're leaving because it must've meant you've done a good job there. We fought that a little bit because we're a very proud family. We're a very strong family, and then to have people try to attack your character just because you left is very tough, but we drew strength from UK fans. They embraced me, my family. They prayed for my wife, which is extremely important to me, and we had a very successful year because of it. I'm excited for what we can be and what we will be, and really getting the tradition of winning over here on the women's side, just like it is on the men's side. It wasn't an easy decision. It's one where some people can doubt, and some people can understand, but all in all, until you walk a mile in a man's shoes, you can't judge him, and I'm the only one that's walking in my shoes, so we're excited about it and looking forward to the future."

During his last season at Virginia Tech, Brooks had a very good team which finished prematurely in the Big Dance with a final record of 25-8 overall. For most of the season, the Hokies had been among the leading contenders to make another trip to the Final Four. "It's a very emotional time because you're always coming off of a season," recalled Brooks. "We had a very successful season, but we had a very tragic ending to our season because my best player (All-American Elizabeth Kitley) had gotten hurt, and so that's why the power of prayer was big for us. We prayed upon it, we talked about it, and all signs said this (UK) is where I needed to be. I'm a man of faith. My wife has a much stronger relationship with God than I do, and I'm working on that, but everything, through the power of prayer, He just led us here.

"There've been no regrets. We've been very excited, very happy. It's been a whirlwind. We haven't really had time to just relax a little bit, but hopefully we can get through this transfer season (in April of 2025) and then we can enjoy Lexington a little bit more. She enjoys it. She goes out and she loves it, and I'm looking forward to getting introduced to Lexington."

After UK's two straight poor seasons, many observers agreed Kentucky made a very impressive hire in Brooks, an experienced coach with proven results. Before coming to Lexington, Brooks posted a 517-204 career record in 22 seasons. His teams have captured five Colonial Athletic Association Tournament titles, four CAA regular season titles, one ACC Tournament title, one ACC regular season title, and 10 NCAA Tournament appearances. Said UK athletics director Mitch Barnhart, "Kenny has a strong history of player development and championship performance at James Madison and Virginia Tech. When you combine his coaching excellence with his vision for this program and his passion to take us there, he is ideally suited to be head coach of the Wildcats."

According to his five-year contract with UK, Brooks' first-year salary was $1.3 million, a nice bump from his $890,000 pay at Virginia Tech. The 16-team SEC features several highest-paid coaches in the nation, including national championship coaches South Carolina's Dawn Staley (reportedly $4 million in 2025) and LSU's Kim Mulkey ($3.264 million).

Asked how he felt about being the one of the highest-paid coaches in the conference, Brooks said, "Obviously, that (pay increase) factors into it, but it's not at the top (of the reasons). When you just said that, it doesn't even ring a bell for me, and obviously, you don't want to go somewhere and take a pay cut, but I knew that they were going to take care of me. I don't look at my bank account and say, 'Oh, this is great.' It was more about the opportunity to be the head coach at UK, and for the desire to try to win a national championship. That's what was most important to me, and everything else, I have people for that. I have agents or whatever, but when you do look at it, it does show you the commitment that they have to invest in women's basketball, and that is very important."

## Growing up in Virginia

During the 1970s and 1980s, Brooks fondly remembers his childhood in Waynesboro in the northern part of Virginia, and he followed sports. He is the oldest child with younger siblings Michael and Sheena.

"Mother and father lived in Waynesboro, but they were separated. So, I lived with my mom and she did most of the caretaking. My father was around so I had loving parents who always supported me in everything that I wanted to do," he said. "My mom would work two jobs so that I could do the sport camps, live my dreams. Even though we struggled from a financial standpoint, I never knew we struggled because we had everything that we needed as far as love, attention. They were great providers in that area and always supporting, being at every sport event that I had, and they're a big reason why I am what I am today, and I'm very, very grateful for their love and the way that they (taught) me how to grow up.

"Growing up in a small town, probably my biggest memories were football. I'm a big Dallas Cowboys fan, and so I can remember vividly in the backyard playing, and always emulating Roger Staubach, Tony Dorsett, Drew Pearson, and they were always the team of choice.

"As we would go to the baseball (season), I was a (Los Angeles) Dodgers fan. So from the '70s and early '80s, I can tell you the lineups for the Dodgers because I loved collecting baseball cards. So, the Steve Garveys, the Davey Lopes, the Bill Russells, the Ron Ceys, (Steve) Yeager, Dusty Baker were guys that I always watched and tried to emulate.

"Then, on the basketball side, it was more college than it was professional. I would look at players (from) the North Carolina teams, like the Dean Smith-coached teams, Kenny Smith, obviously Michael Jordan. Players like that were players I would look to. Sports was a big part of my life, and we always were out in the front yard, the back yard, playing and emulating the sports teams that we loved. Mine were the Dallas Cowboys, the Dodgers, and college basketball, it was the North Carolina teams."

On his younger brother, Michael, Brooks said, "(He's) is my best friend. I talked to him this morning. I talk to him every morning on my way to work. He's my biggest fan, and we look very similar, so a lot of times he'll come to my sporting events and people will mistake him for me."

Brooks, who also has a younger sister Sheena, has a large extended family, and they stay in close touch with each other. "I have lots of cousins that we consider like brothers and sisters," he said. "One of my cousins is Cory Alexander (who is also from Waynesboro), and he does commentating for ESPN right now, for basketball, and he does some NBA games. He played in the NBA and he's like my brother, but he's my cousin. We call each other brothers."

There is an interesting teenage story about Brooks while he was attending Waynesboro High School. When he was a sophomore, Brooks didn't study like he should have. He nearly got dropped from the basketball team as his grades suffered. Why the poor grades? Brooks was spending too much time with a basketball board game in which players roll a die to come up with plays. He was simply fascinated with the game strategies and statistics. Obviously, it showed that Brooks had a coaching mindset during his youthful age. In 1987, he graduated from high school where he was an honorable mention all-state basketball performer.

## College Days

When it was time for him to go to college, Brooks stayed fairly close to home, attending James Madison University in Harrison-burg, a 40-minute drive to the campus. A 6-foot-1 guard, Brooks lettered for four years and eventually became a two-year team co-captain. During his collegiate career at JMU, Brooks averaged 5.7 points and 17.4 minutes in 107 games. A part-time starter, he was deadly from the three-point line, hitting 41 percent (82 of 200). He graduated in 1992 with a degree in business man-agement. His coach at JMU? He was legendary Lefty Driesell, a colorful personality who later was enshrined in several basket-ball hall of fames, including the Naismith Hall of Fame in 2018. At the time of his retirement in January of 2003, Driesell, who also coached at Maryland for 17 years (1969-86), was the all-time fourth-winningest Division I men's basketball coach. While at

JMU, Driesell, who died in 2024 at the age of 92, coached for nine seasons, compiling an overall record of 159-111.

*Legendary Lefty Driesell coached Kenny Brooks at James Madison University. (JMU Athletics Photography)*

Brooks said Driesell has been a big influence in his life. "I say life, not just basketball life," he pointed out. "He taught me so many things other than just what's on the basketball court. When I played for him, I thought he was a crazy madman. Some of his tactics I didn't understand at the time, but as I have gone on to become a father, as I've gone on to become a coach, I find myself doing a lot of the things that he did to me. They were very influential to me, and they made a big impact on my life.

"The biggest thing that he taught me was that you can incorporate family into business. He always had his family around our teams, whether we were coming to his house, whether they were coming on road trips with us, and he taught me that you can do both and be successful at both because a lot of times if you are a strong family man, you're not a good basketball coach because you focus your attention just on one area. Sometimes you can be a really good basketball coach, but not a really good family man because you focus on one area.

"He taught me how to incorporate them into one and then you can win because you're going to be strong with your family. You're going to be present with your family, but you're also going to incorporate the family values into your team. He did that, and I saw that blueprint. That's something that I've emulated, and it's because of him. He showed me that you can do it. Sometimes the lazy narrative is that you can't do both well, and he taught me that you can. He was very, very proud of me. Even into his last years, he was watching me. He would comment on my games, and he would send me notes. He followed me even though I was in women's basketball, and that was something that made me very, very proud."

So, Driesell's family was heavily involved with the basketball program. "Everywhere we went, his family was there," said Brooks. "Mrs. Driesell, even if I was mad at Coach Driesell, Mrs. Driesell would come up and give me a hug and tell me she loved me. That's something that meant a lot to me."

*Kenny Brooks during his playing days at James Madison*
*University. (JMU Athletics Photography)*

Added Brooks, Driesell was a "big personality," who once declared that Maryland would become the "UCLA of the East" during the days when Coach John Wooden and his UCLA teams
were winning consecutive national championships during the late
1960s and early 1970s.

## Lefty's Hall of Fame & 90th Birthday

After Driesell's coaching career, Brooks recalled two of his biggest thrills: celebrating Lefty's induction to the Naismith Basketball Hall of Fame in 2018 as well as his 90th birthday in 2021.

Said Brooks, "When he finally got selected to go into the Basketball Hall of Fame, he was giving his speech. He said 'I have two former players that are head coaches right now' and I'm like 'Okay, here's my moment. He's going to say my name, but then he just stopped and went somewhere else.' Then, I talked to him the very next week and I congratulated him, and he was very grateful. He said, 'Kenny, I was about to say your name during my speech, but I forgot your name.' And that was okay with me because I knew he was thinking about me at some point during his speech, and that was an honor for me. He was very influential in my life, and listening to him tell it, I had some impact in his life, and that makes me feel really, really good. I knew he was very, very proud of me, and that made me feel really good.

In December of 2021, Driesell had a virtual birthday celebration via Zoom with his friends, mostly former players and coaches, as he turned 90 years old. He was the first coach to post more than 100 wins with four different schools, all in NCAA Division I: Davidson, Maryland, James Madison and Georgia State. Brooks was one of his featured guests on the Zoom. The other guests included distinguished folks like Mike Krzyzewski, Billy Packer, John Feinstein, U.S. Congressman and then-House Majority Leader Steny Hoyer, George Raveling, Scott Van Pelt, Albert King, to name several. "They did a Zoom celebration and they had people from all over his past, and just talking about him to him, while he was on the Zoom," said Brooks, who after finishing his talk was followed by Coach K on the Zoom. "I was delegated to represent James Madison."

## Early Coaching Days

Since Brooks played for Driesell, it's no surprise that his coach at James Madison was the one who influenced Brooks the most as far as coaching career is conccrned.

"It was Lefty Driesell, and obviously I had people that I looked up to, but I didn't know them like I knew Coach Driesell, and so he had the biggest impact on me," said Brooks, who began coaching in 1993. "It was always my dream to play professionally, but I think at some point in time, reality sets in, and you know if you're good enough to play professionally or not. I didn't think that I was good enough to play professionally in the NBA, so I told him that I wanted to coach, and my last year, he coached me differently. He taught me how to be a coach, and I watched the game differently, because I always wanted to stay around the game, and so he allowed me to do that.

"He actually was the person who hired me for my very first coaching job, and my interview went like this. He said, 'Kenny,' and I said, 'Yes, sir,' and he said, 'You still want to coach?' I said, 'Yes, sir.' He said, 'Be here Monday.' That was my first coaching interview, but from that point on, he taught me a lot. He taught me just the rigors of coaching, that it wasn't stable, but it taught me how tough it was. He taught me how to develop a work ethic that can be conducive to winning and being a fixture in basketball because it's not very easy. He was a Hall of Fame coach, so I was very fortunate to be able to work for him right out of college."

So Brooks began his coaching career as a part-time assistant for the 1993-94 JMU men's squad that won the CAA Tournament and advanced to the NCAA Tournament. Then, after four seasons as an assistant for the men's program at Virginia Military Institute (1994-98), he moved back to his alma mater as a men's assistant from 1998-2002. In December 2002, he was named interim women's head coach before taking over those duties on a full-time basis in March 2003.

*Kenny Brooks when he was the head coach at James Madison. (JMU Athletics Photography)*

"My start was with Coach Driesell, and I was doing anything and everything," added Brooks. "I might go pick up his lunch one day, I might go pick up his dry cleaning one day, and it had nothing to do with basketball, but it had a lot to do with basketball. It was, if you were willing to sacrifice a lot for a cause that you might not think is going to help, but you still want to be a team player, you have the right mind set to be a coach. Ironically, I wanted to be a women's basketball coach, but all of my contacts were on the men's side, and so when I got the opportunity to coach, I was on the men's side, but I always had an eye on the women's side, and that was because I loved the way the women's game was played. I loved the camaraderie, and I loved the direction that it was going in.

"That was due to the fact that when I was at James Madison as a player, our women's team was really, really good, and I loved watching their practices. I just felt like it was basketball in its purest form, and it was a huge impact on me. For me, unfortunately, my ties, all of my contacts were on the men's side, so I was on the men's side for 10 years, because (I was) trying to make my way, climbing up the ladder to become a head coach, and then I got an opportunity to switch to the women's side and I took it.

"And to the dismay of my mother, she did not want me to do it. She wanted me to be a head coach on the men's side. She said she didn't like women's basketball as much as men's basketball, and I had an opportunity. I turned it down, and then the same opportunity arose two years later and I just talked to my wife. I didn't talk to my mom, and I decided to make that jump. Then, I've been on the women's side for the last 24 years."

## Mars vs. Venus

How different is coaching between the men's and women's teams?

"Well, what's the book? *Men are from Mars*, and *Women are from Venus*? It's very different," said Brooks. "It's very different, but yet the same, and it's kind of like raising children. If you have a son and you have a daughter, you raise them the same, but you raise them differently. You have to get in and you have to really understand the differences. To try to understand the differences from the outside is very difficult, but if you're on the inside, the best way I can relate to it is if you have a son and you have a daughter. You love them both the same. You raise them with the same morals and values, but you raise them a little bit differently because they're boys and they're girls.

"For me, it was an easy transition. I call it my little omens. I kept having daughters, and so it was just a really easy transition for me. I've often said that I don't know if being a father of three daughters has made me a pretty good women's basketball coach or being a women's basketball coach has made me a pretty good father of three daughters, but either way, they go hand in hand, and it's something that I cherish, the opportunity that I do have. I consider myself a women's basketball coach just because I love the women's basketball game, and I'm glad that I've been able to have some sort of impact on the game and helping the game grow. I'm very proud of that growth.

"Again, being a father of three daughters, you just want your children, whether they're boys or girls, to have every opportunity. As a coach of women, I want the same for them. They work hard; they work very hard. They work as hard or harder than their counterparts, and they deserve the same recognition and for it, too. It's not even, and I don't know if it'll ever be even in my lifetime, but you can see the gap is closing a little bit, and you just need to put eyeballs on the sport. If people are open-minded and they come and watch it, you'll have a very good time.

"Now, it's just like any other sport. All women's basketball is not great, but all men's basketball is not great. There's some bad teams out there too, but if you find the right women's basketball team that you want to support, you can really enjoy the games. It just takes an open mind, and when people are open-minded and they allow themselves to go to the games and look at it for what it is, you can really, really enjoy it."

In 2024, women's basketball made history as it was the first time the NCAA women's championship game, featuring Iowa and superstar Caitlin Clark vs. powerhouse South Carolina, had outdrawn the men's title game. The women's showdown posted an average of 18.7 million television viewers while peaking at 24 million viewers. As for men's title game between UConn and Purdue, it drew an average of 14.82 million viewers.

After many years of coaching on the women's side, would Brooks be interested coaching the men's team if the opportunity arises?

"I've had overtures where people have asked me if I was interested," he said. "They wanted me to be their coach on the men's side, but like I said before, I consider myself a women's basketball coach, and I have no interest in switching back over to the men's side, unless the Lakers call. If the Lakers call, then I'm like, 'Yeah,' but I don't think they're calling. I'm very happy on the women's side and very happy to have been a part of the growth, the boom of women's basketball. I got to see it first hand when we went to the Final Four in 2023, and that was the most watched Final Four ever, and proud to have been a part of that. I will watch the men's game, some, not a lot, but I consider myself a women's basketball coach and have no desire to go and coach on the men's side."

## On Three Daughters Playing Basketball

Over a period of time, Brooks' three daughters — Kendyl, Chloe and Gabby — have played or practiced for Virginia Tech with the youngest one, Gabby, also following him to Kentucky after redshirting during her freshman year at VT. In her first year at Kentucky, Gabby, a 5-foot-10 guard, saw brief action in four games. As the Big Blue Nation will recall, the Wildcats had men's teams with starters like Sean Sutton and Saul Smith who played for their dads — coaches Eddie Sutton and Tubby Smith. The youngsters, for the most part, were unfairly criticized for their play even through no fault of their own.

Brooks was asked if he has had any concerns about possible favoritism as seen among the fan base in regard to playing his daughter on his team.

"The lazy narrative is that you will show favoritism to your daughters," he said. "I don't need to show favoritism to my daughters by putting them on the floor so that they will love me. Regardless if they play two minutes or 42 minutes, when we go home, they're going to love me, and so I don't have to have that affection from them just because I played them. What I do is, I am very competitive and I want to win, so I will put the best players on the floor regardless of what their last names are. It can be Brooks or it could be something else, and if they're the best player and I feel like they're giving me the best chance to win, I will play that person.

"What I've had to do, and again, this is the influence by Coach Driesell. He taught me how to incorporate the two. He taught me how to be fair to all sides, and the one thing that I had to learn is how to be fair. I had to learn how to be fair to my daughters because there were several times where they would play extremely well, but I didn't want to look like I was showing favoritism, so that maybe I wouldn't congratulate them. I remember one of my assistant coaches pulled me to the side and they said, 'You need to be fair to her because she's doing well, and you have to congratulate her just like you would any other player.' That stuck with me. It stuck with me big time.

"I had one of my daughters (who) made seven three-pointers in a game against Boston College, and I remember the referee running over to me. He covered his whistle and he said, 'She must get that from her mother.' I laughed, because I was just really so engulfed in the coaching aspect of what was going on that I forgot 'Hey, I'm a proud dad' in that moment, too. Having my daughters around, there's been backlash. There are people who have no fight in the game and they still say it, but that's just the way that this world is now with social media. Everyone wants to try to tear everyone down, but I think it's strengthened me and my family, and my relationship with my family because having my daughters around has really benefited my programs. It has given that family value to the program. It humanizes me because one of the things that I never did was I never made my daughters call me Coach.

"I remember the very first time I was coaching one of my daughters. She came to me and she said 'Dad' and the staff member said, 'That's not Dad right now, that's Coach.' I quickly corrected him and I said, 'The most important title that I'll have in my life, which I'll never relinquish, is Dad. I don't care where we are. I am her dad.' He just had this funny look on his face, and from that point on, no one ever questioned it. I think it humanizes me. It humanizes me because my players can see me as Coach, but they also can see me as Dad. So it's not so regimented. They don't fear me. They come over to my house and sit on my couches because of my daughters. They can be watching *The Bachelor*, they can be making cookies, and that's a comfort level that they develop because a lot of it's my daughters. They're teammates.

"Where some people will try to find fault in it, we've found a lot of good in it, and I think it's been a big part of our success. You just have to drown out the noise. You really do because you're never going to please everyone, and people are always going to find something to be upset with. It's the easy target to go after the daughters, but it's never gotten in the way of our success because I have a strong enough relationship with my daughters that I don't have to play them. I am the coach. I've had my career. I don't have to live vicariously through my daughters to feel good about myself. They are learning a lot. They've learned how to handle adversity. They've learned how to deal with people saying bad things about them, whether it's warranted or not, and that's something that we will value.

"I would not change the opportunity to coach my daughters. It has really shaped my life. It's given me bonus time, because very early in my career, I missed out on so much of what they did because I was so busy trying to build a life that I wasn't living a life. Now I get to live that life with them, and it's something that I don't care who wants to try to discredit it. It's been probably the biggest joy of my coaching career."

## Evolution of Coaching

Over the years, the coaching profession has changed a lot and Brooks agrees. "I think the evolution of coaching has changed," he said. "When I played, 'You do as I say.' We used to grow up and you would question your parents? 'Why do I have to do that?' They would say 'because I said so.'

"I think we're getting into the day and age where kids want to know why, and their expectation is to get an explanation of why. You have to evolve with the generation, and you can't just stay one way. Then you become a dinosaur, and we all know what happened to dinosaurs. They were extinct, so you have to learn how to adapt. Now, I don't give them carte blanche. I don't give them full say, but I think when you have players like Georgia

Amoore and you've developed a very strong relationship with them, that it becomes a little give and take.

"It becomes more of a conversation, when you're talking about schemes, and you value their input because you trust them, and you've been with them for a while and you've developed a relationship, and then it becomes a partnership. It really has to evolve over time, and if that happens, then I'm more than willing to listen because the only person who invented the game was Dr. James Naismith. I'm still learning as much as I can, and this year in particular. I learned a lot from Georgia, just having her in my meetings, because I can coach the game from the sidelines but she's actually on the floor. She understands the feel and what's happening on the floor. If she can articulate it to me, then it's going to help me, and that's a relationship that I will value forever."

## Kim Mulkey

In recent years, LSU coach Kim Mulkey, a member of Naismith Basketball Hall of Fame, and Brooks have faced each other several times and they respect each other.

"Kenny was at James Madison and nobody ever wanted to play him because he was that good a coach and just really did wonderful things there," recalled Mulkey. "I think the world of Coach Brooks. I think he's just a classy guy, a great coach."

Said Brooks, "I love the way she goes about her business. She's a little bit more fiery than I am and her clothes are a little bit louder than mine, but we still are old-school basketball coaches. The way she gets after her kids, I just love watching her perform. We've exchanged pleasantries on the recruiting trail. She's someone that I admire. She's a legend in this game, and it's going to be a lot of fun going against her again."

*Kentucky high school hoops legend and former UK standout
Geri Grigsby, who was Kentucky's Miss Basketball in 1977,
and Kenny Brooks after his introductory press conference at
UK.  (Photo by Jamie H. Vaught)*

## Advice for Aspiring Coach

During the postgame press conference at the 2023 NCAA Final
Four in Dallas, Brooks, then at Virginia Tech, was pleased to
share his coaching career path when a reporter asked how can

an aspiring coach of color look at his story and draw inspiration from it.

"You can work hard. You can be where your feet are because I didn't just get here overnight," said Brooks. "I've been doing this my whole life. I started coaching when I was 23 years old, 24 years old. I had to go pick up Lefty's laundry. I had to go pick up his No. 7 from Wendy's. I had to drive him to Charlotte, North Carolina. I had to answer his phone calls at 12:00 at night to do something, and it's never easy.

"For anyone who ever asks me, I always tell them, don't try to emulate my path because my path is my path. Your journey is your journey. You can take bits and pieces, but the best piece of advice I can tell you is be where your feet are. You've got to do a phenomenal job everywhere you are so that you can move and you can get an opportunity. You can't just say, 'Well, I've been here 10 years, I should get my opportunity.' No, you've got to work. You've got to work hard. If you're somewhere and you're thinking about something else, you're not going to do a good job where you are.

"So I hope — and I'll continue to talk — that my experience and what we've done and where we've gotten our program to, I hope it opens many doors because there are a lot of people who look like me who deserve an opportunity who I think will do a tremendous job. I don't think that we're just recruiters. I don't think that we're just workout guys. I don't think that we're just good assistants. I see a lot of young minds, and a lot of them are assistant coaches, who I think that's all we need is an opportunity. We're not perfect. Just because I say someone is good, yeah, they've got to go prove themselves. They're not going to be a great coach because they're a coach of color. Everyone has to work and work hard.

"I love sharing my experiences, and even though my path is my path, my journey is my journey, maybe people can take bits and pieces of it and try to help their journey."

## Andy Griffith

During the interview at the Joe Craft Center on UK campus, the author informed Brooks that former UK coach Tubby Smith liked to watch the History Channel, and also mentioned that Coach Smith is one of the author's favorite people in sports.

"Well, he's one of my favorite coaches, and growing up, there weren't very many people who looked like me that were coaching, and he was one," said Brooks of Smith. "Him and Coach (John) Thompson from Georgetown, so those are people that I watched. If I was clicking the channels and Tubby Smith was on, I would watch just because he was someone that I wanted to emulate as far as being a coach. 'If Coach Smith can be the head coach at Kentucky, then maybe I can be a head coach, too,' so he's someone that I really admire. He's that special. He's probably a little bit smarter than I am because I don't watch the History Channel.

"I like to watch *The Andy Griffith Show*. I like to watch shows that are nostalgic to me, taking me back to a time that was a simpler time. I like to watch shows that really take my mind off of a lot, and just takes me back to a time when I remember growing up. My daughter will refer to *The Andy Griffith Show*, because I watch it in here every day. Comes on every day at 4:00 (on TV Land), and I watch it, and it'll be background noise for me. I've seen every episode, and my daughter, when she talks about *The Andy Griffith Show*, she just starts whistling the song. You know that show? She'll start singing that, but that's what I like to do.

"It's my comfort show. I can tell you what Barney Fife is going to say before he says it. I take pride in that." Brooks also enjoys *Sanford and Son*.

Speaking of Smith, Brooks finally got to meet the former Wildcat boss during the summer of 2025. It was definitely a special meeting for Brooks.

Brooks also plays some golf. "I can swing it pretty good, but I'm not a big golfer," he said. "I like to relax at home and talk with my family or just kind of unwind because there's so much stresses in my day-to-day job. I'm not a coach that kind of wants to go out and seek attention. You'll see me out eating, doing things of that nature, but I'd rather be at home than to be out in public, just because it's my only time to just really unwind."

## On Meeting His Future Wife

Indirectly through former NBA star and three-time national college player of the year Ralph Sampson whose hometown is Harrisonburg, Brooks met his future wife, Chrissy Stewart, when they were students at James Madison in Harrisonburg. She studied education at JMU, while her boyfriend took business classes. Later, she taught at public schools in Virginia.

"She was actually taking a break from college, so she worked at a local retail store when I was in the store buying some batteries for my Walkman," recalled Brooks. "I later learned that as I was about to check out, a friend of hers which is Ralph Sampson's sister, knew that Chrissy had an interest in me so they traded spots. So I had to go up and interact with Chrissy. When I got there, I looked up and she was just looking at me differently and she was smiling. I'm like, 'Why is she smiling at me?' It's probably not a good thing to say, but I didn't have to pay for the batteries, and I got the batteries. I saw her maybe two days later at a local establishment, a bar, and we talked and we connected. We went out on a couple of dates and we dated for a very long time.

"I like to say that she really hung in there because she was very patient with me. Then one thing led to another, and we got married a few years later. We've been married for 27 years. Like I said, we have three daughters, and I have a stepson (Nicholas) with her, and she's been my rock. She's been my biggest fan. She yells at the referees for me, whether I'm right or wrong. So I guess 'til death do us part and she's really my biggest fan."

*Kenny and Chrissy Brooks with their daughters, Gabby and Kendyl, during a pregame ceremony for UK's annual Play4Kay game at Historic Memorial Coliseum. (UK Athletics Photo by Eddie Justice)*

Mrs. Brooks adores history. "I feel like I had the History Channel in my house because my wife was a history teacher, and so I can never beat her when we play *Jeopardy!*" he smiled. "She retired about eight years ago when we went to Virginia Tech, but she loves history. Sometimes when she tells me stuff, it's too much. It's too smart for me."

Chrissy Brooks recently had to deal with a painful medical issue. She was diagnosed with breast cancer while her husband was coaching at Virginia Tech. Fortunately, she has won the battle after undergoing cancer treatments. In mid-February 2025, the Brookses and two of their daughters participated in a pregame ceremony for UK's annual Play4Kay game where the fans were encouraged to wear pink to raise funds and awareness of breast cancer, and the Wildcat players wore white jersey with pink lettering and trim on it.

In the postgame press conference, after UK's 67-49 setback to Texas, an emotional Brooks added more insight about his wife's cancer struggles. "It really puts it into perspective," said the coach. "This last year has been the hardest year of my life, and to watch my wife walk out there, and when they said she rang that bell on May the 24th. It really put things into perspective because she is the strongest person I know and knows that we did not get to this point by ourselves. The power of prayer. She and I kept it to ourselves throughout the basketball season last year.

"When we told people, it was the biggest weight lifted off my shoulders because so many people helped us, and they prayed for us and helped us get through it. Nights like tonight, when you know what you have gone through, and know that you have gotten through it because of other people, and to be able to bring awareness to this nasty disease and that is what (Texas coach) Vic (Schaefer) and I talked about because he has a son who he almost lost (due to traumatic brain injury many years ago), and nights like tonight really puts things into perspective that you cannot do things by yourself and you have so many great people that are helping you. The University of Kentucky has been great to me. I love when people come up to me before they even ask me anything about basketball, they will ask me how my wife is doing and that means everything, because family means everything. Tonight was special."

Brooks later pointed out his family support is critical. He said his wife, Chrissy, is "the biggest fan that I have. My daughters are the biggest fans that I have. This is an opportunity for me to be able to give some of that time back that I missed when I was a young coach. I felt like I was so busy making a life, I wasn't living a life. And I get an opportunity now to just get bonus time. They're so positive, just such a positive influence on my program.

"Gabby played four games, but she's the life of the party in the locker room. She helps humanize me. The girls would go to her and say, 'Well, is he mad?' And she can interpret all that. She can tell them what's going on. That's really what helped our locker room, other than Georgia (Amoore) knowing me. Kendyl is a big supporter. They're basketball fans, and they have basketball minds, and they're there for the kids. You can't forget Chloe. Chloe is in France. Chloe stays up — I don't know what time it is now — but she watches every one of our games. She calls me, and she'll ask me. She'll preface it and say this is a coaching question or this is a dad question. She'll say, 'Why did you do this? Why did you do that?' But it's just the support. I couldn't do it without them, and I wouldn't want to do it without them because it gives us the opportunity to make this program a family."

## Mark Pope's Introductory Press Conference

What was Brooks' reaction when he learned 20,000 fans had come to Rupp Arena to watch UK introduce its new men's coach at a press conference?

"To be very honest with you, I wasn't really around," said Brooks. "I did see the pictures, and it was impressive. We were here, and we were so engulfed and trying to put our roster together that I didn't even go to the press conference. I think we had a visit, but then when I saw the pictures and saw that it was 20,000 plus, I think everything that I thought about Kentucky came true. I'm like, 'Okay, well, these people are fans,' and to be able to come out and support a press conference, just to introduce the coach. It just showed me that the Big Blue Nation is special. It was very eye-opening. I just didn't get to experience it firsthand."

Smiled Brooks when he spoke at the 2024 SEC Tipoff Media Days, "When I got to Kentucky, (John) Calipari was there. Cal stayed for a week. I told everybody that the talent wasn't big enough for the both of us, so I ran him out."

Brooks said Pope has given his program "an infusion of energy in itself. That's what he is. We've been kind of feeding off each other with that. It's really caused a lot of excitement (around Kentucky).  It's been a blessing to be able to be a part of the excitement. A little pressure because you want to make sure you do your part, but you want those type of situations."

## Memorable First Season at Kentucky

Brooks' first season as the Wildcat boss with a final national ranking at No. 16 was considered a huge success as UK had its first 20-win season since the 2019-20 campaign when then-coach Matthew Mitchell's squad compiled a 22-8 mark.  The 2024-25 edition posted an overall mark of 23-8, including 11-5 in SEC, with five victories over Top 25 teams.

"We were one floater away from going to the Sweet 16," said Brooks moments after Kentucky dropped to Kansas State 80-79 in overtime in a heartbreaking NCAA tourney loss. "But more importantly, we built a foundation. It's been a terrific year. I love Lexington. I love what Big Blue Nation is willing to put into or pour into women's sports. It was a lot of fun."

*All-American Georgia Amoore and Kenny Brooks
discuss during a 2025 game at Historic Memorial
Coliseum. (Photo by Jamie H. Vaught)*

However, about a week later after the season ended, Brooks faced a mild controversy when Pike County native and backup junior guard Cassidy Rowe was told she did not have a roster spot for the upcoming season of 2025-26. Many fans, especially from eastern Kentucky, were emotionally upset the 5-foot-5 Rowe, who had plans to attend UK's Doctor of Physical Therapy program, wouldn't be returning to the team. As the program's head coach, Brooks said he understood that he has to make tough decisions and not everyone is going to be happy. The team's only Kentuckian, Rowe saw action in 67 games, averaging 1.7 points and 0.9 assists, while starting 16 games as a sophomore during her three-year Wildcat career. Brooks also added if any of his former players, including Rowe, called him for help or advice, he wouldn't hesitate. He thanked them for their contributions.

Named the National Coach of the Year by the *Sporting News*, Brooks shared his best and worst moments of the 2024-25 campaign with the author after hitting the ground from scratch in spring of 2024, recruiting 11 players, and hiring 11 coaches and staffers.

"Wow! Our best moment? I have probably three I can think right off," Brooks said. "We beat Louisville (in overtime in mid-November), I think, for the first time in eight or nine years. Obviously, playing in the ACC, we battle with Louisville in my tenure there (at Virginia Tech), but I didn't understand the rivalry when I got here. To me, it was just Louisville.  So when we played the game, the importance of playing and beating Louisville, I didn't understand it until that moment. The next (moment) was Tennessee. Again when I was at Virginia Tech, we played Tennessee and we had success against them, so I didn't understand the rivalry of Kentucky and Tennessee until we were about to play, and we beat them pretty handily (82-58). That was very important, too, and then the third (highlight) is when we had the (NCAA) Selection Show and we made the NCAA Tournament. We were hosting (during) a year which a lot of people considered would be a rebuild.

"(The) other one that you can add to the plus list was watching (sophomore) Clara Strack grow and develop into the SEC Defensive Player of the Year and become all-conference at such an early stage in her career.

"Then add one more to that is when Georgia (Amoore) got drafted. That was a special moment. That was a long time coming. It was five years in the making. She took a blind leap of faith to follow me here (from Virginia Tech), and she followed me here with her dreams in tow. We were able to capture those dreams all the while building a foundation and making Kentucky women's basketball relevant again. So that really put Kentucky back on the map. I was very excited about that.

"Probably, the worst moments (were) we had two young ladies that felt like were going to be major contributors for us this year, and they got hurt last summer. Just watching that situation be put on hold was difficult, and then the other moment was when Georgia had a last-second shot that could have sent us to the Sweet 16. It's a shot that she can make in her sleep, and it just ended up coming off and I have no idea how it didn't go in, but that was a tough moment."

On Brooks being named the National Coach of the Year, Amoore said, "I've been with this man for five years. I think what he's done has been phenomenal. People really don't realize how much he does. I think it's one thing to see how he coaches on the court, the wins and the runs that we've made, but I don't know anyone that does player development the way that he does. We go down to the minuscule of details. He covers all aspects. He teaches us so many off-court lessons as well as on-court. He bet on himself to come here and, within a year, completely turn it around and be competitive, be in a position where Kentucky is back in consideration for top recruits. We're ranked high again. He did that recruiting 11 new girls — girls he's never coached before. And someone like Clara (Strack) who didn't really play much last year. He coached her and his ability to create greatness out of what he has is something that's like truly amazing."

Added graduate guard Dazia Lawrence, "That's something I would never take for granted. He's more than deserving. His development, his coaching, his life lessons that we will take for the rest of our lives is something that a lot of coaches don't do for their players."

# 11

# Italian Magician

## (Rick Pitino)

*(This is a reprint of a chapter about then-Kentucky basketball coach Rick Pitino which appeared in a 1991 book, titled "Crazy About the Cats: From Rupp to Pitino." The 45-minute interview with Pitino took place at his Memorial Coliseum office in 1990 as he prepared for his second season at UK. Since the book was published nearly 35 years ago ago, it's determined a new or younger generation of Big Blue Nation fans would enjoy reading about Pitino while he was coaching at Kentucky. At the time, the Wildcats were still ineligible for postseason tournaments in 1991 due to NCAA sanctions from the Eddie Sutton era.*

*After guiding Kentucky to three Final Four trips, including the 1996 national championship, Pitino left UK in 1997 for the famed Boston Celtics, one of NBA's most glamorous teams. Now a member of the Naismith Basketball Hall of Fame, Pitino, at this writing, is the head coach at St. John's after stops at Louisville and Iona.)*

Kentuckians treat boyish-looking coach Rick Pitino as if he was some Hollywood movie star. In accepting his role, he realizes the exposure — although sometimes irritating — comes with the territory of being the head coach at a very public place like Kentucky. Yet, he enjoys the spotlight. During his first two years at probation-ridden Kentucky, Pitino, labeled as the program's savior, has already appeared as the "cover boy" of several national sports publications, including *The Sporting News.* And it wouldn't be surprising to see him enter the television broadcasting field some day when he quits coaching. With his good looks and personality, the TV job is his if he wants it.

"I think that one thing you can't do in life is look ahead and want for something else," said Pitino, who received good reviews for his brief TV studio role as a basketball analyst on ESPN during the 1991 post-season tournament action. "If you want for something else, you are tired of what you are doing. I am not tired of coaching. I love coaching. I love dealing with young people. I want to enjoy what I am doing now. I just want to concentrate on what I am doing now.

"I have done quite a bit of TV work. I had my own TV show in New York, commenting on the NBA playoffs, and had a lot of coaches shows. I hosted a show for the (NCAA) Final Four out in Denver (in 1990). I have been on the David Letterman show and some talk shows."

Pitino says he admires outspoken Dick Vitale, the colorful TV analyst, for saying what he thinks and for creating enthusiasm in the game of basketball. "There are two ways of looking at Vitale," he commented. "You can admire him for what he has accomplished as an ex-coach or you can be jealous of him and say he speaks too much. I kind of admire him for what he has accomplished."

Pitino, asked if he ever gets upset over Vitale's comments, replied, "No, because you can't throw stones when you make mistakes yourself. There are comments I wish I had not made, but any time you make comments you are going to say things that don't always come out right. You have to respect him not for the bad comments but all the good ones he made."

Both Pitino and Vitale are Italians. They first met in the 1970s when Vitale, then the head coach at the University of Detroit, spoke at a prestigious basketball camp where Pitino was working. In Pitino's second year at Kentucky, Vitale covered the UK-Indiana game at Bloomington for ESPN. The matchup between Pitino and coach Bobby Knight of Indiana intrigued Vitale so much that he said it matched the nation's best young coach against the nation's best veteran coach.

*Kentucky coach Mark Pope and his former UK mentor, Rick Pitino of St. John's, smile during a preseason practice at Joe Craft Center in 2024. On the previous night, an emotional Pitino had made a surprise visit to the Big Blue Madness at Rupp Arena. (UK Athletics Photo)*

## Leaving NYC for Bluegrass

June 1, 1989 marked a new beginning — actually a rebirth — of
Kentucky Wildcat basketball. It was the historic day that UK lured
Pitino away from the bright lights of New York City. The successful Italian had been the head coach of NBA's New York Knicks
for two years. Pitino, who was hired to coach the scar-marred
Wildcats and to restore Kentuckians' pride in UK's roundball
program, became the youngest mentor in the SEC at the age of
36.

Just several days earlier, the NCAA almost hammered Kentucky
with a death penalty for breaking several NCAA rules. Instead, the
Wildcats were hit with with a severe three-year penalty, which
included no live television and two years of no post-season tournament play.

Pitino's highly-publicized arrival in Lexington gave the Wildcat
faithful high hopes that the school's basketball program could
soon return to its age-old status as a national contender. He was
the man the fans had sought to take over the Wildcat helm, vacat-
ed by the departure of Eddie Sutton. Kentucky athletics director
C.M. Newton indicated that if Pitino or someone of similar stature
had not accepted his offer, he would have coached the team
himself until a suitable replacement could be found.

Pitino primarily came to the Bluegrass for three reasons. One,
he loved the challenge of rebuilding a program. Second, he wanted to return to coaching in the college ranks. Third, he wanted an
ideal place to raise his family. And not to mention that Kentucky
has a long tradition-rich history of successful basketball.

"I came to Kentucky because it was right for my family and I am
happy about that," Pitino said.

However, Pitino's wife, Joanne, wasn't too crazy about moving
to Lexington. Not that she didn't like Kentucky's second-largest

city, she just hated to uproot her family again as they had previously moved several times because of her husband's rising coaching career. "She was unhappy about moving, whether it be Florida, Hawaii or wherever because we had moved too much," explained Pitino, who now has four sons. As a family, they made the decision to move to Kentucky. "I was not overly happy and excited with the lifestyle I was leading," Pitino admitted. "I wanted to make a change at this point." Also, Pitino did not enjoy a good working relationship with his boss while at New York. He had some philosophical differences with then-Knicks general manager Al Bianchi.

Pitino didn't come cheap, as he was doing well financially in New York. In addition to outside income, Pitino's salary with the Knicks was reported to be in the $425,000 range. His seven-year pact with UK calls for annual base salary which began at $105,000 with periodic raises. (By comparison, coach Adolph Rupp's last coaching salary was $29,000.) Pitino's outside income coming from various sources such as commercial endorsements and TV/radio shows would push his total income to nearly $1 million. During his first year at Kentucky, Pitino's total income was estimated to be around $800,000. Pitino, however, later said the move to Lexington from New York had cost him a lot financially.

"You make good money in coaching. When you are in the professional limelight, you deserve the money but you give it away to charities and people expect that," said the coach from his refurbished Memorial Coliseum office on the UK campus. "This was a bad move for me economically, and I don't care about that because I enjoy basketball so much but I lost my life savings on my move from New York. It was not a good financial move to come here. People say you will make it back. We'll never make it back. Every time you move, you have to purchase a home and put new things into the home but that is OK with me because I enjoy the place (UK) basketball-wise and that is the only important thing."

## Surprising Seasons

Weeks before Kentucky's 1989-90 season opener with Ohio at
Rupp Arena, the doomsayers predicted the Wildcats would be
very lucky to win perhaps eight games out of a 28-game schedule.
The Wildcats only had eight scholarship players on the squad and
none of them were taller than 6-foot-7. Key players such as Chris
Mills, LeRon Ellis and Sean Sutton had left the campus. Short of
experienced players, the Wildcats only had two proven players in
6-foot-5 senior Derrick Miller and 6-foot-8 junior Reggie Hanson.

Unlike the past, interest in the program had dropped consider-
ably. But still there was plenty of faithful support for the Wildcats
and their new mentor. Kentuckians prepared for a long winter.

As the season progressed, the Wildcat players and the fans
alike started to catch Pitino's fever — his running game, his
three-point offensive bombs, his pressing defense, his work ethic, his optimism, his blazing personality. The Wildcats stunned
observers as they won five of their first seven games with hustle
and heart. Everybody was shaking their heads in wonderment. A
*Sports Illustrated's* article about Kentucky's new beginning with
Pitino was appropriately titled, "The Bluegrass Isn't So Blue." The
Wildcats were on the road to recovery. Pitino had just given the
program a shot in the arm. Interest in Wildcat basketball grew.
Everybody was having fun.

Meanwhile, at Pitino's suggestion, his post-game radio show
with legendary announcer Cawood Ledford was moved to the
courtside of the Rupp Arena floor so the spectators could hear
and see him in the show. Expecting only a small group of faithful supporters to stay around after the Mississippi State game
on Dec. 4, Pitino was stunned when 5,000 showed up for the
radio show. Attendance for the show grew and the radio pro-

gram ended up attracting a season-average of more than 13,000, which by the way, would have ranked 24th nationally in GAME attendance in 1989-90. Moments after UK's last home game of the season with Auburn, Pitino conducted the team's post-season awards ceremony on the radio show with an appreciative crowd of over 20,000 looking on. Describing the event, Pitino jokingly remarked that it was the world's largest awards banquet.

Although there were some rough times, Kentucky nevertheless finished the season on a high note with a remarkable 14-14 record. And the Wildcats even surprised LSU coach Dale Brown and his ninth-ranked Tigers with an exciting 100-95 victory before a then-record Rupp Arena crowd. In SEC action, Kentucky placed fourth with a 10-8 record.

Pitino said he wasn't all that amazed his first Kentucky edition, popularly known as Pitino's Bombinos, was able to finish with a break-even record. "I wasn't surprised," he said. "I thought we would win and I was very pleased with the effort that was put out, so it was a pleasant surprise if anything."

After the NCAA hit Kentucky with sanctions, the school had difficulty in finding a proven coach who was acceptable to UK officials. But they found and grabbed Pitino away from the big city lights, surprising many observers. "To say that I was ecstatic when we hired Rick Pitino was an understatement," said former UK player Bret Bearup. "We couldn't have hired anybody better. I mean, people talked about (NBA coach) Pat Riley, this and that. Pat Riley wouldn't have come in and had the impact that Pitino has. (Georgetown coach) John Thompson and (North Carolina coach) Dean Smith wouldn't have. Nobody would have. It's Rick Pitino. It's him. His style of basketball is fun. It's entertaining. It's fun to talk about. It's fun to watch. He brought magic back to where it should be."

For his miraculous efforts, Pitino received a couple of individual honors in 1990 as he was named the national Coach of the Year by the *Basketball Times* and SEC Coach of the Year by the UPI. Two

Wildcat players also won regional awards as Hanson and Miller received All-SEC recognition. Not to be forgotten were the team's other key contributors, such as sophomores Deron Feldhaus, John Pelphrey, Sean Woods and Richie Farmer, as well as freshman Jeff Brassow. There were others who did not see a lot of action, but they sweated it out in grueling practices. That group included Johnathon Davis, Junior Braddy, Tony Cooper, Skip McGaw and Michael Parks.

This young, three-point shooting team will always be remembered. Playing against incredible odds, the Wildcats were amazing. Even the critics had to agree. And the following season — 1990-91 — saw a much-improved Wildcat squad on the court. Far better than anyone, including Pitino, had anticipated. Finishing with a 22-6 mark and a No. 9 national ranking against a tough schedule, Kentucky once again had become a powerhouse like in its old, glorious days. Although they were ineligible for the SEC regular season championship, the Wildcats, indeed, were the No. 1 team in the SEC as they posted the league's best record with 14-4. Needless to say, it was a fun season.

"A championship is won and lost on the basketball court, and no matter what anyone thinks or what anyone says, we won this (SEC) championship," said Pitino moments after the Wildcats whipped Auburn 114-93 in a regular season finale before a record-breaking Rupp Arena crowd of 24,310. "We had one of the toughest schedules in the nation, and when you come in and play as hard as this team plays, you deserve a championship season."

For the first time since Kentucky's 1977-78 NCAA championship squad, UK had five players who finished the season averaging double figures. Hanson and Pelphrey paced the Wildcat attack with 14.4 points each.

Pitino and his three Wildcats captured individual SEC honors. While Pitino was named Associated Press SEC Coach of the Year, Hanson, Pelphrey and freshman Jamal Mashburn were chosen to

AP's All-SEC second and third teams. In addition, *The Sporting News* selected Pitino as its 1991 national Coach of the Year.

On senior Hanson, Pitino said, "I think I will miss him more than anyone I've ever coached." To show appreciation of what Hanson has meant to Pitino and the Wildcat program while re-covering from Kentucky's ugly scandal, the coach created the "Reggie Hanson Sacrifice Award," to be given annually to a player who makes great personal sacrifice for the sake of the team. The first winner of the new Hanson award went to Feldhaus in 1991. Hanson, a product of Pulaski County High School in Somerset, Ky., completed his UK career with 1,167 points, placing him 27th on the all-time Wildcat scoring chart, behind No. 26 Bill Spivey's 1,213 points.

## Joe B. Hall

During his initial season at Kentucky, Pitino said he didn't seek advice from ex-coach Joe B. Hall about the program. Although they met each other several times in social surroundings, they only once had a serious discussion. It regarded the Joe B. Hall Wildcat Lodge, which primarily houses the basketball players. When Pitino was hired, he had expressed some reservations about the so-called basketball dormitory, which he said "is not a very pretty place. It's run down because of all the things they had to do (in accordance with the NCAA rules several years ago)." He wanted the players to live like regular students. And he even talked about converting the lodge into a weight room.

On his infrequent meetings with Hall about the situation, Pitino explained, "I kind of wanted to develop my own feel of the pro-gram rather than have any preconceived notions of what it was all about. I wanted to establish feelings of my own. Joe felt it (the lodge) was a positive influence. David Roselle, the president, felt it was a negative. In fact, it was a positive. Because now under the jurisdiction of (UK) housing, it is considered a dormitory rather than an athletic lodge. So, now other students live in there. They are monitored by housing. They are under the same guidelines as other dormitories on campus."

Pitino first became aware of the stature of the Wildcat program in the late 1970s when he worked at a basketball camp for Hall on the UK campus. At that time, he was the young head coach at Boston University.

"About 12 years ago, I did a clinic for Joe B. Hall and I got to tour a little bit and understand what Kentucky basketball was all about," recalled Pitino, who later guided Providence College to the Final Four in 1987. "I think in the other places that I lived there were other avenues of interest. There were professional teams. In New York, there were the Giants, the Jets, the Yankees, the Mets, the Rangers and the Devils. In Providence, (R.I.), there were the Red Sox, the Celtics and some New York fans as well, so there were other interests. Here it is more focused on Kentucky basketball. I think there is not as much diversity here, so it makes the concentration level for one program that much better."

So while he was coaching elsewhere, Pitino had to share the media spotlight with other coaches and teams from various sports. But that's not the case in Kentucky where Pitino dominates the news. In the eyes of Kentuckians, he's the top-dog. "I don't mind sharing," said Pitino of his New York days. "I really don't pay too much attention to the fanfare. I try to just focus in on what we are trying to do and the program so really the spotlight is not that important. After a while, it becomes secondary."

However, with Pitino virtually being the sole spotlight in the state, it at first created some hardships for his wife and their sons. They had to adjust to the glare of enormous public attention. "It was more so (of an adjustment) for my family than it was for me," said the coach. "I had a pretty easy adjustment because I am around my job so much. I didn't notice it as much as my wife and family, but now everyone is used to it and have adjusted. Like anything else, you try to make the good as big as the sky and the bad as small as a pea."

One noticeable difference Pitino has found in Lexington is that the Kentucky sportswriters aren't as tough as the ones he faced in New York City. "It is like asking the difference between Atilla the Hun and Mary Poppins," he said. "It is quite different. You are more of a target and there is not as much reverence paid to a New York coach. There you are an open target for anything at anytime. I think the people (in Kentucky) focus more on the team than the individual itself. There is nothing in life more difficult than the New York media. I am not saying that Kentucky is easy. It is just that there is only one major newspaper here (in Lexington). In New York, you have three or four tabloids and seven other newspapers that cover you so any time you have that competition the truth can be stretched a little bit."

## Big Apple

Although Pitino now lives in Lexington, he will always be a New Yorker.

Born on Sept. 18, 1952 in Manhattan, Pitino grew up in Queens. He was the baby of a very close-knit, middle class family with two older brothers. His parents worked extremely hard to support the family. His father, who passed away a few years ago while Pitino was coaching the Knicks, was a truck driver most of his life and he owned a trucking business. Then he became the manager of an industrial building in Manhattan. His mother is a retired nurse.

"Both of my parents grew up in Manhattan," Pitino said, "and both worked over 30 years. They traveled together leaving at 5:30 in the morning and getting home about 6:30 at night so they put in long days. Both were blue-collar workers. We had everything we needed to have. We didn't have much money, but we never starved or wanted for food or clothing. It was a very good family.

Anytime you are from an Italian household, you are very, very close (to your parents)."

Later, when Pitino was a teenager, the family moved to Long Island in Oyster Bay. He attended St. Dominic's High School where he played basketball. He was the captain of the roundball squad and broke several scoring records.

*Then-Louisville coach Rick Pitino jokes with assistant Wayne Turner before a UK-U of L matchup at Rupp Arena in 2013. Turner is a former Wildcat standout who played on the 1996 national championship team. (Photo by Jamie H. Vaught)*

It was during his high school days in the summer between his sophomore and junior year that he met his future wife Joanne Minardi. "I met her while I was playing basketball in the backyard with a group of friends," Pitino said. "We decided to get a bite to eat so we walked to a deli about a mile away and we were throwing a ball with lacrosse sticks. Somebody threw me the ball and it went on her front lawn. She was combing her hair on the steps because she had just come back from the beach. I said hello. I asked my friends who she was. We were having a party that night and I said, 'Why don't you invite her to the party?' and that is how we met."

Pitino said it was not easy to change his New York lifestyle when he moved to the Bluegrass. He still misses the New York life, especially his immediate relatives. "It is difficult just because you miss your family," he said. "One brother still lives in New York. My mother lives in New York. My wife's family still lives in New York, and some of my closest friends live in New York.

"I love the New York sense of humor. New York people are very witty and a lot of fun. They joke around quite a bit. But I think I have enjoyed it as much here with the exception of maybe the all-night diners — a great restaurant that's open 24 hours. I think I miss that aspect.

"People are people wherever you go. Maybe they talk differently in Kentucky. There is good and bad in every place you live and the only thing that is difficult is not acclimating yourself to a new environment. The difficult thing is that you miss your family.

"The pace is much different here (in Kentucky). The lifestyle is much different. You don't stay up as late. There is not as much stress here with traffic. I would like to think I have enjoyed every place I have lived and you adapt to the different lifestyles rather than say one is better than the other. You just adjust and say 'when in Rome do as the Romans,' and that is what I do here in Kentucky."

Pitino, in fact, has added an Italian New York touch to the Bluegrass. Early in the 1990-91 season, he and some 25 investors opened a well-publicized restaurant in downtown Lexington. Called Bravo Pitino, it is modeled after his favorite Italian establishment in New York.

Pitino has a good sense of humor. He frequently jokes with sportswriters at press conferences. He puts on a good show, something that would make Ronald Reagan proud. Describing his outside income, Pitino once jokingly said, "I'm going to be making about $11 million a year." At another press conference, on rumors that his wife wasn't happy in Lexington, Pitino quipped that Joanne had run off with a so-called wealthy New Yorker by the name of Donald Trump.

During an intense Kentucky-LSU game in 1990 in Baton Rouge, an angry shouting match between Pitino and LSU mentor Dale Brown nearly erupted into a full-fledged boxing match with their noses only inches apart. Sportswriters later quizzed Pitino if he and Brown had made up. Pitino responded by saying, "I think he's a great guy. He recruited me as a high school player and offered me things....just kidding."

On a serious note, Pitino said he respects "Dale Brown because he has great love and affection for his players and that is what counts. He treats his players so well and I like him."

Asked where he got his humor from, Pitino replied, "I think when you pick out things about different cultures and different places I think New York because there is so much stress in New York that you have to laugh. You have to smile and joke around to get through the day and week and all this stress. If you don't laugh about going one mile in 45 minutes, then it is going to be very difficult to take and that is how you get through it. I think it (humor) comes from friends more than anything else."

After high school, Pitino moved on to the University of Massachusetts in Amherst where he was a point guard in the early 1970s. While a senior, he served as the team captain in the 1973-74 campaign. Then he began his coaching career in Honolulu, Hawaii, where he was a graduate assistant at the University of Hawaii. As many observers would find out, Pitino was *Born to Coach*, a book he would co-author years later while in the NBA.

## Highs and Lows

The year 1987 had both happy and sad times for Pitino. A season he will never forget.

Making their first NCAA tournament appearance since 1978, his Providence College Friars shocked the nation when they went to the Final Four in New Orleans. By employing the press and three-point shooting, they engineered a couple of big upsets over Alabama and Georgetown in the Southeast Regionals. They were the nation's darlings, playing the role of a Cinderella. Pitino's former boss at Syracuse, Jim Boeheim, knocked the Friars out of the national championship picture as the Orangemen won 77-63 in the semifinals. Providence finished with a 25-9 worksheet, and Pitino earned a couple of awards in winning the John Wooden National Coach of the Year and the *Sporting News* Coach of the Year honors.

Pitino later said that was the happiest moment of his life.

During the Final Four hoopla, the sportswriters as well as TV guys found Pitino's life intriguing. Hundreds of newspaper articles and columns about Pitino were written, many of them on the front page. They were human interest material. His one-night honeymoon. His tragic loss of a baby son. Pitino was good copy.

The coach prefers not to talk about the down moments of his life, especially the death of his infant. "From a sad point of view, those are personal things," he explained.

But it is no question that perhaps the worst moment of his life came after Providence had just finished playing in the Big East Conference tournament in New York. En route to Providence on the team bus on a Sunday afternoon, Pitino and his wife learned that their six-month-old son, Daniel Paul, had passed away. A highway patrolman — with his cruiser's flashing lights on — had stopped the northbound bus on I-95 to inform the Pitinos of the disturbing news. Their babysitter had attempted to contact them, but the squad had already departed. (Daniel Paul had suffered a variety of disorders, including a congenital heart ailment, with his mother making daily one-hour trips to a Boston hospital from their Rhode Island home for several months.)

A hour or two later, CBS-TV announced the NCAA tournament bids and Providence received its first NCAA invitation in almost a decade. Normally, this would have called for a big Sunday night party, watching the tournament pairings on television. But there would be no pizza party for the Pitinos.

A few months later, Pitino left Providence for the NBA, despite the fact he had inked a new five-year contract with the Friars. He was named head coach of the struggling New York Knicks, an organization he had previously worked for as an assistant under coach Hubie Brown in 1983-85. It was a move that Pitino later wished he hadn't made.

"The only move that I have ever regretted was in leaving Providence the way I did because I left for the wrong reason," Pitino admitted. "I loved being that coach and it has made me a better coach today, but I left for the wrong reason and that is why I am bothered by it. I left because my ego got in the way. I just felt my ego could not turn down a big job — especially when you were a boy growing up in New York and you were just 10 blocks from Madison Square Garden — and I left Providence because of my ego and not because of what was right for my family."

Asked if the Providence College officials have forgiven him for leaving them, Pitino said, "I think some people appreciate the fact that Providence went from dead last place to the Final Four in two years, and other people feel like they are jilted lovers or it is a divorce. They love you but they divorce you."

## Marriage and Family

Pitino and his wife were married in the summer of 1976 just after he had completed a two-year coaching stint as an assistant at Hawaii. Staying at a New York City hotel, their honeymoon plans abruptly changed on their wedding night. The couple had planned to leave for San Francisco the next day on the way to Hawaii for their honeymoon. But Syracuse's Boeheim somehow contacted Pitino that night and offered him a job to become an assistant coach for the Orangemen. It took some persuading and an increase in salary on Boeheim's part before Pitino finally accepted. And Pitino was off recruiting the next day and the honeymoon had to be postponed. Of course, Joanne wasn't very happy about the timing of her husband's new job. But she reluctantly understood the situation. Boeheim said in 1987 that he didn't think Pitino's wife will ever forgive him for what he did on their wedding night in offering Pitino a job.

On his wife, who does not grant many interviews, Pitino said, "She is a very social person, but she does not like the limelight — sticking out like a coach would. She likes being one of the people, but not the key person. She doesn't feel that is her place."

Like Joanne, Pitino is a social person. "I am a people person," said the coach. "For instance, I would not like living in a rural area on a farm away from people. I enjoy being around a lot of people and having neighbors. I don't mind crowds. If I had a choice of having solitude or being around people, I would choose being around people."

As far as their religion is concerned, the Pitinos are both Catholics. Her late uncle Martin who happened to be a priest married them.

A new member was added to the Pitino family in June of 1990 when Joanne gave birth to Ryan Martin Pitino in a New York

City hospital. The baby boy weighed 6 pounds and 9 ounces. He joins his three older brothers — Michael, Christopher and Richard. Joanne spent the last several weeks of her pregnancy in New York — not in the Bluegrass — because her physician's office was located there, and she had encountered some problems in a previous birth.

However, she was surprised when she learned she was pregnant with Ryan Martin. The Pitinos didn't expect to have any more children. Pitino says that her pregnancy had created some false rumors about her unhappiness in Lexington and their separation.

"The biggest problem was that she had been told she couldn't have any more children, and here she moves to Lexington and she is pregnant at age 38 in a temporary home," said the coach. "We were building a home, and she just took on a lot at one time. The chances of her getting pregnant were very slim and the doctors were very nervous. She had to go to New York to have the baby, but she didn't want to go to New York. She was told to do so. She was only allowed on her feet for one hour per day. She went to New York for three months, and for eight weeks, she was in a hospital bed just trying not to lose this baby while doctors monitored her. People here (in Kentucky) didn't realize this and that she was in the hospital for eight weeks.

"When she had the baby she had to be around her doctors because they were expecting something to go wrong, so she went through one of the toughest pregnancies you could ever go through. After she had the baby, she needed a lot of help because the circumstances weren't normal due to the loss of our last child. I told people that they just started rumors about her leaving me and not coming back.

"One thing I can say is that I have been a very rich person, not in money but in the type of marriage we have had and our family. People don't realize that here and that is something we can't do anything about.

"We kid around about it (her leaving for Donald Trump) because it is so far from the truth. We wouldn't really care about it too much except for the fact that we are going to make Kentucky our home for a long time. It bothers me that people make up things about me. That is the problem with living in a small town.

"We just thanked God that the baby was healthy."

## UK Hoops Tradition

Pitino knows there are a lot of rival coaches who are jealous of Kentucky's rich tradition in basketball. But he philosophically understands that it is an undesirable part of living.

"Jealously is a word that a lot of people have," he said. "Anytime a person can't have something, he either admires that person or he is jealous of that person. There is very little indifference in people, so jealously is a word that is sad. It is a shame that people are jealous.

"But anytime you are at Kentucky, people are going to be jealous because we have the best fans, the best facilities, the best tradition — so it is normal. Other people admire it and try to copy it and those are the people you try to help. You can't worry about the jealous people. That is a part of life."

## SEC and Country Music

Pitino's favorite SEC place other than Lexington is Nashville, the capital of country music. Vanderbilt has the league's largest city in Nashville with approximately 500,000 citizens. Although Pitino enjoys the city atmosphere, Music City is nevertheless a surprising choice because he doesn't care for country music.

"It is not that I don't like country music, it is just that I don't listen to lot of it," Pitino explained. "I very rarely listen to music. I would listen to a talk show, but if I was going to listen to music, it would not be country. It would be Frank Sinatra, Tony Bennett. I would listen to some Motown music but not country western. It is not my cup of tea."

## Pitino in Olympics?

Pitino an Olympic head coach in the future?

Even if he was eligible for the post, Pitino is definitely not interested. Only a mentor with NBA ties is considered for the prestigious job.

"That is one of the things that I have never concerned myself with because, unfortunately, I don't agree with the way we do it today," Pitino said. "I think an Olympic coach should devote all his time to the team. He should not be a college coach and not a pro coach. It should be maybe a coach who is retired and would devote all his time to the Olympics because, if I become an Olympic coach, I know I am going to throw my heart and mind into it every day and I would take away from the Kentucky program or wherever I am at and I don't think that is right. I think they should take an Olympic coach and make it a paying job so someone can concentrate all his efforts on that.

"I think you should concentrate all your efforts to the University of Kentucky. So I have never really concentrated on that (Olympics). My goal is to win the championship for the University of Kentucky and that is the way it is."

# 12

# Pope Brings Hope & Passion

## (Mark Pope)

Here is a trivia quiz on Kentucky basketball.

—*Who is the oldest basketball head coach ever hired by UK since 1930 when 29-year-old Adolph Rupp took the same position?* Not Joe B. Hall, who was 43 when chosen in 1972 for the head coaching job at Kentucky. Not Eddie Sutton, who was 49. Not Rick Pitino, who was 36. Not Tubby Smith, who was 45. Not Billy Gillispie, who was 47. Not John Calipari, who was 50. It's Mark Pope, who was 51 years old when hired in April 2024.

In a July 2025 interview for this book, Pope was shocked to learn that he was the oldest hoops coach hired by the university. "I did not know that. Is that true?" he said. "Wow. Man, it makes me feel old." Asked how he felt about that, Pope added, "First of all, I didn't know that. I think that I've been really blessed to actually have the background I do to walk into this job. I think in some ways I've been blessed to know Kentucky basketball better than anybody else that's taken this job for the first time, because I got to

24

JAMIE H. VAUGHT

be a player and I got to experience everything that Kentucky basketball is, and then I got to see Kentucky basketball from afar and also see it up close. So, I think I have been really blessed in terms of that preparation to come here and coach in Kentucky because coaching at Kentucky is different than coaching anywhere else in basketball; it's just a different job. The assignment is different, the requirements are different, the expectations are different, and so I think it's really been an incredible advantage for me to be familiar with all those things before I got here."

Here are the other two other trivia questions on Pope the fans can also use for a fun discussion.

—*Other than Joe B. Hall, who was the only Wildcat player who later became the head coach at UK during the modern era?* Pope was a member of the school's 1996 national championship team. Hall played one year of varsity basketball in the late 1940s under Rupp.

—*Who would have been the second coach from UK to earn a graduate degree from prestigious Columbia University in New York City had that person completed his medical studies?* The first person was Rupp, who had a master's degree at Columbia. Other than playing or coaching hoops on national championship teams at UK, the duo of Pope and Rupp nearly had something extraordinary in common.

Back in 2006, when I had an email interview with Pope for my syndicated column, I asked him about his possible medical career after retiring from NBA. At the time, he had been accepted into Columbia's College of Physicians and Surgeons and had begun taking classes. Before entering Columbia, two other institutions — Yale and the University of Colorado — also wanted him. While at UK in 1995, he was nominated as one of UK's two Rhodes Scholarship candidates.

"I never considered medicine as an undergrad at UK. It wasn't until midway through my pro career that I really took the possibility seriously," wrote 34-year-old Pope, who was living in New York

City with his family. "My growing interest was really a confluence of several different factors. I had two good friends while I was playing with the (Milwaukee) Bucks. One was a med student and the other was a resident. I loved the stories that they would tell me about their work and they later encouraged me as I began the process.

"I had always loved the work that we did in hospitals through the NBA. I knew that I loved working with people and hearing their stories. I also loved that the work was all about helping people. Unbelievably cliche? I know, but true nonetheless. In the NBA, I spent 90 percent of my time working on my very limited game and 10 percent of my time working in the community. That 10 percent was the good stuff.

"I'm confident that medicine will flip-flop those percentages so that most of my time will be focused on the good stuff. The heart of medicine is service. The work is personal, intimate and important."

After his NBA career, Pope knew he would need a challenge in his life. "I love that feeling of not being quite sure whether or not you can do it — pushing the envelope. I love to compete on the floor, and I love to compete in the classroom," explained Pope. "I really do look at a test in the same way I look at matching up with Syracuse (in winning the national championship game). I want to kick its tail — take no prisoners — and talk a little trash along the way. I'm sure some of my classmates think I'm nuts, but I love it. I expect that when I'm practicing medicine I will feel the same way about disease. I love the challenge. I love the idea of competing against disease with patients as my teammates."

While playing in the NBA, Pope, who was born in Omaha, Nebraska, took some courses like physics and chemistry to meet the pre-med requirements.

## Early College Days

Pope said he "did not come from a family that was very much into athletics. We had people in the theater, in the arts. My dad was a debate champion, and so we did not have a real athletic background. With that said, I'm still probably the worst athlete of my five brothers and sisters."

But he was tall and ended up playing basketball, starring at Newport High School in Bellevue, Wash., under coach Richard Belcher before signing with the University of Washington. Pope praised Belcher, saying he is like a second father to him. Then, after two years at Washington where his coach, Lynn Nance, a former FBI agent had been a Joe B. Hall assistant for two years, was fired, Pope transferred to Kentucky in 1993. Because of NCAA transfer rules, he had to sit out a year before playing two seasons for Rick Pitino's Wildcats.

While sitting out during the 1993-94 campaign, the 6-foot-10 Pope practiced with a young Kentucky team that had to play without All-American Jamal Mashburn, who left UK after his junior year for NBA. But the Cats adjusted well, capturing their third straight SEC Tournament title and advanced to the NCAA tourney's second round. Under the senior leadership of playmaker Travis Ford, along with talented sophomores like Tony Delk, Jared Prickett and Rodrick Rhodes, Kentucky finished with a 27-7 mark and a No. 7 national ranking. At the time, Pitino praised Pope's work ethics, calling him "by far the hardest worker I've come across in my 20-year coaching career."

The next season saw the Wildcats, a Final Four contender, improve to the final No. 2 national ranking, but they were upset by North Carolina 74-61 in the NCAA regional finals in Birmingham. "That North Carolina Elite Eight game will haunt me forever, courtesy of Coach P, who tortured us for the next year," recalled Pope. As a fourth-year junior, Pope started eight out of 33 games, averaging 8.2 points and 6.3 rebounds. He also shot very well from the three-point line, gunning in 21 of 44 field goals for team-best 47.7 percent. Against Auburn, he had season-high 19 points while grabbing 10 rebounds in UK's 93-81 win in the the SEC Tournament.

*Mark Pope and his mother, Linda, during UK's Senior Day festivities at Rupp Arena in 1996. (Photo by Jamie H. Vaught)*

As a senior during Kentucky's "The Untouchables" national championship season of 1995-96, Pope had his best game — scoring wise — against No. 14 Maryland in the season opener, hitting a career-high 26 points and grabbing six rebounds in top-ranked UK's come-from-behind victory in the Hall of Fame Tip-Off Classic held in Springfield, Mass. Pope, who would play mostly as a backup center, was chosen as the game's MVP. And the dominating Wildcats went through the SEC battles without a scratch, posting a perfect 16-0 league mark, with a glamorous overall record of 34-2. Without a doubt, they were one of greatest NCAA Tournament teams in history. In recent years, *The Athletic* and *Athlon Sports* had ranked Kentucky among the top three in both rankings of NCAA champions. Four Wildcats were chosen in the 1996 NBA Draft with the Indiana Pacers selecting Pope as the 52nd pick overall in the second round. Antoine Walker, Tony Delk and Walter McCarty were picked in the first round. In addition, Pitino earned SEC Coach of the Year honors for the third time at Kentucky.

Looking back, Pope said UK "was such a beautiful experience for me playing here. I got so much better as a player. I improved so much more in practice than I did in games. Facing Walter McCarty and Antoine Walker was harder every day in practice than it was facing just about every frontline player in college except for Marcus Camby (of UMass). He was a problem for me."

Even though he enjoyed basketball, Pope had many other interests. He also loved to read. He loved to write essays. He loved cycling. He loved milking the cows. He received a bachelor's degree in English. As mentioned previously, he was nominated for prestigious Rhodes Scholars program. His professors saw Pope's enormous potential and they encouraged him to apply for the Rhodes Scholar program. Pope said it was an interesting experience to go through the process.

"I had a couple of teachers who had said, 'Listen, this is something you should really seriously consider,' and I did," said Pope, who was one of the more likable players on the team. "I went through this whole long drawn out process — I had to write a full-length essay, as well as getting recommendations from teachers on the campus to going through a series of interviews on campus — and then when I was chosen to do that, I was thrilled. I was really excited. It's one of those things that I can't imagine anything else that I would look forward to more. Of course, it didn't work out, but the procedure itself was interesting and I learned a lot from that. It was something to actually represent the university."

An Academic All-SEC selection and third-team GTE Academic All-American pick as a junior, Pope said he learned a lot more about himself, the culture and the people around the world when he took some literature classes. He really enjoyed these classes. After a practice, Pope would often lie down on his bed and read. "It's a great leisure for me," he said.

## Professor Pope?

During his early days, Pope had expressed a strong interest in teaching a English Literature class on the college level. He was asked in 2025 if that was still an attractive option. Even though he doesn't have a PhD degree, he still might be able to teach a lower level — freshman or sophomore — class because of his past graduate work and academic honors such as Rhodes Scholar candidacy, as well as having a degree in English. Generally speaking, a college instructor will need at least 18 graduate hours in a subject area to teach a freshman or sophomore class to meet the school's accreditation requirements. Of course, teaching an online course certainly would give Pope the schedule flexibility he needs while coaching if the opportunity ever arises, but the Wildcat boss prefers a face-to-face class.

"I would love to be an English-lit teacher. Absolutely love it," said the UK coach. "I wouldn't enjoy it as much as coaching, but there are so many things I would love to get a shot at doing, but I just happen to be able to do the thing I want to do most right now. I don't think I would like teaching online. I think I love being in the classroom with students where you have that direct face-to-face interaction so much where you can be in a classroom where the ideas just start bouncing off of each other, then you get different immediate impact of feedback, of different points of view as you unravel a text all together. So, I don't know that I would love teaching online, but I do think I would absolutely love teaching in a classroom."

Pope was asked if he would like teaching after he retires from coaching. "Well, I'm hoping that I coach until the day I die," he smiled.

And he still loves to read. Pope was asked about his favorite books that he has read. "I'm in this American history vibe right now," he said. "I love this so much. I just finished *1861: The Lost Peace* by Jay Winik, and it's awesome because it's a light read. And then right now I'm slogging through *Team of Rivals* (by Doris Kearns Goodwin), which I'm falling in love with. It's interesting. Of course, I'm fascinated by Lincoln. Then William Seward, who was the two-time governor of the state of New York and then was the Secretary of State for President Lincoln, who also ran against him in the presidency election. I think these people and what they lived through and how they navigated the times were incredible.

"I just finished *Ego is the Enemy*. The author is Ryan Holiday. I really, really enjoyed it and I think it's incredibly relevant to the head coach to Kentucky and any player that ever played in Kentucky, and just understanding the interplay between how ego can be functional for us and how it can actually really, really hurt us. So, that's where I've been reading the last few weeks."

As the author began reading the next question, Pope interrupted the conversation. "And then, Jamie, the other thing on my reading list would be your first six books. All of them, fantastic," he added. Personally, I sure didn't know what to think but that was very nice to hear and I thanked him.

## Rick Pitino

While at UK when he was the team's two-time co-captain, Pope had previously said his greatest moment in sports took place during a practice session at Memorial Coliseum when Pitino stopped the practice and angrily screamed at him in front of his teammates. "I was in practice one day and I can't even remember what we were doing, but I said something," Pope recalled, "and Coach just stopped the playing, yelled at me, and said, 'Would you stop talking so much? You're wasting your oxygen! Save your oxygen!' Coach would say strange things every now and then. He would come up with some great lines and you know that was the kind of things that happen when you're in such an intense atmosphere.

"We practiced twice a day, every day, and during the winter, we practiced sometimes three times a day. After the first practice in the morning, you are so tired and you don't think you can even walk to class. You got to walk to class and come back and have another full-blown practice. So, working that hard together and spending that much time together, funny things are bound to happen. You know you're under this intense scrutiny. There's so much pressure and you're so tired and busy all the same time. You're just squeezed in this little area and it's bound to cause strange things to happen. So, those are the times that you really treasure.

"The guys were giving me a hard time about it. But the thing is that Coach gets on everybody. What Coach does is he makes you stronger."

Fast forward to 2024. On February 20, after Pope's No. 25 Brigham Young team upset No. 11 Baylor before 17,978 fans at the

Marriott Center, Pitino, now the head coach at St. John's, posted a message on X (formerly Twitter), congratulating his former player. "So proud and happy for BYU coach Mark Pope with his great win vs. 11th ranked Baylor," the former UK coach wrote on social media. "Our captain of one of the greatest college teams ever assembled - 1996 Champions!!! We love you Mark, so happy for you!!"

After seeing Pitino's message on X, an emotional Pope was quoted as saying in a story by Kevin Reynolds in *The Salt Lake Tribune*, "It is really sweet to me. I love that man. Like, he changed me as a person. I don't know — he doesn't hand out compliments all the time."

The victory gave BYU its first-ever regular season with wins over three different ranked opponents.

Pope, who first met Pitino at his parents' home in Bellevue around 1990 or so during a two-hour recruiting visit, had more to say about Pitino several months later after becoming the head coach at Kentucky. And Pitino was among the first people to endorse or support Pope shortly after his former player got the UK job with a video on X. "Coach Pitino is really personal to me," he said. "If you think about your life, you count on one hand maybe the people that really, really, really change you forever, and I love Coach Pitino for that.

"I'll be forever grateful for him. He changed the way that I see the world, and he changed the way that I walk into a room, and he changed the confidence that we approach challenges with. And on top of all that, we got to share as a team under his leadership just the most extraordinary of extraordinary experiences together.

"He is a coach that also is on the Mount Rushmore of Kentucky basketball coaches, and that's really saying something. He took a program when it was in a really, really, really difficult spot and took it to back where it belongs, at the top of the college basketball mountain, and he did it with all of his style and intensity and everything that he brings to the game.

"I love him so much, and it was really special for him to be able to walk into Rupp Arena (at 2024 Big Blue Madness) and feel that from BBN, to feel their gratitude. We talk about gratitude every single day on our team. It's a really important part of what we do. For Coach to be able to feel the gratitude of BBN for him I thought was really special."

*Coach Mark Pope signs autographs during a break from his postgame radio show at Rupp Arena in 2025. (Photo by Jamie H. Vaught)*

Another Pitino memory. After Kentucky's 93-85 victory over rival Louisville at Rupp Arena in mid-December 2024, Pope was asked about how he felt about coaching the Cats against the Cards. As a Wildcat player, Pope twice had played U of L, winning one and losing one. The night before the 2024 matchup, since he couldn't exactly remember these two games in the series, he and his wife looked up the games he faced against coach Denny

Crum's Cardinals: "My junior (year) we lost by two (88-86) at Louisville. When I saw it, I was like 'Wait, what?' So, I remember now. The bus ride home from Louisville. I was in a full-on, teary-eyed sweat last night. I blocked it out of my memory. And all of a sudden, it all came rushing back. I'm starting to sweat right now. You get locked in the bus with Coach P for an hour and a half after the two-point loss against Louisville. I don't wish that on any of you, actually. I bet only half of you guys would come out alive, I kid you not. And our senior year, we had a runaway win."

Asked if many legendary stories about Pitino's conditioning sessions are true or exaggerated, Pope smiled, "They are true. It would be impossible to exaggerate them."

In 2025, Pope was asked if he thought Pitino has mellowed a lot over the years since his coaching days at Kentucky. "I wouldn't use the word mellowed," he said. "I would say that Coach is every bit as intense and demanding and focused as he's ever been. Maybe more so. I think he goes about it differently, but I think he's got all the intensity that he ever had."

## Faith Journey

During his early days as a kid, Pope admitted that he didn't have much interest in his Mormon faith even though his parents were members of the Latter-day Saints and his three older brothers served missions. Pope said he was "pretty apathetic" about his faith, according to BYU's *Y Magazine*, an alumni publication, in 2021.

While at UK, Pope was still searching for his faith as he attended numerous religious affiliations and studied the New Testament. As mentioned in *Y Magazine*, his feelings, however, began to change during a road trip. Pope and his father, Don, had driven an old Nissan across the nation so the younger Pope would have a car on campus. Along the way, they stopped at a historic Mormon site called Adam-ondi-Ahman in Missouri. In a peaceful moment, Pope was struck by the Spirit. "The words of Heavenly Father were imprinted on my mind in an undeniable way," he said. Pope's faith grew and became stronger after reading the Book of Mormon and listening to a tape by a BYU professor that a friend had sent him.

## Last Year at Brigham Young

In basketball, as the Cougers prepared for the 2023-24 season in their first year in the Big 12 Conference, they were not expected to do much. In a preseason poll by the coaches, BYU was picked to finish at No. 13 in the 14-team league. After leaving the West Coast Conference, Pope was asked if the low preseason ranking took some pressure off his team. "I was super excited about the 13th pick," he said. "I have four daughters, and we managed to make it to a couple of the Taylor Swift concerts this year, and her favorite number is 13, and I think that bodes well for BYU basketball this season.

"We're really excited about that. I think the pressure is always there. If you're running from pressure, you shouldn't be in athletics. Actually, we love it. I think you're pressure picked at 13 and pressure picked at 1 and pressure picked everywhere, but certainly we are very humble moving in this league, but we're very confident....I don't know if anybody puts a lot of stock in the preseason picks, but we're excited to come compete."

When the regular season ended, BYU surprised many observers as it tied Kansas with a 10-8 conference mark, finishing at No. 5 in Big 12. Overall, BYU finished the year with a 23-11 record with a trip to the NCAA Tournament. The Cougars, who ranked third in the nation with 11.1 made three-pointers per game, also had victories over No. 7 Kansas, No. 11 Baylor and No. 24 Iowa State.

One huge highlight for the Popes during the season was guiding the Cougars — who were making the trip to iconic Allen Field-house in Lawrence, Kansas for the first time since 1971 — to a major upset, beating the Jayhawks 76-68. Future Wildcat Jaxson Robinson, coming off the bench, was a major contributor with 18 points in leading the BYU attack. "I think the guys agree that everybody knows what this place is," said Mark Pope after the game. "This was my first time walking into a game like this where I've never seen an atmosphere quite like this. It's actually really special. This is a great team. We're grateful we got an opportunity to come compete here." BYU became the first unranked team to beat a Kansas team ranked in the Top 10 at Allen Fieldhouse since 2018.

*With his wife, Lee Anne Pope, looking on in the background, Mark Pope discusses his BYU team's road victory over No. 7 Kansas during a postgame radio show in 2024. (BYU Photo)*

Pope said the victory over Kansas "is really special. I think it's special because we all have such a deep respect for this program and this venue. It's the all-time Mecca. I think what makes it most special for me is faith. We talk all the time about faith in our program, and it's certainly an important part of our university. Watching our guys' faith in each other tonight and their faith in the process, of their abilities and their work, was really special to watch."

With Lee Anne sitting nearby, Pope said on his postgame radio show that he discussed the faith with his players about the highs and lows, among others. It was a historic and wild night the Cougars will never forget.

## John Calipari

On his predecessor, "You'll never hear me say a negative word about Coach Cal because there's not a lot to say to," said Pope not long before the 2024-25 campaign began. "He's a Hall of Fame coach. As a die-hard Kentucky fan and alumnus and former player, I am grateful for everything, all the incredible things that Cal accomplished at the University of Kentucky.

"And he's also been a good friend. He's been a terrific mentor, and he's always been generous to Lee Anne and I as we've gone through our coaching journey. So, we wish him the best in everything that he does, and I will forever be grateful for everything that he did at Kentucky. And we'll be cheering for him every day like crazy — except for February 1st."

For the rabid Big Blue Nation, it was that memorable date in February of 2025 when Calipari returned to Rupp Arena as his Razorbacks visited the Wildcats. It was surreal to witness Calipari entering the floor from the visitor's dressing room on the other side and greet first-year Kentucky coach Mark Pope and others, receiving mixed reaction from a boisterous crowd of 21,266. Some fans hadn't been too happy with Calipari's coaching performance in recent years at UK, especially during the postseason tournaments.  He became the third former Wildcat to coach at

Rupp Arena, joining Pitino (Louisville) and Tubby Smith (High Point).

*ESPN's Alyssa Lang interviews Arkansas coach John Calipari after his team's 89-79 win over Kentucky at Rupp Arena on Feb. 1, 2025. (Photo by Jamie H. Vaught)*

It was an emotional time for Calipari as he had so many fond memories during his 15 years in Lexington, including the 2012 national championship and the Final Four season of 38-1 in 2015. And you can add his unranked Razorbacks' 89-79 upset win over the No. 12 Wildcats to a long list of Calipari's memorable moments at Rupp Arena with Arkansas supporter John Tyson, the CEO of Tyson Foods, sitting in the front row behind the visitor's bench.

"We needed to win a game. It didn't matter who it was against. I made it clear," Calipari said of his emotions in a postgame news conference. "It was a privilege and an honor to coach here. We had 15 unbelievable years and a great run. The fans supported us, the families that trusted us with their sons. I got 190 texts by the time the game ended. I'm guessing a bunch of them are former players, not that they are ever going to cheer against Kentucky. They went to school here, but they also have a relationship with me. The only emotion I had was to win the game."

It should be pointed out Pope returned to Rupp Arena in 2017 as the head coach of the Utah Valley Wolverines where his team dropped to Kentucky 73-63 in the season opener, spoiling his homecoming. "I've always respected him," said Calipari after that game. "He's obviously, being a graduate from here, you keep an eye on stuff, but the one thing that really disappointed me is that his ovation was better than mine."

## Faith and Basketball

Fun-loving Pope is a philosophical and faith-oriented person who is also good with humorous one-liners. He tries to be a positive influence in his surroundings even though, like everyone else, he has frustrating moments at times. And he believes God has a plan for our lives.

"I'm a member of the The Church of Jesus Christ of Latter-day Saints. My faith is really, really important to me," Pope told the author. "I am so grateful to be centered in my faith. It's a brilliant thing. The fact that the atonement of Jesus Christ is a real thing, and the fact that we can receive grace and peace, that we can mess up and know that we have second chances built into the program, that we can walk in faith knowing that. The journey is actually we know what the finish line is, what's interesting is the path we're going to take to get there.

"With our players, we talk about two things all the time, urgency and faith. So, there's the urgency of approaching every moment with complete desperation, but all of that is laid on the foundation of this faith that you know at the end of the day things are going to work out better than you could ever imagine. And so combining those things, that urgent desperation to do everything we can knowing that the race has already been won is an incredibly empowering thing for me, for sure."

During the 2025 NCAA Tournament, Pope also discussed his coaches and faith in a media session while previewing the Kentucky-Illinois game. "I think that I've had the greatest mentors in all of basketball," said Pope. "I mean, I've been exposed to the greatest coaches from my high school coach Rich Belcher to my first college coach, Lynn Nance, to Rick Pitino to the great Larry Bird, and along the way Billy Donovan and a whole slew of incredible coaches. I'm leaving out 25 coaches that have been so great. I got to work for Dave Rose (as assistant) at BYU who was one of my great teachers and mentors. I've been really blessed.

"I think that my life view, most of it comes from my faith. And I'm a believer. It just makes you see the world different. It really does. I think it's actually real that the world is what we see and what we look for. I think that we are active creators in the world that we live in. I mean, I really believe that. I believe that if we really want to see the goodness of the world, if we work hard, we can see it. I really believe we can see it, right?

"I think that my faith is — a foundational principle is gratitude, and I think it's really hard to not be positive, not be joyful, not be happy if you work really hard at gratitude. If we all take the time in our day to sit down and start listing the things that we could be grateful for, starting from the very basic level, how can we not love life and be so incredibly full of joy and positivity. Because it's just miracle after miracle, just the fact that we get to wake up every morning.

"I'm giving you a long answer because I actually love this. I believe in this. You guys have heard this kind of story of if I gave you $10 million right now, would it make you happy? And most people would be like 'Yeah, I would take that in a second.' No strings attached. Are you kidding? And if I said well, here's the deal. If I was going to give you $10 million today or you could wake up tomorrow, which would you choose? And you would choose to wake up tomorrow, right? So waking up tomorrow is worth way more than $10 million. That's a fact, and it's a reality. It's just sometimes we don't actually take the time to look at it and understand it that way. And when we actively do that, I think our lives get really, really good really, really fast.

*Coach Mark Pope*

"So, I think that I want my guys to be challenged. I want them to face all of the struggles and trials and adversity that this game and this experience can offer them, because it gives them a chance to grow. But I also want them every single day to remember how blessed they are to have the opportunity to wake up, to be basketball players at the University of Kentucky. It's just incredible. I love it, man. I love the whole thing, and it's not hard. It's not hard to find joy in life."

Before UK's NCAA Sweet 16 matchup with Tennessee, Pope was asked about the happiness among the players in the locker room. "I think joy in the gym is a principle that's really, really important to us," he said. "I think we play better when we work hard to find joy in the process because this can be a grind also. It can be mentally and emotionally taxing and exhausting. And the pressure can be immense. But finding the joy in it, I think, actually helps us perform better. It helps us be more focused. I think it helps us be looser. It helps us, enables us to be better decision makers. It takes us from our limbic system to our frontal cortex literally, in a real sense, and helps us be decision makers, which is such a crucial part of what we do on the court.

"Also, it is what's the point? What's the point of all this if you're not building relationships that are going to last forever and if you're not enjoying every moment? If you can't be here in this city (Indianapolis) in the Sweet 16 with this group of guys, if you can't enjoy that, then you need to find another thing to do.

"I love that the guys are enjoying it. And I love that they're taking in every single moment. They came here for a reason. They're very focused on that reason. But their love of each other is showing through is actually a strength for us."

## First Date with Future Wife

"It was a very inauspicious first date, so it was busy like it always is," Pope recalled. "She (Lee Anne) was flying to Indianapolis for work. And we had never met in person before, although we'd been talking on the phone and emailing at a high clip. My brother and sister-in-law were in town, and I was watching their baby, and it was just a madhouse. So, I actually picked Lee Anne up for the first time at her hotel at the Canterbury Inn in downtown Indianapolis and I had a baby in the back of the car. So, that was our first introduction. And then we ended up racing around town trying to get everyone where they were.

"We were running late, stopped at a gas station, and told her that she could get anything she wanted for dinner at the gas station. So, it was actually a beautiful first night. We had so much fun and it was so awkward and weird, and nothing worked out exactly right, but it was so easy to feel connected to her. She's different than anybody I've ever met. And it was probably pretty symbolic for the rest of our life. It's just been sheer chaos and madness every day since, and we've loved every segment of it."

Added Pope, "I don't know if I ate anything. I think she probably grabbed some vegetables from the tiny little refrigerated food area at the gas station."

## Pope's Parents

Don and Linda Pope made a trip to Lexington from Idaho to watch their son coach the Wildcats for the first time in 2024. It was about a week before Thanksgiving, and UK was playing an early regular season game against Lipscomb. It was an easy win for the Wildcats, who won 97-68.

"They came out for a game early in the season, and it was so fun to have them out here," said the younger Pope. "They hadn't been in Lexington for 30 years, so it was actually really fun to have them come out.

"Mom and Dad are living in Nampa, Idaho. They're doing well. They're getting older, they're not quite as mobile as they once were, but they're doing great. They've actually found a community there that they just love that's really embraced them with great neighbors and a great church community and they're living a good life right now."

## NBA Dancer Layla Pope

Wearing her father's 1996 Kentucky jersey with No. 41 on it, Layla Pope, the second-youngest daughter, made a surprise visit to Rupp Arena when she performed with the members of the UK dance squad during the halftime of Kentucky's 75-64 victory over Tennessee in mid-February 2025. It was definitely a special night for the Pope family.

Shortly after the game, reporters asked Coach Pope about his daughter's performance. "Actually it's super sweet to me," he said. "I had three of my four daughters here tonight, which we don't get to be together that much. And my other daughter is out serving the world in El Salvador right now. It's really actually pretty incredible. I got to have my daughter wearing my national championship jersey on our court in this game. And you know it's not about me or about us. In a really personal way, it was a super special moment for me."

Layla, who is a student at BYU, is a dancer for NBA's Utah Jazz. "She's a lifelong dancer," Pope later told the author. "She always wanted to be a professional dancer. She's having the time of her life. She's on a team that probably spends hours of the day, more time together than our basketball team is allowed to. They work incredibly hard and they rely on each other, and she's having an incredible experience."

In 2020, Layla had to have a spinal surgery but she recovered nicely. "She had over a 70-degree curvature in her spine," said her father. "She had to have surgery. She was afraid that she would never be able to dance again. And just through sheer guts and determination worked her way back to be an elite level dancer."

## NIL & Transfer Portal

In recent years, Pope has seen a lot of significant changes taking place in college athletics with the NIL (Name, Image and Likeness) and transfer portal giving more control and freedom to the players who have become almost like free agents in the professional ranks. Not surprisingly, the Kentucky mentor said the coaching job is harder now.

"It's more difficult now," he said. "One of the things that's interesting about NIL is these kids that we get to mentor and teach and grow through the experience, they've always had incredible challenges. They had challenges of dealing with the physical, mental and emotional aspects of the game. They have a challenge of dealing with the opposition, dealing with referees, dealing with fans, dealing with people in the community, deal with all the pressure, and now we've just added one more massive burden on them, which is that they have some finances that they have to deal with and deal with responsibly.

"And it comes with incredible opportunity, but it also comes with massive responsibility. My guys are now on their list of things to do is to start their own foundation, is to find what charities they're interested in supporting, is to find out how they're going to invest their finances and actually be responsible with the money that they're making, how are they going to make determination on who in their family they can give what help financially, how are they going to be disciplined with these resources.

"So, good problems, but it's more challenging for these players than ever before, and therefore it's more challenging for us as coaches, which is a good thing. With those challenges comes more opportunity to learn. So, at the end of the day, it's a great thing, but it makes the job more demanding."

Would Pope like to go back coaching like it was before the days of NIL and transfer portal? Does he have a preference?

"I like them both," he said. "I think there's good and bad that comes with both. I think one of the great things about coaching is that you get to coach in different environments all the time and it's what makes the job so fascinating. So, every different change in the organization and the environment that we have as coaches I think is something that makes the job even more interesting. So, I like coaching in both eras."

While at Brigham Young, did Pope ever think about retiring like many other well-known coaches because of the changing landscape in college sports even though he was still many years away from his retirement age?

"Well, the short answer is no, because I love this job so much," said Pope. "I do think there's been a lot of time reflecting on how the job is different. Before the transfer portal and before NIL, the way we approached our job and the way we approached mentoring these kids and growing a team was significantly different than the way it is now. So, there was a beauty to the way that we used to do this, for sure. There was something wonderful about it where you planned your roster by class, you had your seniors, juniors, sophomores and freshmen, and you actually had a freshman and you were planning out your roster all the way for the next four years to when they would be a senior and plugging in all those pieces. There's a real challenge in having that continuity because you don't get to change as much, so it's just different.

*Coach Mark Pope listens at a press conference during UK's annual Media Day festivities in 2024. (Photo by Jamie H. Vaught)*

"But there's a beautiful part of that about having a player and knowing that you have for two, three or four years, and getting to grow a team every year where it's grown from the inside of a core of returning veterans that have been competing there for two or three years. And they can share with the rest of the team what that means. Then you just see the game different when you become a senior, your fourth year in a program. We don't have much of that any more in the current environment, but there are other opportunities and challenges that are great."

## Weetabix

During the 2025 NCAA Tournament, Amari Williams, a 7-footer from Nottingham, England, and his teammates had fun with the one of the United Kingdom's most popular cold cereals, Weetabix. Some of his team members, including Coach Pope, tried out the cereal for breakfast and they liked it pretty good after a staff member found Weetabix at an international store in Milwaukee. According to the company's website, Weetabix Food Company had been a family-owned business since 1932 when the first box of Weetabix came out before it became a subsidiary of St. Louis-based Post Holdings, Inc.

When Williams was growing up in the United Kingdom, he said his parents forced him to eat Weetabix. "It's like shredded wheat," said Williams. "I had about three of them this morning. I feel like that helped my performance today, for sure. " Just moments earlier, he had helped the Cats to a second-round tournament victory over Illinois with 10 rebounds, eight points and six assists. "Incredible energy on the floor," Pope said of Williams.

A couple of days earlier, Williams said he had four pieces of toast for breakfast. "They thought that wasn't enough," he said. So, Pope asked him what do you usually eat? Williams said, when he was growing up, "I had something called Weetabix, which is from England."

On the cereal, Williams said, "It doesn't taste too bad. Depends how you make it. It definitely tastes amazing, and it gives you a lot of energy throughout the day, for sure. Ever since coming to America, I've never seen people have cereal with warm milk. So, I feel like that's something you've got to try if you have Weetabix and warm milk."

Pope said, "The Weetabix were extraordinary, actually. So it comes in a biscuit that looks very untasteful. But I learned today that you crumble it up into tiny little things, and then you put some warm milk. I've never had cereal with warm milk. Shout out to

Xaymara (Gonzalez Adams), our nutrition specialist, for making that happen. Then Amari gave me permission to put some sugar on it. He was nervous. He put four packs of sugar, I put one, because if I put more than one Lee Anne was going to kill me. It was actually fantastic. I like it so much more right now than I did this morning."

Even the Kentucky fans had fun with the cereal and bought them at stores and online as well as posting pictures on social media. "This whole Weetabix thing has been super fun, man," said Pope. "The videos that we're getting sent to us are really special, sweet and delightful." In early April, Williams posted a picture of himself on the cereal box in Instagram, saying, "Woke up a cereal box legend. Huge shoutout to @WeetabixOfficial for stepping up my breakfast game! Not gonna lie ... this would look good on shelves."

In the 2025 NBA Draft, Williams was selected at No. 46 overall by Orlando before he was dealt to the Boston Celtics. His 6-foot-7 teammate, Koby Brea, was chosen at No. 41 overall by Golden State before the Phoenix Suns obtained him in a trade.

## Oscar Combs

A member of Kentucky Journalism Hall of Fame who founded popular *The Cats' Pause* magazine in 1976, Combs praised the hiring of Mark Pope as the new coach at UK. "Naming Mark Pope as head coach may turn out to be Mitch Barnhart's most popular coaching hire in his 20-plus years at UK. No, Pope wasn't Mitch's first choice, but the former Wildcat was always on Mitch's short list," said Combs, a native of Hazard who retired as co-host of the UK Radio Network pregame show in 2016. "From the minute Pope stepped to the microphone in front of 20,000 screaming fans at his first press conference in Rupp Arena, you knew he had the Commonwealth wrapped around his finger, the one right next to his 1996 NCAA championship ring. His mission is to add another one soon, the school's 9th.

"The enthusiasm generated at that initial press conference had fans so excited that one of their very own was now in charge. Pope understood what wearing a jersey with 'KENTUCKY' plastered on the front means, just like 30-plus years ago when he transferred to UK from Washington."

On Friday morning on April 12, 2024, shortly before Pope was officially hired by the university, Combs was disappointed with the reaction by many folks on the possible hiring of Pope.  On X (formerly Twitter), Combs wrote, "Here's my last word and I'm going to slide away from Twitter a few days. I feel very saddened that the possible hiring of Mark Pope has brought so much vile from so many UK fans the past 12 hours. I thought BBN was better than this. Disagreement is fine, but this has been way overboard.

"If Pope is hired, there will be a day when lots of fans who 'know it all' will discover they really didn't 'know it all.' Mark brings to the program hope that UK factions can come together while winning at a high level. Just look at his support from ex-UK. players. Peace."

And Combs enjoyed watching Pope's first UK team as the Wildcat boss. "His first team, literally put together in just a few weeks, was so entertaining and though there were some numbing losses to Georgia, Vanderbilt and Texas, UK advanced to second weekend of NCAA for first time in five years," he said. "Wins over Duke, Gonzaga, Florida, Texas A&M and Tennessee gave promise as to what to expect this winter (2025-26)."

## First Season as Wildcat Boss

Even though the 2024-25 Wildcats were loaded with experienced newcomers, many fans and the media were pleasantly surprised with the coaching success by Pope, who had to build the team from scratch. After going through UK's disappointments in recent years, especially in the NCAA Tournament, it was finally an exciting and fun season for the Big Blue Nation. The so-called "Big Blue" spirit has returned to the hungry fan base. They saw the Cats roar all the way to NCAA Sweet Sixteen despite injuries to key players, finishing with a 24-12 record, including several victories over ranked opponents.

On a scale of 1 to 10, how would Pope grade his first coaching year at Kentucky? "I'd rate it as a 10 because it's the greatest job in the world, so there's nothing else in the world I'd rather be doing," he told the author. "It's my favorite thing, so for me it's always a 10 every day I get to be a coach here."

With Pope as the head coach, his first UK team will never be forgotten. He praised their work ethic and attitude for setting up a strong foundation. "They set a really high standard," said Pope. "They set a high standard on the court and a higher standard in the locker room and off the floor. They set an incredibly high standard representing the University of Kentucky, representing BBN, and representing this jersey, and I'm grateful for that. That standard will carry us for a long time. We'll be talking about these guys 10 years from now as the guys that came in here and set a standard of what this is supposed to be, how you're supposed to carry yourself as a Kentucky basketball player, how you're supposed to connect yourself with your teammates. We'll set this as a standard for the future. I'm very proud of these guys.

"I do believe that God has a plan for our lives. I do believe God brought all of us together with this extraordinary group. I think he brought us together so each of us individually could grow. I think he brought us together so we could build relationships that are going to last forever. I'm pretty sure one of these guys will be slumming at my house some time in the next years. I don't know who it's going to be. I think that these guys have had an incredible impact. They've gone out of their way to have an incredible impact on BBN and the state of Kentucky and the community around them, whether it's been their regular hospital visits, or Ronald McDonald House visits, or meeting with fans before or after games, finding other ways to serve, and serving each other. I think this group was brought together to serve as best they can. And these guys did it in an incredible fashion."

Said playmaker Lamont Butler, who once hit the game-winning field goal while at San Diego State in the 2023 NCAA Final Four, "I think it's really cool we were able to set the culture for Pope's first year."

Senior writer Mike DeCourcy of the *Sporting News* covered college basketball for nearly 40 years, and he has seen significant changes taking place in college basketball. DeCourcy has been very impressed with the work Pope has done with the Wildcats. "The challenge for the first-year coach in the current era of college basketball is greater than it's ever been," he told the author. "There was a time when a coach taking over a program with what I came to call an 'empty gym' — no players on the roster, or almost none — was almost as rare as a LeBron-level talent. Mick Cronin entered such a situation when he took over Cincinnati in 2006, and Tom Crean at Indiana two years later. And that was about it. Those coaches were not expected to win immediately, and they didn't. It took Cronin five years to reach the NCAAs, and Crean four years.

"Now, it's almost more common than not for a coach to need to install a completely new roster upon arrival. And at a place like Kentucky, the coach isn't likely to encounter a great deal of patience from the fan base. Even in these different circumstances, and even with significant injuries impacting the rotation from the middle of the season on, Mark Pope exceeded what might have been demanded from him. The Wildcats beat elite opposition, including a non-conference win over Duke, the rivalry game against Louisville, a home game against eventual NCAA champion Florida, and a regular season sweep of Tennessee. They reached the Sweet 16. Perhaps more germane, Pope established an entirely new identity for his version of Kentucky basketball. Not better or worse than what came before, but distinctly Pope's. One honestly couldn't have asked more from his first season."

Kentucky author and sportswriter John Huang has an interesting observation about Pope and his first season as the UK boss. "What's most surprising to me — and frankly, most fascinating — about Mark Pope isn't just his relentless energy or encyclopedic knowledge of the game. It's the way he thinks *about* the game. Not just strategy, not just plays, but the *structure* of basketball itself. Pope is one of the rare coaches who doesn't merely accept the rulebook as a given — he studies it, questions it, and even finds creative ways to exploit it. He dives into the bylaws and nuances the way a constitutional scholar might analyze the Federalist Papers, searching for overlooked truths and underutilized advantages. Most coaches game plan; Pope questions the architecture of the game itself. This mindset gives Pope a kind of basketball savant's edge. It's not just X's and O's with him — it's metaphysics. He's fascinated by tempo not simply as a style of play, but as a philosophical lever of control. He talks about spacing and movement as if choreographing a symphony, where every player is a note in motion.

"And because he's played at the highest levels — championship-caliber college ball and a stint in the NBA — Pope doesn't romanticize the game. He reveres it *intellectually*. That depth of thought is what allows him to innovate without gimmickry, to modernize without losing the soul of the sport. For a fan base steeped in tradition and focused on hanging banners, that might just be the most hopeful surprise of all."

As ESPN's Dick Vitale would say about Kentucky's newly revived passion, "It's awesome, baby!"

# About the Author

Veteran sportswriter Jamie H. Vaught has covered the University of Kentucky's basketball program since his early college days, including the team's NCAA Final Four appearances in 2012 and 2015. He is a longtime credentialed sportswriter in Kentucky, whose columns or articles over several decades have appeared in numerous outlets and daily newspapers. Vaught, who is also a photographer, has now written seven books about UK basketball, including *Crazy About the Cats: From Rupp to Pitino.* A member of the U.S. Basketball Writers Association (USBWA), Vaught is the founder and editor of the growing *KySportsStyle.com Magazine.*

While a college student at UK during the late 1970s, Vaught served as a sportswriter and sports editor of *Kentucky Kernel,* the campus daily newspaper, before graduating with two degrees — a bachelor's in accounting and a master's in business administration (MBA). He also attended Somerset Community College for two years before transferring to UK. During the 1980s and early '90s, he worked for *The Cats' Pause* as a sports columnist for 13 years. His articles also have appeared in *The Cats' Pause Kentucky Basketball Yearbook.*

For 33 years, Vaught taught at Southeast Kentucky Community and Technical College in Middlesboro as a tenured professor before retiring in 2024. The author is also severely hard of hearing. He was prematurely born (of nearly two months), and it was likely the cause of his severe hearing impairment — near deafness. He and his wife, Deanna, live in Middlesboro, and they have two grown children, Janna and Warren.

Made in the USA
Middletown, DE
02 December 2025

23735026R00198